We have a *rendez-vous* with the BNA Act.   F. R. SCOTT

The Future of
Canadian Federalism

L'Avenir du
fédéralisme canadien

edited by / *édité par*

P.-A. CREPEAU &
C. B. MACPHERSON

UNIVERSITY OF TORONTO PRESS
LES PRESSES DE L'UNIVERSITÉ DE MONTRÉAL

© *University of Toronto Press 1965*
Reprinted in paperback 2015
ISBN 978-0-8020-1356-9 (cloth)
ISBN 978-0-8020-6043-3 (paper)

AVANT-PROPOS

1964. Centenaire de la Conférence de Charlottetown. La Société royale du Canada et, à sa suite, les Sociétés savantes, avaient décidé de tenir leurs assises dans la capitale de l'Ile du prince Edouard.

Occasion toute trouvée pour parler de fédéralisme. L'Association canadienne des professeurs de droit a pour cela voulu que le programme de son congrès fût entièrement consacré à l'étude de ce régime constitutionnel conçu à Charlottetown, en septembre 1864, façonné à Québec, quelques semaines plus tard, mis au point à Londres, à l'automne de 1866, ratifié par le parlement de Westminster au printemps suivant, et proclamé en vigueur le 1er juillet 1867.

Mais, afin d'élargir les bases de la discussion et de donner au débat ses justes dimensions, les responsables du congrès ont sollicité la collaboration de l'Association canadienne des Sciences politiques. Et c'est ainsi que durant la journée du 11 juin, des spécialistes du Canada anglais et du Canada français avaient l'occasion d'exposer leurs vues sur les aspects économiques, politiques, et juridiques des divers problèmes que soulève aujourd'hui la nécessaire adaptation de notre régime constitutionnel aux conditions nouvelles et naguère insoupçonnées de notre société politique. Les professeurs de droit consacraient, de plus, la journée du lendemain, le 12 juin, à l'examen de questions plus spécifiquement juridiques concernant, d'une part, l'interprétation et l'application de l'Acte de l'Amérique du nord britannique et, d'autre part, la réforme des structures et des organes du régime fédératif.

Ces deux associations sont ainsi heureuses d'avoir provoqué un dialogue serein et animé, non seulement entre spécialistes, mais aussi entre des représentants autorisés des deux principales communautés ethniques du pays.

La rencontre de Charlottetown, 1964, constitue, à n'en pas douter — et cet ouvrage qui groupe les travaux du congrès en fournit une preuve éloquente — une contribution utile au grand débat qui s'ouvre sur l'avenir du fédéralisme canadien.

INTRODUCTION

By the beginning of 1964 public debate about the terms on which French and English cultures could continue to co-exist within a single Canadian federal state had become intense. Many causes could be assigned for the intensity of the debate, but one of them evidently was the lack of clear formulation of the problems.

It was in these circumstances that two of the Canadian learned societies—the Association of Canadian Law Teachers and the Canadian Political Science Association—believing that their fields of competence gave them some special responsibility, undertook to use their 1964 meetings to begin to repair this "défaut des clercs." Papers and commentaries were commissioned, and in June the series of four sessions, each comprising two papers and some commentaries, took place in Charlottetown.

It will be clear to those who read the papers and commentaries here published that the contributors to the two days' sessions were given a free hand within a very accommodating general design. Indeed, those who were organizing the meetings were as much concerned to accommodate the known talents of the sort of contributors they wanted to invite as they were to fit papers into an over-all plan. The general intention was to get, on each of four aspects of the current problem of Canadian federalism, a vigorously reasoned statement, by a French-Canadian and an English-Canadian scholar, of the essentials of the problems as he saw it, and then, by way of invited commentaries and discussions from the floor, bring the ideas more fully into play. The four aspects, which drew on the talents of lawyers, political scientists, and economists, were: competing concepts of federalism, economic problems peculiar to our federal state, legal and political attitudes towards the BNA Act, and institutional problems of a revision of the Act.

The arrangement of the book follows roughly the arrangement of the sessions at Charlottetown. Section I examines, from two different points of view, the main notions that have been competing for predominance in Canada, as to what federalism is or should be. Professor Mallory sorts out five such notions, shows how they have been and are related to the changing demands made on the political system by Canadian society generally and Quebec society in particular, and argues that our federal constitution stands in need of some revisions if the present social demands are to be adequately met. Professor Trudeau opens with an analysis of the basic relation between state and nation in the modern world, shows how the modern nation-state uses the emotional appeal of nationalism to preserve the identity of the state, and points out that in federal states this use of nationalism is both especially needed and especially apt to be self-defeating. But he holds out some hope that politicians in Canada will see the auto-destructiveness of nationalism, and will prefer pragmatic reason as the more assured road to success. Thus, it might be said that of the two main papers in Section I the first shows the breadth of the Canadian political problem and the second the depth. Principal Corry's commentary indicates the common ground in the two papers, states the (rather few) points on which he dissents from each, and concludes with a plea for not treating economists as statesmen.

Section II introduces the economists, who make it clear that they do not wish to be treated as statesmen but prefer to stay within the limits Principal Corry would assign to them, "clarifying analysis, and ingenuity." Professor Parizeau, distinguishing between the kinds of policies that are needed for economic stabilization and for economic growth, treats separately the problems that have arisen, in each of these respects, from the fact of the post-war shift in economic and budgetary weight from the federal to the provincial governments. The federal government has been mainly concerned with *stabilization* policies, which are rendered precarious by the growing economic weight of the provinces. The provinces have taken the initiative about *growth*, and the problems of uneven growth, and their actions have probably forestalled any grand federal design of growth. Professor Parizeau concludes that there is no way of dealing with these problems except by continuous negotiation between governments, and that a full-dress revision of the constitution would hinder rather than help the rational solution of the urgent economic problems.

Professor Hood emphasizes problems of economic growth and pleads for a mean between two criteria of growth, one being aggregate growth in the country as a whole, the other being equal welfare per head in each region. He then reviews the development of federal-provincial fiscal and financial relations, especially since the war, with special notice of the implications of the Canada Pension Plan, and examines the problems that lie ahead, with some warning of the inflationary potential of the shift of investment funds from the private to the public sector of the economy. After allowing the economists to open Section II, the balance was redressed, as one might expect in a joint project of the Law Teachers and Political Science Associations, by having two lawyers as well as one economist make comments on the two main economists' papers. Professor La Forest puts in a strong claim for regional equality. Professor Lalonde pleads for an end to the balkanization of economic policies, in which he sees the welfare of the individual citizen being lost to sight beneath the power struggle between provincial and federal politicians. Professor Gordon takes sharp exception to the assumption he finds in Professor Hood's paper, that the investment of capital by governments is less wise or efficient than private investment, and to Professor Parizeau's assumption that the interventionist policies of the Quebec government are necessarily more to the left than Ottawa policies.

In Sections III and IV the lawyers have full sway, but they speak in terms intelligible to laymen. In Section III, Dean Lederman concentrates on the ways the BNA Act has been interpreted by the courts, bringing out the complexities and the hopeful flexibility of what is known as the "aspect theory." He sees no need for a change in the present constitution of the Supreme Court of Canada, although he would not object to a constitutional entrenchment of its independence. Professor Beetz points to the paradoxical character of the BNA Act: it requires a broad liberal interpretation, yet it is drawn up in a style which calls for narrow literal interpretation. He draws attention also to the change from the traditional Québécois fear of the state, to their appreciation that they could use the powers of their own state for their own ends. Against this he puts a warning that, in spite of the trend of constitutional interpretation which favoured the provinces for so long, the general tendency in federal states for the central government to get more and more power is not at all inhibited by anything in Canadian law or constitutional interpretation. Co-operative federalism appears to him as another form of integration of powers in federal hands, and he doubts that Quebec will stay in the federation if nothing better is offered to it.

Section IV pursues the question whether a substantial revision of the constitution is now required, and what kind of revision would be feasible. Professor Morin argues that a fundamental revision *is* necessary, and makes some striking claims as to what would be feasible. He believes that the best way to restore a Canadian federal equilibrium is by giving a special constitutional status to Quebec, and he suggests that this would best be guaranteed by (among other things) a new role for the Senate and a change in the structure of the Supreme Court. Professor McWhinney, by contrast, suggests that the informal methods of revision of the constitution that have been effective so far—judicial ingenuity, and executive and administrative action—can suffice in the future, and that there is a positive advantage in relying on them: they avoid the direct political confrontation between Quebec and the rest of Canada which, with the present hostility in English Canada towards Quebec, might be disastrous to the continuance of Canada. Of the three commentators on these papers, Dean Azard opens with an emphasis on the role of the jurist as initiator of legal change, Dean Mackay points out that English-Canada is not as monolithic as Professor Morin had implied, and Dean Cohen sets out a fortright statement of his own and Professor Morin's prejudices, which leads him to a sharp rejection of most of Professor Morin's position.

In all these papers and commentaries there is no consensus, nor was there expected to be one. Nor is there a French consensus and an English consensus. What there is, which is more important, is a series of statements of essentials, statements which reveal what some of the most perceptive, most informed, and in some cases most committed, scholarly analysts hold to be the essentials of the Canadian problem.

The formulation and publication of these views is, we believe, a significant step towards a rational and peaceful solution of the problem.

The two days of meetings concluded with a dinner for the members of the ACLT and CPSA, presided over jointly by the presidents of the two associations, at which the after-dinner speaker was the distinguished former Dean of the Faculty of Law of McGill University, Frank R. Scott, also a member of the Royal Commission on Bilingualism and Biculturalism. We publish the text of his speech as a fitting, if light-hearted, coda to the proceedings. The problems of Canadian federation are serious, but they are not yet, we may hope, beyond the possibility of solution by such rational efforts as those of the Royal Commission whose work is so appealingly portrayed in Dean Scott's knowledgable and not so frivolous address.

The Association of Canadian Law Teachers and the Canadian Political Science Association are grateful to the Canada Council for a grant which has enabled these papers to be published, and to the Premiers of New Brunswick, Nova Scotia, and Quebec for grants for the simultaneous translation service which contributed greatly to the efficiency of the meetings.

PAUL-A. CRÉPEAU, Président sortant
Association canadienne des professeurs de droit

C. B. MACPHERSON, Past President
Canadian Political Science Association

Contents / Table des matières

CONTRIBUTORS / COLLABORATEURS

J. R. MALLORY — *Professor of Political Science and Chairman of the Department of Economics and Political Science, McGill University*

PIERRE E. TRUDEAU — *Professeur agrégé à la Faculté de droit de l'Université de Montréal*

J. A. CORRY — *Principal of Queen's University*

RAY FORRESTER — *Dean of the Cornell Law School, Ithaca, N.Y.*

JACQUES PARIZEAU — *Professeur à l'Ecole des Hautes Etudes commerciales de Montréal*

WM. C. HOOD — *Professor of Economics, University of Toronto*

G. V. LA FOREST — *Professor of Law, University of New Brunswick*

M. LALONDE — *Membre du Comité de direction de l'Institut de recherches en droit public de l'Université de Montréal*

SCOTT GORDON — *Professor and Chairman of the Department of Economics, Carleton University*

W. R. LEDERMAN — *Dean of the Faculty of Law, Queen's University*

JEAN BEETZ — *Professeur de droit constitutionnel à la Faculté de droit de l'Université de Montréal*

JACQUES-YVAN MORIN — *Professeur de droit international public à la Faculté de droit de l'Université de Montréal*

EDWARD MCWHINNEY — *Professor of Law, University of Toronto*

P. AZARD — *Doyen de la Faculté de droit de l'Université d'Ottawa*

W. A. MACKAY — *Dean of the Faculty of Law, Dalhousie University*

MAXWELL COHEN — *Dean of the Faculty of Law, McGill University*

F. R. Scott   *Former Dean of the Faculty of Law, McGill University*

P.-A. Crepeau   *Associate Professor à la Faculté de droit de l'Université McGill*

C. B. Macpherson   *Professor of Political Science, University of Toronto*

CONCEPTS OF FEDERALISM

CONCEPTIONS DU FEDERALISME

The Five Faces of Federalism

Canadian federalism is different things at different times. It is also different things to different people. This is not the result of widespread error but of simple fact, for political institutions which accommodate diversity will reflect the dimensions which are vital to the actors who work them.

In the past century it is possible to see five different forms of Canadian federalism which may be described roughly as follows: the quasi-federalism (to use Dr. Wheare's description) which was most marked in the Macdonald era; federalism of the classic type characterized by the co-ordinate and autonomous relationship of the central and regional organs; emergency federalism, most obviously in being during the periods of extreme centralization in wartime; the co-operative federalism which reached its zenith in the period since 1945; and the "double-image" federalism which includes both the straightforward central-regional relationship between the central and provincial organs and a special relationship between French and English which to some extent transcends the other. While these various forms can be made to fit approximately into different historical periods, they overlap one another and do not in fact conform to a clear stage-by-stage development.

QUASI-FEDERALISM

In 1867, the new Dominion of Canada did not begin to operate as a full-blown federal structure. There were several obvious reasons for this. Canadians are always sensitive to the influence of the United States, and the American federal system was at that time in some disarray. The peril of state's rights and secession was manifest, and there were not a few of the Fathers of Confederation who noted with concern that state's rights afforded an opportunity for such democratic excesses as the spoilation of the vested rights of property. The new federal government in the first blush of its power in Ottawa was both a national coalition and a concentration of political talent which was bound to leave little political weight in the provinces. Furthermore, the opening of the West led to the creation or admission of new provinces whose early relationship with Ottawa was a colonial one.[1]

The influence of the forms of government on political action should never be underestimated. The "colonial" relationship with the provinces was a natural one—much more natural than the "co-ordinate and autonomous" relationship more appropriate to a federal system. Macdonald and his ministers had grown up politically in a system in which the governor still played a role as an imperial presence difficult to appreciate today. Most of them had been in politics long enough to remember when the governor still actively participated in policy discussion with his council, and before the cabinet had completely split off from the formal executive. For a wide range of matters that were beyond the reach of local self-government or were ones in which there was an imperial interest, they were accustomed to the idea that the governor possessed power as well as influence. In the British North America Act, the lieutenant-governor was just as much an agent of the federal government as the governor general was an agent of the British government.

It therefore seems more appropriate to think of the dominion-provincial relationship at that time as similar to the relationship of the imperial government with a colony enjoying limited self-government. This was most obviously true in provinces like Manitoba and British Columbia where the weakness of political parties and the lack of political and administrative experience meant that the provincial governments were in a state of tutelage. The difference between these provinces and the older provinces in this matter was a difference of degree.

Dr. Wheare, in discussing the nature of Canadian federalism, attaches some importance to the ambivalent role of the lieutenant-governor and concludes that the Canadian constitution is in form only quasi-federal.[2] During the first couple of decades after Confederation, when the federal government frequently resorted to disallowance and reservation to curb the growth of provincial powers of self-government, "quasi-federal" understates the case. The relationship was much more like that of mother-country and colony, and the institutions of control were essentially those

[1]An excellent discussion of the theme that the relationship was essentially colonial is found in V. C. Fowke's *Canadian Agricultural Policy* (Toronto, 1947).
[2]K. C. Wheare, *Federal Government* (3rd ed., London, 1953), pp. 19–21.

of colonial rule. But there was the inescapable fact that the constitution was indeed federal, and the federal distribution of power nourished the strength of the provinces as the strains brought about by race, religion, economic exploitation, and the sheer impossibility of running such a disparate country further diffused power in the system.

Nevertheless, this quasi-imperial relationship was a long time dying. The long retention by the federal government of administrative control over the natural resources of the western provinces emphasized their colonial status. The rise of agrarian populism through the progressive movement was a revolt against the exploitation of the west by the banks, the railroads, and the tariff-protected industries of the east. When populism went too far, as it did under William Aberhart's Social Credit administration in Alberta, it was curbed by the old imperial remedies of reservation and disallowance.

CLASSICAL FEDERALISM

A federal constitution is in essence a division of jurisdiction between equally autonomous bodies. But no constitution can express, in precise detail, a distribution of authority so exact that no doubts can arise about which of the two legislative structures, central and regional, is within its powers in a particular regulatory statute. Some agency, external to both legislatures, must hold the balance between them. It was natural in Canada, as it was in the United States, that this role should be assumed by the courts, for both countries are part of a constitutional tradition that insulates the judicial process from the politics of the day. Furthermore, disputes of this kind—about the powers of constituted authorities —are justiciable.

This is not the place to consider this large and intricate subject, but only to make some general observations on its effect on the system and the boundaries within which it operates. There is one important difference between the role of the Supreme Court of the United States and the role of the Judicial Committee of the Privy Council, and that is in their approach to the problem of adjudication. Following the bold initiative of Chief Justice Marshall, the Supreme Court has approached its role in a spirit of constructive statecraft. "We must never forget," said Marshall in *McCulloch* v. *Maryland*, "that it is a constitution we are expounding."[3] Accordingly the Court has not hesitated to reverse itself in the light of changed circumstances, and to play the major role

[3]Wheat. 316, at p. 407 (1819).

in adapting the constitution to the changing needs of succeeding generations.

A Canadian court might well have followed the same path. Much of the law is experience, and Canadian judges would no doubt have been more sensitive to the strains and the changing patterns of Canadian life than the Privy Council.[4] To the remoteness of the Privy Council and its reluctance to engage in judicial statecraft was added a further difficulty —the inability of English judges to understand the basic fact about federal constitutions, i.e., that a distribution of power written into the constitution is fixed and almost unalterable. In the United Kingdom it was a perfectly proper exercise of judicial self-restraint to take the view that, if the purpose of Parliament was frustrated by lack of foresight in drafting so that the courts found a section to be meaningless, it was not the business of the courts to interpose themselves and to say, "This is what Parliament meant to accomplish by this act, and we shall interpret it accordingly," but rather to interpret the words narrowly and as they found them. If this is not what Parliament wanted, then it has the right to amend the act itself. This is all very well in a unitary state, but in a federal system, a construction of the constitution which is too narrow, or wrong-headed, may do great harm, since constitutional amendment is extremely difficult.

There is no general agreement about the general effect of the interpretation of the Canadian constitution by the Judicial Committee of the Privy Council. It has been argued that the very wide meaning given to property and civil rights, together with the emasculation of the federal power of trade and commerce and the relegation of the "peace, order and good government" concept to a wartime emergency power, was clearly contrary to the intention of the Fathers of Confederation to create a strong central authority and to confine the provinces to local matters.[5] Whether this was the result of ignorance or high imperial policy is no longer of much importance. It is more than likely that the narrow construction placed on federal powers was the only reaction which could have been expected from common law judges in a period

[4]This has often been argued, but never more persuasively than by Alexander Smith in *The Commerce Power in Canada and the United States* (Toronto, 1963) where by reference to early cases he shows the Canadian courts appealing to history and experience in a way which would horrify "black-letter" lawyers.
[5]Thus Sir John A. Macdonald said, "The primary error at the formation of their constitution was that each state reserved to itself all sovereign rights, save the small portion delegated. We must reverse this process by strengthening the General Government and conferring on the Provincial bodies only such powers as may be required for local purposes." Sir Joseph Pope, ed., *Confederation Documents* (Toronto, 1895) p. 14, n. 4.

when the courts, in the United States as well as the United Kingdom, were responding sympathetically to the litigious pressure of powerful economic interests intent on resisting the growing role of the state in limiting economic liberty.[6] In any event, by the inter-war period the courts by using a "watertight compartment" theory of jurisdiction, had succeeded in interdicting effective action by the federal authorities to deal with the economic problems of the depression.

Whatever its consequences, what had evolved was federalism of the classic type, if I may borrow Principal Corry's phraseology, in which power is allocated to the central and provincial authorities so that each enjoys an exclusive jurisdiction, with disputes about the margins of power settled finally by the courts. This has certain advantages. It entrenches provincial rights, and at the same time it confines the provinces to their sphere. Disputes are settled by the impartial arbitration of the courts, as guardians of the constitution. It has its disadvantages. Since federal constitutions are notoriously hard to amend, the only dynamic element is the extent to which the courts are able to adjust the meaning of the constitution to face the facts of social change. That is what Dicey meant when he said that federations substitute litigation for legislation. But the courts are not the first to perceive the outlines of social change. And while the Supreme Court of the United States has shown considerable capacity to "follow the election returns," the Judicial Committee of the Privy Council was so deficient in both sense and sensibility that the allocation of power in the constitution, by the end of the 1930's, had achieved a remarkable incongruity between the resources, capacities, and responsibilities of the federal and provincial governments.

EMERGENCY FEDERALISM

But the Canadian constitution in one respect was totally lacking in the rigidity of its federal arrangements. This had not been by design, for there is nothing in either the Confederation Debates or the BNA Act itself which addresses itself to the distribution of power in an emergency. It was the courts themselves which made this dangerous opening in the system. Nobody before 1914 foresaw the effect of modern war on constitutional government or on the settled Victorian notions of propriety about the role of government in economic affairs. But when war came and Parliament abdicated to the executive the vast powers to make

---

[6]Cf. J. R. Mallory, *Social Credit and the Federal Power in Canada* (Toronto, 1954), *passim*.

regulations for the peace, order, and good government of Canada, the federal government assumed a wide range of powers over matters of civil rights and property which in peacetime belonged to the sacrosanct powers of the provinces. And the courts gave their blessing to the proposition that the federal distribution of power was a peacetime luxury which must be forgone in wartime. Building on a dictum of Lord Watson in the *Local Prohibition Case*, they found that wartime was a situation which transcended the terms of sections 91 and 92 altogether and one which, in effect, made Canada a unitary state for the duration.

When the First World War was over the courts hurriedly began to erect a fence around this dangerous doctrine, to the exasperation of many Canadian lawyers during the depression years, and they stubbornly refused to seek a more flexible formula which would allow the central authorities power to deal with lesser emergencies. For the trouble with the emergency doctrine was that it went too far. It seemed to be all or nothing. And it went so far that it is not difficult to sense their reluctance to apply it. This is no doubt why Lord Haldane was led into the entertaining speculation in the *Snider Case* that the Judicial Committee had upheld federal jurisdiction in *Russell* v. *The Queen* only on the assumption that the country was confronted by such an epidemic of intemperance as to constitute a national disaster.

The emergency doctrine, in the form in which Lord Haldane left it, is one that we can well do without. For events have shown that it was of little value in conferring necessary jurisdiction on Parliament except in wartime and in the short period necessary to wind up wartime controls after the end of hostilities. From this difficulty we were extricated by the unexpected wisdom of Lord Simon who demonstrated, in the *Canada Temperance Federation Case*, that "emergency" is not just a rather frightening source of absolute federal power in wartime, but rather an aspect of things. Categories of the constitution are not absolutes which are mutually exclusive, as between the federal and provincial authorities. Each in its own way, and for its own purposes, may legislate about things which properly concern it. The facts have always been this way, but they have sometimes been neglected. For example, the courts early rejected the idea (in *Bank of Toronto* v. *Lambe*) that a province could not tax a bank just because it was a bank and therefore under federal jurisdiction.

In any event, the elaborate reasoning of the emergency doctrine may have been unnecessary since Parliament has exclusive power to legislate for defence, and it is obvious today that this is a concept that goes far beyond military arrangements for defence against an enemy. It is concerned with a very wide range of economic activity and, in these days of subversion on a massive scale, with internal order as well. It is note-worthy that the Essential Materials (Defence) Act (1950–51) was founded on a broad view of the defence power, and so was its successor, the Defence Production Act of 1951. In the federal constitutions of Australia and the United States the defence power has turned out to be the most powerful centripetal force in the constitution.[7]

One of the most striking developments of the past quarter of a century has been the decline in the role of the courts as arbiters of the balance of the federal constitution. "The courts are retiring, or being retired, from their posts as the supervisors of the balance," as Principal Corry notes in a perceptive analysis of modern Canadian federalism.[8] He attributes this change to an alteration in the interests and attitude of the business élites. The central role of the courts in the half-century before was brought about, as I have argued elsewhere,[9] by the persistent resistance of the business community to regulation by the state. Great aggregations of economic power have a strong vested interest in stability; they have come to accept the primacy of the federal government in regulating their affairs, and they find it better to exert influence at the summit of the political system rather than to fight every extension of state power in the courts. Since they cannot beat the welfare state, they have decided to join it.

CO-OPERATIVE FEDERALISM

At the same time there has been, as a result of a spectacular refinement of the techniques of economic and fiscal policy since the war, a quiet revolution in the structure of Canadian federalism. A whole new set of institutional arrangements has grown up under the name of "co-operative federalism." In spite of the separate and co-ordinate division between the authority of the provinces and the central government enun-ciated in the law of the constitution, the demands of modern government and the immense financial resources of the central authority have forced an incestuous relationship in which administrative co-operation has become an effective device for control and initiative from the centre. This system is the only effective answer to the size and complexity of modern economic institutions and everyone now has such a strong vested interest in this system that no one, Dr. Corry argues, can afford to rock the boat.

The essence of co-operative federalism in Canada is this: while the

[7]Cf. Bora Laskin, *Canadian Constitutional Law* (2nd ed., Toronto, 1960), pp. 242–3.

[8]J. A. Corry, "Constitutional Trends and Federalism," in Paul Fox ed., *Politics: Canada* (Toronto: 1963), p. 36.

[9]*Social Credit and the Federal Power in Canada.*

central and regional legislatures nominally retain their separate jurisdictions over different aspects of the same subject, there is close contact
and discussion between ministers and civil servants of both levels of
government so that even changes in legislation are the result of joint
decisions. Since 1945, says Professor Smiley, the most obvious characteristic of Canadian federalism has been "a process of continuous and
piecemeal adjustment between the two levels of government, which is
still going on. To an overwhelming degree, these adjustments have come
about through interaction between federal and provincial executives."[10]
There are three principal areas of co-ordination. The first is through
continuous consultation of officials on joint programs. In these consultations there appears to be a surprising degree of harmony, partly, no
doubt because there is a broad consensus among the economists about
the goals of economic policy and partly because all officials are inclined
to see problems in a practical and pragmatic way. The second area of
co-operation is through the delegation by Parliament of regulatory functions to provincial agencies, a technique which gets around the bar
against delegation of legislative authority from one level of government
to another. The third "device of flexibility" is through federal spending
on matters which fall within provincial and/or municipal jurisdiction.

The advantages of these arrangements are apparent. The "artificial"
division of powers in the constitution, conceived before the dawn of
the welfare state, can be ignored in achieving progress and uniformity
comparable to that normally realizable only in a unitary state. The
higher administrative skills and deeper purse of the federal government
result in better schemes. Finally, the obstruction to geographical mobility
imposed by tying the citizen—like a medieval serf—to the area of land
from which his pension, his hospitalization, and his other welfare benefits
come, is removed.

The benefits of co-operative federalism are not achieved without
serious costs. The joint-cost schemes involve the federal government in
very heavy fixed commitments, though, since the Dominion-Provincial
Conference at Quebec in April 1964, discussions have begun for ultimate federal withdrawal from some of them. A further disadvantage is
that the financial and constitutional context of the arrangements has
made it impossible to take into account differing provincial fiscal
capacity so that, while rich provinces can participate readily, the poorer

[10]D. V. Smiley, "The Rowell-Sirois Report, Provincial Autonomy, and Post-
War Federalism," *Canadian Journal of Economics and Political Science,* vol.
XXVIII, no. 1, p. 54.

provinces must divert a substantial share of their resources to providing their share of the cost. Lastly, the main drift of these programs has been in the direction of health and welfare services.

The result has been seriously to limit provincial autonomy. Provincial priorities are distorted by the inability of a province to forgo, for political reasons, a program which may inhibit financing its other obligations. The result has been to starve areas of provincial jurisdiction in which the federal government is not, for various reasons, interested. While a vast amount of time is spent in intergovernmental consultation, it nevertheless remains true that provinces find long-term budgeting virtually impossible, because they cannot foresee where the lightning of federal generosity will strike next.

A reaction against these cosy arrangements is now in train. Significantly it is led by Quebec, but Quebec is not alone in seeking to reverse the trend to centralize all economic and social policy in Ottawa. It is not improbable that the practical advantages of centralization, which English-speaking Canadians would probably accept, would have led—as it had done in the United States and Australia—to the growing obsolescence of federalism. But Canada is not the same kind of federal state as the United States or Australia, where the growing homogeneity of the population is likely to lead inevitably to national integration. The difference is what is now usually described as the French-Canadian fact.

DOUBLE-IMAGE FEDERALISM

The survival of French Canada as a fact has depended more on a sustaining national myth and on political power than it has on constitutional guarantees. For the Canadian constitution does not, except to a very limited extent, support the claims which French Canadians regard as necessary to their survival as a distinct group. In the matter of their rights in the Manitoba school question, or in their claim to retain French as a language of instruction in Ontario separate schools, they were either over-ridden by an unsympathetic majority or told by the courts that minority educational rights in the constitution were essentially questions of religion and not of language.

Indeed, one of the most striking things about French-Canadian rights and aspirations in the constitution is that the courts have played little or no role in protecting them. This is one of the striking differences between the American and Canadian constitutions. Where the American constitution extends its guarantees across the whole range of the social order, so that it is the Supreme Court which is presiding over the orderly assimilation of Negroes to full equality as citizens, the Canadian constitution provides no such protection. It confines itself essentially to the distribution of power between two levels of sovereign legislatures, and has little to say on any other rights than the rights of legislatures. In this respect it is indeed a constitution "similar in Principle to that of the United Kingdom." As de Tocqueville said of the British constitution, "elle n'existe point."

It is for this eminently practical reason that French Canadians have adopted as a national strategy the building up and guarding of the security of their fortress-province. The constitution has made such a strategy unavoidable, and the only possible defence against the aggressive nationalism of the dominant English-speaking majority. For even the most liberal of English-Canadians have seldom accepted the "French fact" as more than a transitory source of trouble and discomfort.

There has been among English-speaking Canadians an element of deep-seated Protestant suspicion of the Roman Catholic Church, a feeling that the French tongue is an anomaly in an English-speaking continent, a feeling that the French are both backward and reactionary and therefore an enemy to the forces of progress, and a touch of the North American radical belief that a good state could be built in the New World only by destroying the cultural roots of "foreigners" who must be assimilated in order to build a new Canada.

Against this persistent pressure the French-Canadian reaction was to husband their political strength, to limit as far as possible the impact of the twentieth century on the *habitant* whose backwardness and ignorance —it was thought—would be a solid political barrier against the secular and integrating forces of urban industrial society. Thus Duplessis pursued a policy of immobilism, staying aloof from federally sponsored welfare programs, leaving the educational system in a state of inanation on the grounds that it was bound to develop the kind of social leadership which would destroy him, and harrying those organizations, such as the trade unions, that seemed to be enemies of the traditional centres of community authority.

And yet in the end he could not stem the tide. At his death an irreversible political change began. The most striking change is the alteration in the pattern of power relations in the French-Canadian community. New élite groups of managers and technicians are challenging the traditional leaders. The intellectual of an earlier generation could accept the romantic myth of the mystical virtue of subsistence agriculture as the source of the political and moral strength of French

Canada. The intellectual of today has no patience with a dream of bucolic *survivance*. The French-Canadian community has developed a new set of expectations from government, and looks to the power of the state to satisfy their new wants and to bring the economic development which will enlarge opportunities for all. For them, these things must be done by their own French-Canadian state of Quebec, and not by Ottawa. For this there are two reasons: the new élites wish to share in the management of the new society, and—as they say—Quebec has much ground to make up in order to pull level with the rest of Canada.

It is these new forces which have created the latest crisis in Canadian federalism. The growing centralization of the past fifty years created no great problems in Quebec as long as the province was seeking to contract out of the twentieth century. But with the French-Canadian community determined to use to the full the resources of the provincial government to achieve a national revival a whole range of problems has emerged in Canadian federalism which will require substantial readjustments in the system. The mechanics of this readjustment will not be easy, and the issues at stake are very large indeed.

The federal government must not lightly weaken its fiscal and monetary powers, for it alone has the capacity and the constitutional right to deal with problems of major economic policy—foreign trade, stability, economic growth. It alone can prevent us becoming, as Mr. Pearson said, "a country of developed and underdeveloped areas—Cadillac areas and cart areas."[11] So it must confront the provinces by a clear-headed and hard-headed negotiations, but with a sympathetic and imaginative grasp of the difficulties which confront them. This is, in the last analysis, not a political problem at all, but one that can be solved by the ingenuity and sophistication of the economists.

There must be, at the same time, some recognition that Quebec is not a province like the others. Section 94 of the BNA Act already does so by providing for uniformity of laws relating to property and civil rights in all provinces except Quebec—a tacit recognition that the different needs of Quebec must in any event be accomplished within a conceptually different legal system. This is the contracting-out formula in reverse and should give some comfort to those who regard any special treatment of Quebec as both immoral and unconstitutional. For Quebec must always rate somewhat special treatment from the facts of countervailing power.

However, one of the lessons of constitutional government in its federal form is that the protection of interests by political means is a source

[11]Canada, *House of Commons Debates* (unrevised) April 14, 1964, p. 2142.

of instability and uneasiness. The atmosphere is better if these basic interests become constitutional rights, so that conflicts about them become justiciable. It is difficult in these days not to admire the broad sweep of the American constitution which extends its protection not only to states but also to people. We should consider seriously a similar extension of our own constitution to include rights—including individual rights—to language and within reason to access to the courts and other community services in one's mother tongue whether it be French or English.

This will perhaps require a reconsideration of our present judicial structure to ensure adequate machinery for a constitution which protects not only the rights of government organs but also the rights of individuals and of minorities. It may be that a constitutional court, more fully representative than the present Supreme Court, should be created. A good case on practical grounds can also be made for limiting appeals in civil law questions, unless they raise important questions of public and constitutional law, from the courts of Quebec. Common lawyers cannot get their minds around the concepts of the civil law and, since the function of a court of appeal is to clarify the law, it seems obvious that where possible civil law should be dealt with by civilians.[12]

There is a major danger in the present situation, which is the calculated risk inherent in the public discussion of anything. French Canadians, excluded for so long from the power élite except at the price of becoming wholly English-speaking and operating in a wholly English-speaking environment, tend to attach enormous importance to symbols. The extent to which the debate about the refusal of Trans-Canada Air Lines [Air Canada] to adopt the Caravelle dominated Quebec politics, is a case in point. It is perhaps not surprising that Hon. René Lévesque got into the act, but he was not alone. Just as ministers of the Crown and newspaper editors adopt extreme positions about status symbols, those outside the fringes of power will show their frustration by reacting more violently.

Meanwhile, as they read in their newspapers of the latest outrageous speech or act from Quebec, English-speaking Canadians will become increasingly impatient and will in turn say things which moderate men will later regret. And as a consequence the fund of goodwill towards French Canada, founded on lack of interest and ignorance, will slowly

---

[12]Anyone who doubts this should contemplate the effect of a century of House of Lords decisions on modern Scots law. Whatever the gains in apparent uniformity with English law they were more than offset by a blurring of concepts and a misunderstanding of the system.

be dissipated and the climate for negotiation slowly congeal. There is a too easy assumption about that what is needed to solve outstanding misunderstandings is a "dialogue." These exchanges are not a dialogue. Dialogue there must be. But first there should be some agreement on the subject matter.

It needs to be said that the crisis is real. One cannot turn one's back on two centuries of history. French Canadians have survived as a distinctive group by a series of overt and tacit acts. Canada is in fact a country based on the co-existence of these two cultures, and is the better for it. There has been a delayed revolution within the social structure of French Canada, and this social revolution has political implications. There will have to be some readjustment of the machinery of the constitution. We may even have to modify some of our out-of-date symbolism because symbolic gestures are important as an earnest of good faith. Just because the position of French Canada within confederation has never been clearly defined it is bound to be a source of unease in a group which is a permanent minority. There has been a comfortable and, on the whole, mutually satisfactory liaison between French and English for all these years, and we should not complain too much if one partner would now prefer more formal marriage lines.

Federalism, of all the forms of government, is the most difficult to work. The fact that we have been able to work it at all for nearly a century should be a matter of pride, and sustain our belief that it will continue to work. The fact that the Canadian federal system has materialized in so many forms is proof of its essential vitality, but the survival of any system depends on a consensus that it is worth while and worth paying for.

Federalism, Nationalism, and Reason*

PIERRE E. TRUDEAU

I. *STATE AND NATION*

The concept of federalism with which I will deal in this paper is that of a particular system of government applicable within a sovereign state; it flows from my understanding of state and nation. Hence I find it necessary to discuss these two notions in part one of this paper, but I need only do so from the point of view of territory and population. Essentially, the question to which I would seek an answer is: what section of the world's population occupying what segment of the world's surface should fall under the authority of a given state?

Until the middle of the eighteenth century, the answer was largely arrived at without regard to the people themselves. Of course in much earlier times, population pressures guided by accidents of geography and climate had determined the course of the migrations which were to spill across the earth's surface. But by the end of the Middle Ages, such migrations had run their course in most of Europe. The existence of certain peoples inhabiting certain land areas, speaking certain languages or dialects, and practising certain customs, was generally taken as data—*choses données*—by the European states which arose to establish their authority over them.

It was not the population who decided by what states they would be governed; it was the states which, by wars (but not "people's wars"), by alliances, by dynastic arrangements, by marriages, by inheritance, and by chance, determined the area of territory over which they would

*I wish to thank my friends Albert Breton, Fernand Cadieux, Pierre Carignan, Eugene Forsey and James Mallory who read the manuscript and helped me clarify several ideas. Since the paper was read, on June 11, 1964, other friends have been very helpful with their comments; I dare not acknowledge them by name until I have had time to work their suggestions into some further edition of this paper.

govern. And for that reason they could be called territorial states. Except in the particular case of newly discovered lands, the population came with the territory; and except in the unusual case of deportations, very little was to be done about it.

Political philosophers, asking questions about the authority of the state, did not inquire why a certain population fell within the territorial jurisdiction of a certain state rather than of another; for the philosophers, too, territory and population were just data; their philosophies were mainly concerned with discovering the foundations of authority over a *given* territory and the sources of obedience of a *given* population.

In other words, the purpose of Locke and Rousseau, not unlike that of the medieval philosophers and of the ancient Stoics, was to explain the origins and justify the existence of political authority *per se*; the theories of contract which they derived from natural law or reason were meant to ensure that within a given state bad governments could readily be replaced by good ones, but not that one territorial state could be superseded by another.

Such then was the significance of social contract and popular sovereignty in the minds of the men who made the Glorious Revolution, and such it was in the minds of those who prepared the events of 1776 in America and 1789 in France. As things went however, the two latter "events" turned out to be momentous revolutions, and the ideas which had been put into them emerged with an immensely enhanced significance.

In America, it became necessary for the people not merely to replace a poor government by a better one, but to switch their allegiance from one territorial state to another, and in their own words, to

declare, that these United Colonies, are, and of right ought to be, free and independent states; that they are absolved from all allegiance to the British crown, and that all political connection, between them and the state of Great Britain, is and ought to be totally dissolved; and that, as free and independent states, they have full power to levy war, conclude peace, contract alliances, establish commerce, and to do all other acts and things which independent states may of right do.

Here then was a theory of government by consent which took on a radically new meaning. Since sovereignty belonged to the people, it appeared to follow that any given body of people could at will transfer their allegiance from one existing state to another, or indeed to a completely new state of their own creation. In other words, the consent of the population was required not merely for a social contract, which was to be the foundation of civil society, or for a choice of responsible rulers, which was the essence of self-government; consent was also required for adherence to one territorial state rather than to another, which was the beginning of national self-determination.

Why the theory of consent underwent such a transformation at this particular time is no doubt a matter for historical and philosophical conjecture. Perhaps the prerequisites had never been brought together before: a population (1) whose political traditions were sufficiently advanced to include the ideology of consent, (2) subject to a modern unitary state the centre of which was very remote, and (3) inhabiting a territory which was reasonably self-contained.

Be that as it may, it appears to be at this juncture in history that the word "nation" became charged with a new potential. In the past, the *word* had meant many things, from Machiavelli's "ghibelline nation" to Montesquieu's "pietistic nation"; its broadest meaning seems to have been reached by the *Encyclopédistes* who understood thereby "une quantité considérable de peuple, qui habite une certaine étendue de pays, renfermeé dans de certaines limites, et qui obéit au même gouvernement." The *idea* of nation also had roots which plunged deep in history[1]; and a sentiment akin to nationalism had sometimes inspired political action, as when French rulers reacted against Italian popes. But the idea, like the word, only took on its modern meaning during the last quarter of the eighteenth century.

Consequently, it might be said that in the past the (territorial) state had defined its territorial limits which had defined the people or nation living within. But henceforth it was to be the people who first defined themselves as a nation, who then declared which territory belonged to them as of right, and who finally proceeded to give their allegiance to a state of their own choosing or invention which would exercise authority over that nation and that territory. Hence, the expression nation-state. As I see it, the important transition was from the *territorial state* to the *nation-state*. But once the latter was born, the idea of the *national state* was bound to follow, it being little more than a nation-state with an ethnic flavour added. With it the idea of self-determination became the principle of nationalities.

Self-determination did not necessarily proceed from or lead to self-government. Whereas self-government was based on reason and proposed to introduce liberal forms of government into existing states, self-determination was based on will and proposed to challenge the legitimacy and the very existence of the territorial states.

[1]For a history of the use and meaning of the term, see Elie Kedourie, *Nationalism* (New York, 1960), and Hans Kohn, *The Idea of Nationalism* (New York, 1944).

Self-determination, or the principle of nationalities (I am talking of the doctrine, for the expressions became current only later) was bound to dissolve whatever order and balance existed in the society of states prevailing towards the end of the eighteenth century. But no matter; for it was surmised that a new order would arise, free from wars and inequities. As each of the peoples of the world became conscious of its identity as a collectivity bound together by natural affinities, it would define itself as a nation and govern itself as a state. An international order of nation-states, since it would be founded on the free will of free people, would necessarily be more lasting and just than one which rested on a hodge-podge of despotic empires, dynastic kingdoms, and aristocratic republics. In May 1790, the Constituent Assembly had proclaimed: "La nation française renonce à entreprendre aucune guerre dans un but de conquête et n'emploiera jamais de forces contre la liberté d'aucun peuple."

Unfortunately, things did not work out quite that way. The French Revolution, which had begun as an attempt to replace a bad government by a good one, soon overreached itself by replacing a territorial state by a nation-state, whose territory incidentally was considerably enlarged. In 1789, the *Déclaration des droits de l'homme et du citoyen* had stated: "Le principe de toute souveraineté réside essentiellement dans la Nation. Nul corps, nul individu ne peut exercer d'autorité qui n'en émane expressément." But who was to be included in the nation? Danton having pointed out in 1793 that the frontiers of France were designated by Nature,[2] the French nation willed itself into possession of that part of Europe which spread between the Rhine, the Pyrenees, the Atlantic Ocean and the Alps.

France was indeed fortunate, in that her natural frontiers thus enabled her to correct the disadvantage which might have arisen in Alsace, for example, from a will based on linguistic frontiers. Fortunately for German-speaking peoples, however, Fichte was soon to discover that the natural frontiers were in reality the linguistic ones; thus the German nation could will itself towards its proper size, providing of course that the language principle be sometimes corrected by that of historical possession, in order for instance to include Bohemia. Other nations, such as Poland, enlightened their will by greater reliance on the historical principle, corrected when necessary by the linguistic one. Then finally there were nations who, spurning such frivolous guide-lines as geography, history, and language, were favoured by direct communication with the Holy Ghost; such was the privilege of the United States of

[2]The Abbé Gregoire had spoken of the "Archives de la nature" in 1792. See Kedourie, *Nationalism*, p. 122.

America who saw the annexation of Texas, California, and eventually Canada as—in the words of O'Sullivan—"the fulfillment of our manifest destiny to overspread the continent alloted by Providence for the free development of our yearly multiplying millions."[3]

The political history of Europe and of the Americas in the nineteenth century and that of Asia and Africa in the twentieth are histories of nations labouring, conspiring, blackmailing, warring, revolutionizing and generally willing their way towards statehood. It is, of course, impossible to know whether there has ensued therefrom for humanity more peace and justice than would have been the case if some other principle than self-determination had held sway. In theory, the arrangement of boundaries in such a way that no important national group be included by force in the territorial limits of a state which was mainly the expression of the will of another group, was to be conducive to peaceful international order. In practice, state boundaries continued to be established and maintained largely by the threat of or the use of force. The concept of right in international relations became, if anything, even more a function of might. And the question whether a national minority was "important" enough to be entitled to independence remained unanswerable except in terms of the political and physical power that could be wielded in its favour. Why did Libya become a country in 1951 and not the Saar in 1935, with a population almost as great? Why should Norway be independent and not Brittany? Why Ireland and not Scotland? Why Nicaragua and not Quebec?

As we ask ourselves these questions, it becomes apparent that more than language and culture, more than history and geography, even more than force and power, the foundation of the nation is will.[4] For there is no power without will. The Rocky Mountains are higher than the Pyrenees but they are not a watershed between countries. The Irish Sea and the Straits of Florida are much narrower than the Pacific Ocean between Hawaii and California, yet they are more important factors in determining nationhood. Language or race do not provide, in Switzerland or Brazil, the divisive force they are at present providing in Belgium or the United States.

Looking at the foregoing examples, and at many others, we are bound to conclude that the frontiers of nation-states are in reality nearly as arbitrary as those of the former territorial states. For all their anthropologists, linguists, geographers, and historians, the nations of today cannot justify their frontiers with noticeably more rationality than the kings of

[3]Reading no. 12 in Hans Kohn, *Nationalism* (New York, 1955).
[4]Cf. A. Cobban, *Dictatorship* (New York, 1939), p. 42, and Hans Kohn, *The Idea of Nationalism* (New York, 1944), p. 15.

two centuries ago; a greater reliance on general staffs rather than on princesses' dowries does not necessarily spell a triumph of reason. Consequently a present-day definition of the word nation in its juristic sense would fit quite readily upon the population of the territorial states which existed before the French and American revolutions. A nation (as in the expressions: the French nation, the Swiss nation, the United Nations, the President's speech to the nation) is no more and no less than the entire population of a sovereign state. (Except when otherwise obvious, I shall try to adhere to that juristic sense in the rest of this paper.) Because no country has an absolutely homogeneous population, all the so-called nation-states of today are also territorial states. And the converse is probably also true. The distinction between a nation-state, a multi-national state, and a territorial state may well be valid in reference to historical origins; but it has very little foundation in law or fact today and is mainly indicative of political value judgments.

Of course, the word nation can also be used in a sociological sense, as when we speak of the Scottish nation, or the Jewish nation. As Humpty Dumpty once told Alice, a word means just what one chooses it to mean. It would indeed be helpful if we could make up our minds. Either the juristic sense would be rejected, and the word "people" used instead (the people of the Soviet Union, the people of the United States; but what word would replace "national"? People's? Popular?); in that case "nation" would be restricted to its sociological meaning, which is also closer to its etymological and historical ones. Or the latter sense would be rejected, and words like linguistic, ethnic, or cultural group be used instead. But lawyers and political scientists cannot remake the language to suit their convenience; they will just have to hope that "the context makes it tolerably clear which of the two (senses) we mean."[5]

However, for some people one meaning is meant to flow into the other. The ambiguity is intentional and the user is conveying something which is at the back of his mind—and sometimes not very far back. In such cases the use of the word nation is not only confusing; it is disruptive of political stability. Thus when a tightly knit minority within a state begins to define itself forcefully and consistently as a nation it is triggering a mechanism which will tend to propel it towards full statehood.[6]

That of course is not merely due to the magic of words, but to a

[5]Eugene Forsey, "Canada: Two Nations or One?" *Canadian Journal of Economics and Political Science*; vol. XXVIII, Nov. 1962, p. 488. Mr. Forsey's discussion is as usual thorough and convincing.

[6]Compare Max Weber, *Essays in Sociology* (London, 1948), p. 176: "A nation is a community of sentiment which would adequately manifest itself in a

much more dynamic process which I will now attempt to explain. When the erstwhile territorial state, held together by divine right, tradition, and force, gave way to the nation-state, based on the will of the people, a new glue had to be invented which would bind the nation together on a durable basis. For very few nations—if any—could rely on a cohesiveness based entirely on "natural" identity, and so most of them were faced with a terrible paradox: the principle of national self-determination which had justified their birth, could just as easily justify their death. Nationhood being little more than a state of mind, and every sociologically distinct group within the nation having a contingent right of secession, the will of the people was in constant danger of dividing up—unless it were transformed into a lasting consensus.

The formation of such a consensus is a mysterious process which takes in many elements, such as language, communication, association, geographical proximity, tribal origins, common interests and history, external pressures, and even foreign intervention, none of which, however, is a determinant by itself. A consensus can be said to exist when no group within the nation feels that its vital interests and particular characteristics could be better preserved by withdrawing from the nation than by remaining within.

A (modern) state needs to develop and preserve this consensus as its very life. It must continually persuade the generality of the people that it is in their best interest to continue as a state. And since it is physically and intellectually difficult to persuade continually through reason alone, the state is tempted to reach out for whatever emotional support it can find. Ever since history fell under the ideological shadow of the nation-state, the most convenient support has obviously been the idea of nationalism. It becomes morally "right," a matter of "dignity and honour," to preserve the integrity of the nation. Hence, from the emotional appeal called nationalism is derived a psychological inclination to obey the constitution of the state.

To say that the state uses nationalism to preserve its identity is not to say that the state is the inventor of nationalism. The feeling called nationalism is secreted by the nation (in whatever sense we use the word) in much the same way as the family engenders family ties, and the clan generates clannishness. And just like clannishness, tribalism,

---

state of its own; hence, a nation is a community which normally tends to produce a state of its own." And R. MacIver, *Society* (New York, 1937) p. 155: "There are nations then which do not rule themselves politically, but we call them nations only if they seek for political autonomy."

and even feudalism, nationalism will probably fade away by itself at whatever time in history the nation has outworn its utility: that is to say, when the particular values protected by the idea of nation are no longer counted as important, or when those values no longer need to be embodied in a nation to survive.[7]

But that time is not yet; we have not yet emerged from the era of the nation-state when it seemed perfectly normal for the state to rely heavily—for the preservation of the national consensus—on the gum called nationalism, a natural secretion of the nation. In so doing, the state (or the political agents who desired a state) transformed the feeling into a political doctrine or principle of government. Nationalism, as defined by history, is a doctrine which claims to supply a formula for determining what section of the world's population occupying what segment of the world's surface *should* fall under the authority of a given state; briefly stated, the formula holds that the optimum size of the sovereign state (in terms of authority and territory) is derived from the size of the nation (in terms of language, history, destiny, law, and so forth).[8]

It might be remarked here that history is not always logic; and in the case of nationalism it has embarked upon a type of circular reasoning which leaves the mind uneasy. The idea of nation which is at the origin of a new type of state does not refer to a "biological" reality (as does, for instance, the family); consequently the nation has constantly and artificially to be reborn from the very state to which it gave birth! In other words, the nation first decides what the state should be; but then the state has to decide what the nation should remain.

I should add that some people who call themselves nationalists would not accept this line of reasoning. Nationalism to them has remained a mere feeling of belonging to the nation (in a sociological or cultural sense); they liken it to a dream which inspires the individual and motivates his actions, perhaps irrationally but not necessarily negatively. I cannot, of course, quarrel with people merely because they wish to drain two centuries of history out of a definition. I can only say that is not about *their* nationalism that I am writing in this paper; it is only fair to remind them, however, that their "dreams" are being converted by others into a principle of government.

---

[7]On those values, see P. E. Trudeau, "La nouvelle trahison des clercs," *Cité libre*, avril 1962, p. 15.

[8]Compare Kedourie, *Nationalism*, p. 1: "The doctrine (of nationalism) holds that . . . the only legitimate type of government is national self-government."

Let us then proceed to see what happens when the state relies on nationalism to develop and preserve the consensus on which it rests.

II. *NATIONALISM AND FEDERALISM*

Many of the nations which were formed into states over the past century or two included peoples who were set apart geographically (like East and West Pakistan, or Great Britain and Northern Ireland), historically (like the United States or Czechoslovakia), linguistically (like Switzerland or Belgium), racially (like the Soviet Union or Algeria). Half of the aforesaid countries undertook to form the national consensus within the framework of a unitary state; the other half found it expedient to develop a system of government called federalism. The process of consensus formation is not the same in both cases.

It is obviously impossible, as well as undesirable, to reach unanimity on all things. Even unitary states find it wise to respect elements of diversity, for instance by administrative decentralization as in Great Britain,[9] or by language guarantees as in Belgium; but such limited securities having been given, a consensus is obtained which recognizes the state as the sole source of coercive authority within the national boundaries. The federal state proceeds differently; it deliberately reduces the national consensus to the greatest common denominator between the various groups composing the nation. Coercive authority over the entire territory remains a monopoly of the (central) state, but this authority is limited to certain subjects of jurisdiction; on other subjects, and within well defined territorial regions, other coercive authorities exist. In other words, the exercise of sovereignty is divided between a central government and regional ones.

Federalism is by its very essence a compromise and a pact. It is a compromise in the sense that when national consensus on *all* things is not desirable or cannot readily obtain, the area of consensus is reduced in order that consensus on *some* things be reached. It is a pact or quasi-treaty, in the sense that the terms of that compromise cannot be changed unilaterally. That is not to say that the terms are fixed forever; but only that in changing them, every effort must be made not to destroy the consensus on which the federated nation rests. For what Ernest Renan said about the nation is even truer about the federated nation: "L'existence d'une nation est . . . un plébiscite de tous les

---

[9]Since the *Government of Ireland Act, 1920* it might be more exact to think of Great Britain and Northern Ireland as forming a quasi-unitary state.

jours."[10] This obviously did not mean that such a plebiscite could or should be held every day, the result of which could only be total anarchy; the real implication is clear: the nation is based on a social contract, the terms of which each new generation of citizens is free to accept tacitly, or to reject openly.

Federalism was an inescapable product of an age which recognized the principle of self-determination. For on the one hand, a sense of national identity and singularity was bound to be generated in a great many groups of people, who would insist on their right to distinct statehood. But on the other hand, the insuperable difficulties of living alone and the practical necessity of sharing the state with neighbouring groups were in many cases such as to make distinct statehood unattractive or unattainable. For those who recognized that the first law of politics is to start from the facts, rather than from historical might-have-beens, the federal compromise thus became imperative.

But by a paradox I have already noted in regard to the nation-state, the principle of self-determination which makes federalism necessary, makes it also rather unstable. If the heavy paste of nationalism is relied upon to keep a unitary nation-state together, much more nationalism would appear to be required in the case of a federal nation-state. Yet if nationalism is encouraged as a rightful doctrine and noble passion, what is to prevent it from being used by some group, region or province within the nation? If "nation algérienne" was a valid battle cry against France, how can the Algerian Arabs object to the cry of "nation kabyle" now being used against them?

The answer, of course, is that no amount of logic can prevent such an escalation. The only way out of the dilemma is to render what is logically defensible actually undesirable. The advantages *to the minority group* of staying integrated into the whole must on balance be greater than the gain to be reaped from separating. This can easily be the case when there is no real alternative for the separatists, either because they are met with force (as in the case of the US Civil War), or because they are met with laughter (as in the case of the *Bretons bretonnisants*). But when there is a real alternative, it is not so easy. And the greater the advantages and possibilities of separatism, the more difficult it is to maintain an unwavering consensus within the whole state.

One way of offsetting the appeal of separatism is by investing tremendous amounts of time, energy, and money in nationalism, *at the federal*

[10]Ernest Renan, *Discours et conférences* (Paris, 1887), p. 307. See also p. 299.

level. A national image must be created that will have such an appeal as to make any image of a separatist group unattractive. Resources must be diverted into such things as national flags, anthems, education, arts councils, broadcasting corporations, film boards; the territory must be bound together by a network of railways, highways, air-lines; the national culture and the national economy must be protected by taxes and tariffs; ownership of resources and industry by nationals must be made a matter of policy. In short, the whole of the citizenry must be made to feel that it is only within the framework of the federal state that their language, culture, institutions, sacred traditions, and standard of living can be protected from external attack and internal strife.

It is, of course, obvious that a national consensus will be developed in this way only if the nationalism is emotionally acceptable to all important groups within the nation. Only blind men could expect a consensus to be lasting if the national flag or the national image is merely the reflexion of one part of the nation, if the sum of values to be protected is not defined so as to include the language or the cultural heritage of some very large and tightly knit minority, if the identity to be arrived at is shattered by a colour-bar. The advantage as well as the peril of federalism is that it permits the development of a regional consensus based on regional values; so federalism is ultimately bound to fail if the nationalism it cultivates is unable to generate a national image which has immensely more appeal than the regional ones.

Moreover, this national consensus—to be lasting—must be a living thing. There is no greater pitfall for federal nations than to take the consensus for granted, as though it were reached once and for all. The compromise of federalism is generally reached under a very particular set of circumstances. As time goes by these circumstances change; the external menace recedes, the economy flourishes, mobility increases, industrialization and urbanization proceed; and also the federated groups grow, sometimes at uneven paces, their cultures mature, sometimes in divergent directions. To meet these changes, the terms of the federative pact must be altered, and this is done as smoothly as possible by administrative practice, by judicial decision, and by constitutional amendment, giving a little more regional autonomy here, a bit more centralization there, but at all times taking great care to preserve the delicate balance upon which the national consensus rests.

Such care must increase in direct proportion to the strength of the alternatives which present themselves to the federated groups. Thus when a large cohesive minority believes it can transfer its allegiance to a neighbouring state, or make a go of total independence, it will be inclined to dissociate itself from a consensus the terms of which have been altered in its disfavour. On the other hand, such a minority may be tempted to use its bargaining strength to obtain advantages which are so costly to the majority as to reduce to naught the advantages to the latter of remaining federated. Thus a critical point can be reached in either direction beyond which separatism takes place, or a civil war is fought.

When such a critical point has been reached or is in sight, no amount, however great, of nationalism can save the federation. Any expenditure of emotional appeal (flags, professions of faith, calls to dignity, expressions of brotherly love) at the national level will only serve to justify similar appeals at the regional level, where they are just as likely to be effective. Thus the great moment of truth arrives when it is realized that *in the last resort* the mainspring of federalism cannot be emotion but must be reason.

To be sure, federalism found its greatest development in the time of the nation-states, founded on the principle of self-determination, and cemented together by the emotion of nationalism. Federal states have themselves made use of this nationalism over periods long enough to make its inner contradictions go unnoticed. Thus, in a neighbouring country, Manifest Destiny, the Monroe Doctrine, the Hun, the Red Scourge, the Yellow Peril, and Senator McCarthy have all provided glue for the American Way of Life; but it is apparent that the Cuban "menace" has not been able to prevent the American Negro from obtaining a renegotiation of the terms of the American national consensus. The Black Muslims were the answer to the argument of the Cuban menace; the only answer to both is the voice of reason.

It is now becoming obvious that federalism has all along been a product of reason in politics. It was born of a decision by pragmatic politicians to face facts as they are, particularly the fact of the heterogeneity of the world's population. It is an attempt to find a rational compromise between the divergent interest-groups which history has thrown together; but it is a compromise based on the will of the people.

Looking at events in retrospect, it would seem that the French Revolution attempted to delineate national territories according to the will of the people, without reference to rationality; the Congress of Vienna claimed to draw state boundaries according to reason, without reference to the will of the people; and federalism arose as an empirical effort to base a country's frontiers on both reason and the will of the people.

I am not heralding the impending advent of reason as the prime mover in politics, for nationalism is too cheap and too powerful a tool

to be soon discarded by politicians of all countries; the rising bour-
geoisies in particular have too large a vested interest in nationalism to
let it die out unattended.[11] Nor am I arguing that as important an area
of human conduct as politics could or should be governed without any
reference to human emotions. But I would like to see emotionalism
channelled into a less sterile direction than nationalism. And I am
saying that within sufficiently advanced federal countries, the auto-
destructiveness of nationalism is bound to become more and more
apparent, and reason may yet reveal itself even to ambitious politicians
as the more assured road to success. This may also be the trend in
unitary states, since they all have to deal with some kind of regionalism
or other. Simultaneously in the world of international relations, it is
becoming more obvious that the Austinian concept of sovereignty could
only be thoroughly applied in a world crippled by the ideology of the
nation-state and sustained by the heady stimulant of nationalism. In the
world of today, when whole groups of so-called sovereign states are
experimenting with rational forms of integration, the exercise of
sovereignty will not only be divided within federal states; it will have
to be further divided between the states and the communities of states.
If this tendency is accentuated the very idea of national sovereignty will
recede, and with it, the need for an emotional justification such as
nationalism. International law will no longer be explained away as so
much "positive international morality," it will be recognized as true law,
a "coercive order . . . for the promotion of peace."[12]

Thus there is some hope that in advanced societies, the glue of
nationalism will become as obsolete as the divine right of kings; the
title of the state to govern and the extent of its authority will be conditional upon rational justification; a people's consensus based on reason
will supply the cohesive force that societies require; and politics both
within and without the state will follow a much more functional approach
to the problems of government. If politicians must bring emotions into
the act, let them get emotional about functionalism!

The rise of reason in politics is an advance of law; for is not law an
attempt to regulate the conduct of men in society rationally rather than
emotionally? It appears then that a political order based on federalism
is an order based on law. And there will flow more good than evil
from the present tribulations of federalism if they serve to equip lawyers,

---

[11]On the use of nationalism by the middle classes, see Cobban, *Dictatorship*,
p. 140. And for a striking and original approach, see Albert Breton, "The
Economics of Nationalism," *Journal of Political Economy*, Aug. 1964.

[12]Hans Kelsen, *Law and Peace* (Cambridge, Mass., 1948), pp. 1 and 7.

social scientists, and politicians with the tools required to build societies of men ordered by reason.

Who knows? humanity may yet be spared the ignominy of seeing its destinies guided by some new and broader emotion based, for example, on continentalism.

III. *CANADIAN FEDERALISM: THE PAST AND PRESENT*

Earlier in this paper, when discussing the concept of national consensus, I pointed out that it was not something to be forever taken for granted. In present-day Canada, an observation such as that need not proceed from very great insight. Still I will start from there to examine some aspects of Canadian federalism.

Though, technically speaking, national self-determination only became a reality in Canada in 1931, it is no distortion of political reality to say that the Canadian nation dates from 1867, give or take a few years. The consensus of what is known today as the Canadian nation took shape in those years; and it is the will of that nation which is the foundation of the state which today exercises its jurisdiction over the whole of the Canadian territory.

Of course, the will of the Canadian nation was subjected to certain constraints, not least of which was the reality of the British Empire. But, except once again in a technical sense, this did not mean very much more than that Canada, like every other nation, was not born in a vacuum, but had to recognize the historical as well as all other data which surrounded its birth.

I suppose we can safely assume that the men who drew up the terms of the Canadian federal compromise had heard something of the ideology of nationalism which had been spreading revolutions for seventy-five years. It is likely too that they knew about the Civil War in the United States, the Rebellions of 1837–1838 in Canada, the Annexation Manifesto, and the unsatisfactory results of double majorities. Certainly they assessed the centrifugal forces that the constitution would have to overcome if the Canadian state was to be a durable one: firstly the linguistic and other cultural differences between the two major founding groups, and secondly the attraction of regionalisms, which were not likely to decrease in a country the size of Canada.

Given these data, I am inclined to believe that the authors of the Canadian federation arrived at as wise a compromise and drew up as sensible a constitution as any group of men anywhere could have done. Reading that document today, one is struck by its absence of principles,

ideals, or other frills; even the regional safeguards and minority guarantees are pragmatically presented, here and there, rather than proclaimed as a thrilling bill of rights. It has been said that the binding
force of the United States of America was the idea of liberty,[13] and
certainly none of the relevant constitutional documents let us forget it.
By comparison, the Canadian nation seems founded on the common
sense of empirical politicians who had wanted to establish some law and
order over a disjointed half-continent. If reason be the governing virtue
of federalism, it would seem that Canada got off to a good start.

Like everything else, the Canadian nation had to move with the times.
Many of the necessary adjustments were guided by rational deliberation:
such was the case, for instance, with most of our constitutional amend-
ments, and with the general direction imparted to Canadian law by the
Privy Council decisions. It has long been a custom in English Canada
to denounce the Privy Council for its provincial bias; but it should
perhaps be considered that if the law lords had not leaned in that
direction, Quebec separatism might not be a threat to-day: it might be
an accomplished fact. From the point of view of the damage done to
Quebec's understanding of the original federal compromise, there were
certainly some disappointing—even if legally sound—judgments (like
the New Brunswick, Manitoba and Ontario Separate School cases) and
some unwise admendments (like the BNA no. 2 Act, 1949); but on
balance, it would seem that constitutional amendment and judicial interpretation would not by themselves have permanently damaged the fabric
of the Canadian consensus if they had not been compounded with a
certain type of adjustment through administrative centralization.

Faced with provinces at very different stages of economic and political
development, it was natural for the central government to assume as
much power as it could to make the country as a whole a going concern.
Whether this centralization was always necessary, or whether it was not
sometimes the product of bureaucratic and political empire-builders
acting beyond the call of duty,[14] are no doubt debatable questions, but
they are irrelevant to the present enquiry. The point is that over the
years the central administrative functions tended to develop rather more
rapidly than the provincial ones; and if the national consensus was to
be preserved some new factor would have to be thrown into the balance.
This was done in three ways.

First, a countervailing regionalism was allowed and even fostered in

[13]Kohn, *Nationalism*, p. 20.
[14]As an example of unjustifiable centralization, J. R. Mallory mentions the
federal government's policy concerning technical schools (*Montreal Star*, Feb. 4,
1964).

matters which were indifferent to Canada's economic growth. For instance, there was no federal action when Manitoba flouted the constitution and abolished the use of the French language in the legislature[15]; and there was no effective federal intervention[16] under paragraphs 3 and 4 of section 93 (BNA Act) or under paragraphs 2 and 3 of section 22 (Manitoba Act) when New Brunswick, Ontario, and Manitoba legislated in a way which was offensive to the linguistic or religious aspirations of their French-speaking populations.

Second, a representative bureaucracy at the central level was developed in such a way as to make the regions feel that their interests were well represented in Ottawa. A great administrative machine was created, in which "the under-representation of Quebec can be considered an ethnic and educational factor rather than a regional one."[17] It was this efficient bureaucracy, by the way, which was unable to convert the machinery of government to the production of bilingual cheques and letter-heads during the forty years it took to debate the subject in Parliament; then suddenly the reform took place in five minutes without help even from the cabinet. But such are the miracles of automation!

Third, tremendous reserves of nationalism were expended, in order to make everyone good, clean, unhyphenated Canadians. Riel was neatly hanged, as an example to all who would exploit petty regional differences. The Boer War was fought, as proof that Canadians could overlook their narrow provincialisms when the fate of the Empire was at stake. Conscription was imposed in two world wars, to show that in the face of death all Canadians were on an equal footing. And lest nationalism be in danger of waning, during the intervals between the above events Union Jacks were waved, Royalty was shown around, and immigration laws were loaded in favour of the British Isles.

Need I point out that in those three new factors, French-Canadians found little to reconcile themselves with centralization. First, regionalism as condoned by Ottawa meant that the French-Canadians could feel at home in no province save Quebec. Second, representative bureaucracy for the central government meant that regional safeguards would be entrusted to a civil service somewhat dominated by white Anglo-Saxon

[15]The French language was also abolished in the territories. See F. R. Scott, *Civil Liberties and Canadian Federalism* (Toronto, 1959), p. 32.

[16]The operative word here is "effective." It will be remembered that Bowell's government in Ottawa did try to remedy the situation, first by order-in-council—the dispositions of which Manitoba refused to obey—and then by a bill in the House of Commons—which was obstructed by Mr. Laurier's Liberals, who went on to win the 1896 election.

[17]John Porter, "Higher Public Servants and the Bureaucratic Elite in Canada," *Canadian Journal of Economics and Political Science*, vol. XXIV, Nov. 1958, p. 492.

Protestants. And third, nationalism as conceived in Ottawa was essentially predicated on the desirability of uniting the various parts of the nation around one language (English) and one flag (the Union Jack).

I readily admit that there are elements of oversimplification in the four preceding paragraphs. But I am prepared to defend quite strenuously the implications which are contained therein: that the rational compromise upon which the nation rested in 1867 was gradually replaced by an emotional sop; and that this sop calmly assumed away the existence of one-third of the nation. In other words, the French-Canadian denizens of a Quebec ghetto stripped of power by centralization were expected to recognize themselves in a national image which had hardly any French traits, and were asked to have the utmost confidence in a central state where French Canada's influence was mainly measured by its (not inconsiderable) nuisance value.

Under such circumstances, Canadian nationalism—even after it ceased looking towards the Empire, which took quite some time—could hardly provide the basis for a lasting consensus. So time and time again, counter-nationalist movements arose in Quebec which quite logically argued that if Canada was to be the nation-state of the English-speaking Canadians, Quebec should be the nation-state of the French-Canadians. But these warning signals were never taken seriously; for they were hoisted in years when Quebec had nowhere to go, and it obviously could not form an independent state of its own. But a time was bound to come—"Je suis un chien qui ronge l'os"—when French-Canadian national self-determination could no longer be laughed out of court; a time when the frightened Quebec and Ottawa governments (albeit in obvious contempt of their respective constitutional mandates) found sense in making "scientific" studies of separatism.[18]

In short, during several generations, the stability of the Canadian consensus was due to Quebec's inability to do anything about it. Ottawa took advantage of Quebec's backwardness to centralize; and because of its backwardness that province was unable to participate adequately in the benefits of centralization. The vicious circle could only be broken if Quebec managed to become a modern society. But how could this be done? The very ideology which was marshalled to preserve Quebec's integrity, French-Canadian nationalism, was setting up defence mechanisms the effect of which was to turn Quebec resolutely inward and backwards. It befell the generation of French-Canadians who came of age during the Second World War to break out of the dilemma; instead of bucking the rising tides of industrialization and modernization in a

[18]*La Presse*, 12 mai 1964. *The Gazette*, May 21, 1964.

vain effort to preserve traditional values, they threw the flood-gates open
to forces of change. And if ever proof be required that nationalism is a
sterile force, let it be considered that fifteen years of systematic non-
nationalism and sometimes ruthless anti-nationalism at a few key points
of the society were enough to help Quebec to pass from a feudal into
a modern era.

Technological factors could, practically alone, explain the sudden
transformation of Quebec. But many agents from within were at work,
eschewing nationalism and preparing their society to adapt itself to
modern times. Typical amongst such agents were the three following.
Laval's *Faculté des sciences sociales* began turning out graduates who
were sufficiently well equipped to be respected members of the central
representative bureaucracy. The *Confédération des travailleurs catholiques du Canada* came squarely to grips with economic reality and
helped transform Quebec's working classes into active participants in
the process of industrialization. The little magazine *Cité libre* became
a rallying point for progressive action and writing; moreover it understood that a modern Quebec would very soon call into question the
imbalance towards which the original federal compromise had drifted,
and it warned that English-Canadian nationalism was headed for a rude
awakening; upholding provincial autonomy and proposing certain constitutional guarantees, it sought to re-establish the Canadian consensus
on a rational basis.

The warnings went unheeded; Ottawa did not change.[19] But Quebec
did: bossism collapsed, blind traditionalism crumbled, the Church was
challenged, new forces were unleashed. When in Europe the dynasties
and traditions had been toppled, the new societies quickly found a new
cohesive agent in nationalism; and no sooner had privilege within the
nation given way to internal equality than privilege *between* nations fell
under attack; external equality was pursued by way of national self-
determination. In Quebec today the same forces are at work: a new
and modern society is being glued together by nationalism, it is discovering its potentialities as a nation, and is demanding equality with
all other nations. This in turn is causing a back-lash in other provinces,
and Canada suddenly finds herself wondering whether she has a future.
What is to be done?

If my premises are correct, nationalism cannot provide the answer.

[19]Who would have thought it possible, five years ago, that a prime minister of
Canada, after giving in to various provincial ultimata, would go on to say: "I
believe that the provinces and their governments will play an increasingly
important role in our national development. I for one welcome that as a healthy
decentralization. . . ." (*Montreal Star*, May 27, 1964) Too much, too late . . .

Even if massive investments in flags, dignity, protectionism, and Canadian content of television managed to hold the country together a few more years, separatism would remain a recurrent phenomenon, and very soon again new generations of Canadians and Quebeckers would be expected to pour their intellectual energies down the drain of emotionalism. If, for instance, it is going to remain *morally wrong* for Wall Street to assume control of Canada's economy, how will it become *morally right* for Bay Street to dominate Quebec's or—for that matter —Nova Scotia's?

It is possible that nationalism may still have a role to play in backward societies where the *status quo* is upheld by irrational and brutal forces; in such circumstances, *because there is no other way,* perhaps the nationalist passions will still be found useful to unleash revolutions, upset colonialism, and lay the foundations of welfare-states; in such cases, the undesirable consequences will have to be accepted along with the good.

But in the advanced societies, where the interplay of social forces can be regulated by law, where the centres of political power can be made responsible to the people, where the economic victories are a function of education and automation, where cultural differentiation is submitted to ruthless competition, and where the road to progress lies in the direction of international integration, nationalism will have to be discarded as a rustic and clumsy tool.

No doubt, at the level of individual action, emotions and dreams will still play a part; even in modern man, superstition remains a powerful motivation. But magic, no less than totems and taboos, has long since ceased to play an important role in the normal governing of states. And likewise, nationalism will eventually have to be rejected as a principle of sound government. In the world of tomorrow, the expression "banana republic" will not refer to independent fruit-growing nations but to countries where formal independence has been given priority over the cybernetic revolution. In such a world, the state—if it is not to be outdistanced by its rivals—will need political instruments which are sharper, stronger, and more finely controlled than anything based on mere emotionalism: such tools will be made up of advanced technology and scientific investigation, as applied to the fields of law, economics, social psychology, international affairs, and other areas of human relations; in short, if not a pure product of reason, the political tools of the future will be designed and appraised by more rational standards than anything we are currently using in Canada today.

Let me hasten to add that I am not predicting which way Canada will turn. But because it seems obvious to me that nationalism—and of course I mean the Canadian as well as the Quebec variety—has put her on a collision course, I am suggesting that cold, unemotional rationality can still save the ship. Acton's prophecy, one hundred years ago, is now in danger of being fulfilled in Canada. "Its course," he stated of nationality, "will be marked with material as well as moral ruin, in order that a new invention may prevail over the works of God and the interests of mankind." This new invention may well be functionalism in politics; and perhaps it will prove to be inseparable from any workable concept of federalism.

COMMENTARIES / COMMENTAIRES

J. A. CORRY

In their papers, both authors have tried to look at federalism, and particularly Canadian federalism, in perspective, in a way that is appropriate to the time and place of our meeting. Professor Trudeau has thrown a powerful searchlight on the present dilemma of the Canadian federation. Professor Mallory has focused on the several faces Canadian federalism has revealed in the hundred years of its existence. In his paper, he has deferred to me several times and said so much I agree with that I fear my judgment of his paper may be distorted. So I have looked very hard for points of disagreement.

I agree with Mr. Trudeau about the compound of reason and feeling that have provided the glue or cement for federal union in the past. As one who still likes to think of himself as a rationalist, I yearn for the moment of truth that will show "that the mainspring of federalism cannot be emotion but must be reason." But I am somewhat short of high hope, because all human association so far has been based partly on feeling.

Mr. Trudeau quotes Ernest Renan. I paraphrase his (Renan's) definition of a nation as a group of people who are conscious of having done great things together in the past and want to stick together to do other and more great things in the future. To me, this definition states the general conditions on which a nation comes into being and continues to exist. It gives due place to sentiment and feeling. So the "national image" remains of vital importance for the Canadian nation. I agree with Mr. Trudeau that it has not been easy to detect French features in it. This is something English-speaking Canadians must work to repair. The difficulty of doing so is not lack of good-will, but rather lack of imagination (Anglo-Saxon stolidity, if you will), the fact of nine wholly or predominantly English-speaking provinces, and a continental nation of 180,000,000 people lying along side with an English-style rather than a French-style culture.

But, of course, the people in the nation will not want to stick together in the future unless the main groups in it are satisfied that the terms of association are fair and just, or can be made so by negotiation. Here, as Mr. Trudeau says, emotional sops will not do: reason must satisfy itself of just recognition of regional rights and of fair compromise of competing regional claims.

For the honouring of these requirements, Mr. Trudeau proposes a bill of rights[1] binding on all governments in Canada guaranteeing to individuals and to regional and cultural groups not only individual liberty but also social welfare and cultural equality. The purpose is to enable every Canadian to feel that he is an equal member of the nation. This is our constant objective, and I agree that we should be studying seriously the appropriate content of such a bill of rights.

Given such guarantees, Mr. Trudeau said, we would take the emotional heat out of the issues of Canadian federalism and make them amenable to rational solution. No doubt such guarantees would help but I am not sure they would enable us to find rational solutions for the most acute problems of Canadian federalism. It has seemed to me that what large elements of Quebec opinion want passionately is to establish within the province a large and secure economic base for "a great leap forward." The purpose, unless I misunderstand, is to enlarge Quebec's share of material goods and to use these ampler means to secure, and develop further, a distinctive cultural identity. Current dissatisfaction in Quebec with the structure of Canadian life arises, I believe, from a fear that preservation of a distinctive culture is not feasible on the lines on which we have been proceeding.

This surely is the nub of the matter. We have created here over the last half-century or so a highly integrated national economic and social structure. (Whether we like it or not, it is this integrated structure that gives us our high standard of living.) The essential nature of the structure has put the main initiatives into relatively few hands, those of large national corporations, large trade unions, and the national government in Ottawa. Perhaps those initiatives can be more widely shared than in the recent past, perhaps centralization can be somewhat reduced. But, at best, the integrated national economy sets sharp limits to decentralized initiatives. Critical decisions that are beyond the control of any one province have to be taken, and all the provinces, including Quebec, have to live with the consequences. This massive interlocked economic and social system puts some confinement on us all and presses us to seek our satisfactions, cultural as well as material, along such lines as it leaves open to us.

Severing of the integrated national economy for the purpose of securing to Quebec the economic and fiscal independence needed as a base for quite untrammeled cultural autonomy would, I am satisfied, reduce very seriously the material means available for cultural satisfactions in all provinces, including Quebec. If Canada sat somewhere in Asia or Africa, such a drastic reduction might be thought not to be too high a price for large cultural autonomy. With the contrast of the richest nation on earth flourishing at our doorstep, the price would be thought too high, even in Quebec once it became clear how high it really was. The challenge to reason, a very severe one in our developing circumstances, is to find an accommodation that gives

[1]After presenting his paper as now published, Mr. Trudeau sketched informally a functional approach to Canadian politics, and suggested that a federal Canada would be seen (on balance of costs and benefits) to be preferable to either separation or annexation, but that a workable federal Canada would require a new constitutional bill of rights guaranteeing economic security and cultural equality as well as individual liberties.

fair assurance to the aspirations of Quebec without disrupting the highly productive national economy. It is the old question, put in a new form, of finding room for a rich and desirable diversity within a frame of unity.

Mr. Mallory wants the frame of unity to be strong, supporting a clear pre-eminence for the national government even if it has to be contrived through the incestuous relationships of which he speaks. I judge he would like to see more authority and less contrivance because he regrets the lines of interpretation of the British North America Act set by Lord Watson which were highly favourable to the provinces and which led to serious embalance between constitutional responsibility and fiscal capacity in the nineteen-thirties.

I shall not argue the juristic question of the correct interpretation of ss. 91 and 92 of the British North America Act. I will say, in defence of Lord Watson that, *for his time*, he adjusted the constitution to the important political realities. As Mr. Trudeau says, if the Privy Council had not leaned in favour of the provinces at that time, events might well have taken a turn Mr. Mallory would have found extremely distasteful.

Nor am I sure that, even in the long run, the bias of Privy Council interpretation has really worked as adversely to the effective power of the national government as he thinks. If this interpretation had been consistently much more favourable to Parliament in assuring it of a wider range of power, it is open to question whether we would have had the spectacular refinement of the techniques of economic and fiscal powers after the war, of which Mr. Mallory speaks. Politicians and civil servants are much like the rest of us: they don't like to think unless they have to. It was certainly the deficiency of specific powers in the hands of Parliament that set them thinking furiously, from 1943 on, about how to use the more far-reaching fiscal and monetary powers. Perhaps the Privy Council interpretations have, in the sequel, pushed effective centralization further and faster than it would otherwise have gone. Certainly a more centralizing course of interpretation would not have prevented the revulsion from centralization we are now experiencing. For this, there are many causes, among them weakness of the federal government in the last few years because of general political instability.

On the question of legal power under the constitution, there is one particular point I wish to note. Mr. Mallory said that the federal government alone had the "constitutional right" to deal with problems of economic stability and economic growth. Such rights as Parliament has in these fields, of course, have to be derived mainly from its fiscal, monetary and foreign trade powers. These are considerable, and may be the only really effective ones. But the provinces also have a panoply of powers that can at least be exerted on such problems. The federal government is far from having a monopoly of the powers that bear on economic stability and economic growth.

In the same part of this paper, Mr. Mallory said that the problems of major economic policy confronting us are not political problems at all but ones that "can be solved by the ingenuity and sophistication of the economists." With so many lawyers and political scientists here today, I throw myself on their protection and tell the truth: all significant problems of federalism are political in the deepest sense, and the "reason" of which Mr. Trudeau speaks must be the reason of statesmen and not the ratiocinations of economic science.

I have the highest respect for the clarifying analysis and ingenuity of economists. Attempts at political solutions that do not take into account the calculations of the economists will succeed only by a fluke. Yet the function of science, economic or otherwise, is to tell us the material price of the various alternatives within which we and the politicians must choose. A prerequisite of all rational choice is to know the cost of what is proposed. But cost does not determine choice, unless we assume that the supreme national purpose is to maximize the national income.

Given what is true, that we *do* put a very high valuation on increasing our command of material means, it is clear why Mr. Mallory said what he said. Economists are the best experts for telling us how political tinkering with the integrated national economy can drastically lower the national income, how intervening in one aspect of this interlocked structure can have disruptive effects on the whole structure. Because we put such a high value on constantly increasing the national income, we do come close to treating economists as statesmen. But let us be clear that in so far as we do defer to economists as statesmen, we narrow the ground for political manoeuvre. And we do need a lot of room for political manoeuvre if we are to deal with the challenge I spoke of earlier, of finding, within a frame of effective national unity, fair scope for the aspirations of Quebec.

RAY FORRESTER

I am speaking as an American on a subject that has substantial significance at present in Canada; but it has also substantial significance in the United States. We have heard several references to co-operative federalism. The US has a long way to go on that subject: we have not yet solved the problem of co-operative Republicanism.

In responding to what Professor Trudeau and Professor Mallory have said, I feel, certainly, an element of humility. I do not pretend to know much about the Canadian situation, certainly not from any sophisticated point of view, but there is something alluring and enticing about speaking on a subject in which you are completely unfettered by specific information. There is, of course, no problem which looks as simple as one viewed from afar, and in which you are not personally concerned. And I do believe that Oscar Wilde was correct to some extent when he said that a person with an objective view really has no place in the discussion of a difficult problem. You need to be involved to understand the full overtones. But even Oscar's thought, clever as it is, may be carried too far.

I agree with Mr. Mallory that we should not underestimate the forms of government, but there is a measure of truth, though overstated, in the well-known quotation of Pope: "For forms of government let fools contest; whate'er is best administered is best." There is significance in both aspects of the problem. Form clearly has its effect on us; administration, the human element, has its effect also, and if I were choosing between the two, I certainly would prefer the quality of good administration. The quality of the people and the quality of the leadership which administers for the people are most important.

The basic concept of federalism is a contradiction. Within one word we have an antinomy. It is a contradiction between unity on the one hand and diversity on the other, between the nation and the province. It is dialectical: the thesis and the antithesis give us a synthesis. This process is constantly with us in federalism, constantly unpredictable, but always expected and always prepared for if the federalism works.

I hope that in the US we have learned something of the fact that you must be prepared for the synthesis, and I suggest that the preparation must take recognition of the following points. 1: There must be a willingness to conciliate, to accommodate new facts with new federalism, to compromise. 2: I think that we must adopt the unemotional and calm approach when we are surprised by a new problem emerging in federalism. 3: We must not carry a position to its logical extreme, particularly when it is mixed with sentimentality. 4: We must be prepared to weigh alternatives, and be willing, as wise men, to accept the less painful alternative.

Again let me say that it is the quality of the people involved in the particular federalism which is going to determine whether a problem is solved or whether it will be permitted to carry the group to disaster.

Examples drawn from American history bear out these considerations, I believe. Let me mention a few. Firstly, the Constitutional Convention of 1787. Here was gathered a group of people with sharply different points of view and contrasting values. Yet, over a period of months, they drafted a constitution which has been referred to as the great compromise between local autonomy and centralization. They also reached a compromise between the rule of the majority and the protection of the individual from majority control. These results were obtained because the people involved were willing to weigh alternatives and to accept the form of federalism which was possible at the particular time.

The second issue was that of judicial supremacy, which arose in 1803 in the case of *Marbury* v. *Madison*. John Marshall interpreted article 3 of the US Constitution to give power to the Supreme Court to nullify federal laws. Thomas Jefferson was firmly opposed to this concept. The court was in the hands of the Federalists and he was a Republican. He could have ignored the decision, but he did not. Why? Because in weighing the alternatives he decided to accept defeat from John Marshall and the Federalists on this issue in order to move forward to more important objectives for the nation.

The third example is one of failure: the Civil War. Here we did not remain free from emotionalism. Here we indulged in sentimentality and in the fallacy of carrying a position to a logical extreme. The South had a logical argument, the right to be left alone, to secede. The North also had a logical position. And the hard-headed logic of the two camps carried the nation to disaster. Why? Because, at that time, the leadership failed in the weighing of alternatives.

In conclusion, I would like to say that I agree with the statement of Abbé O'Neill of Quebec City in which he recently declared that Canada must combat prejudice and hatred, and seek compromise where tensions are prone to increase. And I agree with Mr. Trudeau in his recent statement "Prudence indeed will dictate that Governments long established should not be changed for light and transient causes."

I ask: if the men of Canada cannot work out a civilized solution, where are the men who can?

PROBLEMS OF CANADIAN
ECONOMIC POLICY

LA POLITIQUE ECONOMIQUE DANS
LA FEDERATION CANADIENNE

Prospects for Economic Policy in a Federal Canada

JACQUES PARIZEAU

I find it rather difficult to discuss, as a theoretical problem, economic policy in a federation. No doubt models of economic policy, of a general character, have been developed and are well known; but to define the meaning of a federation in terms of economic theory is more than difficult; it is downright impossible.

The same federal constitution can lead and, in fact, does lead to very different economic structures. In effect, even though the constitution might be unambigious on the subject of the fields over which the federal government on the one hand, the states or provinces on the other will have full jurisdiction, we still have no idea as to how these jurisdictions will be exercised, how much money will be channelled into each field, how, in other words, the game will be played. In fact, society as a whole develops, during a given period, a scale of values that sooner or later will be reflected in the structure of public spending. In so far as national defence, external affairs, and foreign aid are accepted as priorities of the highest order, then it is likely that the economic size and weight of the federal authorities will be considerable in relation to the size and weight of junior governments. If education and highways have priority and if both these sectors are under provincial jurisdiction, then the economic dimension of junior governments will grow.

Indeed, each of the two levels can have its own set of priorities. And in a typical federation even conflicting priorities can be carried out sometimes by parallel authorities. Yet sooner or later under public demand, the pendulum is shifted and one set of priorities becomes more important than the other. To that extent we can therefore envisage all kinds of spending patterns on the basis of the same constitution. And for each of these spending patterns, appropriate tools of economic policies will have to be devised.

The division of public spending between central and regional authorities is not, however, the only relevant variable. Surely the way in which public spending is linked at various levels of government will influence appreciably the way economic policies must be envisaged. For instance, a political structure that would imply full control of municipal and school board expenditures by the provinces which in turn would channel a large part of their expenditures into joint programs initiated and developed by the federal authorities, is a very different animal from a political structure where joint programs hardly exist and where local autonomy is prevalent. The constitution may be the same, but economic policies that can be applied to each certainly are not.

In the light of this analysis, Canada has not changed its constitution appreciably during the last twenty years, but the federal rules of the game have been revolutionized. Because of this, most economic policies devised after the war have either been rejected or have been neutralized. To understand the extent of the revolution that has taken place, it is necessary to quote a few figures.

During the last year of the war, the current income of the federal government was more than three times that of junior governments. In 1948, it was still more than twice as large and that proportion was still valid until about 1953. Ten years later, junior governments have a total current income that is 15 per cent above that of the federal authorities.[1] Similarly at the end of the war, the federal debt was five times the total of provincial and municipal outstanding debts. At the end of 1963, the debt of the central government was, in spite of seven years of deficits, only a third larger than that of junior governments. At the present rates of increase the latter should be equal to the former within, say, six or seven years. It would, of course, be possible to find all sorts of other series to prove the same point, but the two that have been mentioned will suffice to illustrate not only the nature, but also the scope and magnitude, of the shift that has occurred in the relative weights of governments.

The factors involved in this shift are well known. The rise of personal income and rapid technological progress have created a considerable demand for a number of social services that are either new or have been improved and developed. The requirements of education, city and intercity transportation, housing and particularly suburban housing, city planning and health have brought about enormous capital expenditures as well as a steep rise in current outlays. Nearly all these fields fell under provincial or municipal jurisdiction. Irrespective of the financial

---

[1]Federal transfers to provinces and municipalities are added to the income of junior governments and deducted from federal total income.

formulas that could be devised, junior governments were bound to become economic units of large magnitude.

However, at the same time that income flows were changed, an attempt was made to connect them much more closely than had ever been the case before. School boards were forced into acceptance of definite spending patterns; provincial control over municipalities was extended and federal financing was opened to them. Finally, cost-sharing agreements or joint programs—a relatively new feature of the Canadian political game—emerged as an efficient technique to project into provincial spending the patterns, priorities, and criteria evolved by the federal government.

Among the developments which I have just described, some seem to be irreversible, while others are much less secure. Thus the shift of resources to junior governments and the control over local authorities will not be easily reversed, while the nature and extent of joint programs are political issues of growing acuteness.

Be it as it may, I suggest that discussions of economic policies in a federal state must, if they are to be at all precise, be based on a set of observable facts such as those I have just mentioned rather than on the letter of the constitution. They, furthermore, must be based on a knowledge of a less technical but possibly just as important a phenomenon which, for the lack of a better label, I should call the degree of identity in social and economic doctrines. In a politically centralized state, the diversity of dogmatic opinion manifests itself in different political parties. And the party in power has at its disposal the tools required to have its own set of doctrines or prejudices prevail.

A federal state provides another outlet for such divergences. Different governments may reflect very different dogmatic positions with respect to economic or social thought. Economic policies may then either be imposed by the larger governments on the weaker and unorthodox ones or they may become a sort of half-baked compromise between all of them.

This sort of analysis has very relevant implications to the present situation in Canada. In this respect, I am not thinking of, say, the former socialist government of Saskatchewan, because that province was never economically large enough to be a real hindrance to national unanimity. But the situation in Quebec is a much more difficult one. The fact that it is populated by a different ethnic group has well-known repercussions. One of these repercussions, possibly the most important, springs from the fact that French Canadians can control in Quebec nearly all the avenues that lead to power, except large business. They dominate or play an essential role in the government, the civil service, mass media, the labour unions, the academic world, but they are completely absent from the management of large firms. This state of affairs was bound to imply that, sooner or later, policies evolved in Quebec would be much more to the left than any of the policies which would emerge from the atmosphere of Ottawa. This is exactly what has happened in the last few years, and the results are already striking. Measures that would be rejected outright by a federal or a provincial government psychologically conditioned by the fragrance of the modern oligopoly can be accepted very quickly in a province where numerous politicians, civil servants, or journalists can easily consider the business lobbyist not as a former student of LCC, UCC, or RMC, not as a former comrade-in-arms, nor as a fellow club-member, but as a foreign and possibly shady character, even though an essential one.

The development of economic policies must take into account such differences of atmosphere that usually tend to expand into articulate and fundamental choices with respect both to the structure and to the growth of the economy. While one may feel that such exogeneous considerations are injurious or insulting to economic theory—although a lot could be written on the historical links between theory and national interests—they cannot be excluded from a discussion of policies.

This being said, we can now proceed to examine the economic policies not of any federation but of the federation we live in at the present time. There are, in this matter, appreciable advantages to distinguishing between the two traditional classes of policies: those that are aimed at the stabilization of the economy, and those that are oriented towards growth. They raise different problems which cannot be solved in quite the same way.

Stabilization policies have given rise in the last quarter of a century to detailed textbooks of recipes. They belong to the toolbox that any student of economics is likely to acquire quite early. In the fields of monetary and fiscal policies particularly, the ways and means by which a recession or a boom can be kept within tolerable limits have ceased, at an elementary level, to be controversial. In the fields of balance of payments policies and debt management, the consensus is possibly not as great but the problems involved are well circumscribed.

It has furthermore usually been recognized that, particularly in view of the short duration of modern cycles, the levers should, in a federation, be handled by the central government. In this way a policy designed, say, to raise transfer payments and public works, to increase the money supply, to change over from the issue of long-term bonds to short-term bonds, and possibly to devalue the currency can be carried out quickly in answer to a cyclical downturn.

In view of the responsibilities of modern governments towards full employment, it is essential that they have a free hand to operate with a minimum of delay and with all possible efficiency. In fact, in the years that followed the war, these requirements were used to prove that the federal government should centralize as many economic tools as possible even at the expense of the spirit or the text of the constitution. What came to be called in French-Canadian political literature the era of centralization was described by some analysts as the coming of age of efficient government as opposed to antiquated provincialism.

However, it was soon recognized that there were huge difficulties in the proper timing of anti-cyclical measures. Too often, they came too late and their effects were in full swing when the economic situation had already changed and called for opposite measures. But better forecasting techniques, better co-ordination between federal agencies, and a keener recognition of what these techniques involved, by politicians who were not passed the point where they could be educated, could in the end improve the timing and increase the efficiency of policies. To a certain extent, some of these hopes were validated by experience. Although it was difficult to have politicians replace the electoral cycle by the business cycle when it came to raising social security benefits, forecasting techniques did improve somewhat. Furthermore, it was recognized that the extent to which Canada could follow a stabilization policy independent from that of the US was limited, but, after some exploring, the margins of tolerance came to be known with some accuracy.

In other words, as time went by, the limits and possibilities of centralized stabilization policies started to appear concretely. Yet, in one respect at least, a whole set of facts was not incorporated in the framework that was slowly emerging. The shift of spending powers towards junior governments was taking place without drawing much attention and certainly without having much impact on the basic principles of federal economic policies.

Because stabilization policies were seen for so long as the exclusive responsibilities of the central government, not only have junior governments never been, since the war, associated with them, but they have not even been permeated by the basic concepts of such policies. Provincial civil servants who eventually administered several hundred million dollars of local borrowing a year, had no notion of what contracyclical measures might mean. In fact, most junior governments acted as if they were private companies.

After the war, this was unfortunate but not tragic. At the present time, however, junior governments are responsible for three-quarters of all public capital expenditures in the country; they account for four-fifths of all public purchases of non-defence goods and services: the lack of co-ordinated management has far-reaching repercussions.

I am not at all sure that all the implications of such a situation have yet been fully explored. One can, at least, distinguish three levels of impact; firstly, it creates a considerable amount of disorder that reduces largely the efficiency of federal policies; secondly, it tends to freeze the use that could be made of certain tools; and, thirdly, it puts an impossible burden on some strictly federal tools such as monetary policy.

The disorder is apparent in a number of fields. The fact that provinces can have absolute priorities just as well as the central government, combined with the shift in social preferences, has increased considerably the size of the public sector of the economy. As all levels of government cannot be faced with large deficits all the time, taxes must be raised, according to pressures and circumstances that have had in the recent past little relationship to the business cycle. At a time when the US government has managed to cut its tax level, the Canadian government can at best hold on to its tax structure, let provincial government raise more resources if they dare, and let the rest of the adjustment be rolled down to the local level, where its effects are exceedingly different from one area to the other.

As another example of similar disorder, the fact that the federal government controls so little of total public works implies in turn that should the central government wish to offset, even if only in the limited way, excess spending by junior governments, it would be compelled to reduce enormously the expenditures involved in the few fields where it still plays an important role, irrespective of the social importance of these sectors.

Secondly, the present situation tends to freeze the use of what could be anti-cyclical instruments. In their search for more funds, provinces must try to get hold of as many sources as possible and gear them towards their own objectives. Thus, for example, the original federal pension scheme based on a pay-as-you-go formula would have required, over a long period, several increases in the rates of contributions. These could have been closely connected with the stabilization policies of the government. In so far as provinces wanted a funded scheme with constant contributions, all possible flexibility in the level of rates vanished.

Thirdly, as a central government finds itself more and more restricted in most of its fiscal operations, it follows that it must put more emphasis on monetary policy to stabilize the economy. And, in fact, we have seen this happening in Canada for several years. Most of the flexibility remaining in our present system lies in that field of operation. A considerable burden was thus put on the Bank of Canada.

As a matter of fact, while there might have been at times very good grounds to criticize the operation of the Bank of Canada, it may well be that, in a historical perspective, the serious crisis that occurred in 1961 between the governor and the cabinet was the logical outcome of a badly managed public sector that expected far too much from monetary policy, that expected in other words that the administration of the money supply would be sufficient to counteract the increasing shortcomings and disorder of a federal system that was changing so rapidly that it tended to destroy or neutralize all previous principles of operation.

The difficulties involved in the general area of stabilization policies must be seen alongside similar and possibly more serious problems that have arisen with respect to growth. At the risk of oversimplification, it might be held that as a capitalist government of the North American variety, the Canadian government has had, in the recent past, very sketchy policies with respect to the growth of the economy.[2] While it was the accepted responsibility of the federal authorities to implement a broad system of social security and to manipulate the essential tools of stabilization, the shape and rate of growth remained the ultimate responsibility of the private sector. To a limited extent, commercial policy and, particularly, the tariff had some influence, since the war, in so far as they helped the development of sources of raw material at the expense of entire segments of secondary industries. But, on the whole, at least until 1957, commercial policy was used in close co-ordination with noticeable trends in private investment and, particularly, in foreign investment.

Generally speaking, the federal authorities were content to establish a climate conducive to growth and to administer as wisely as possible global instruments such as monetary and fiscal policies or the exchange rate. The regional distribution of growth, the rate of expansion of different sectors, were not a federal responsibility. Such an attitude was logical and coherent. As long as the mobility of labour was an accepted dogma, regional policies could only hamper the operations of that wonderful "invisible hand" which—as we all learned at school—guarantees the most efficient use of resources.

[2]This has not always been true. As is well known the federal government did play a strategic role during the nineteenth century in establishing the basic framework of the national economy.

As long as the great post-war expansion lasted, prosperity was usually so overwhelming (if we except two short recessions) that it hid some rather ugly structural developments. However, by 1957, the boom in resource industries ended abruptly. At the same time, the incoming recession revealed to its full extent the disruption of several sectors in secondary industry. Unemployment was widespread but very unequal from one area to the other. In fact, from 1957 to the end of 1961, real income per capita declined in Canada while Europe was on the contrary experiencing a remarkable rate of growth.

Because of the acuteness of unemployment in some areas, a much closer analysis was made of the standard of living and the standard of services across the country. Awareness of regional discrepancies became widespread. It was realized also that labour mobility was much lower than had been hoped. At the most, mobility applied to only a fraction of the population increase. In large areas where there had been very strong incentives to move, population still went on rising, slowly possibly but significantly. Obviously, we had been much too optimistic about the perfection of markets and about factor mobility. Furthermore, social security and housing policies of the federal government tended to reduce further the incentive to move.

In this context of negative or slow growth, of considerable unemployment, and of diverse regional problems, the federal authorities were slow to react not only because they had few of the required instruments but also because it meant a complete change in the traditional approach to the development of the economy and the responsibility of the central government.

On the other hand, provincial authorities which by now had become very large economic units were not only in close contact with such regional problems as had developed but had the means to do something about them. Furthermore, they had no tradition as far as economic policies were concerned. They had not been touched appreciably by the Keynesian revolution which had had so much influence in Ottawa during the 1940's and the early 1950's. They were not, in other words, prisoners of a past and they could not be but impressed by the new powers that large budgets implied.

Thus it came about that provincial governments started to have economic policies of their own that went much further than anything that had been envisaged in the past. In a matter of a few years, coordinated programs were set up that varied enormously from, say, the purely indicative planning of Manitoba to the federal-provincial rehabilitation program of the Maritimes and to active state intervention in the financial or industrial sectors of Quebec. For the reasons explained above this involvement of provincial authorities in regional economic growth was probably inevitable. While considerable emphasis has been put on the French-Canadian issue, it would be quite wrong to assume that decentralized economic policies of growth originated in this political problem. Indeed, it hastened their emergence; but structural economic developments were heading the same way.

Be that as it may, in a matter of a few years, a number of well-known rules of the federal game were changed beyond recognition. Commercial preferences applicable to purchases of provincial governments, Crown corporations, school boards, and municipalities were established in certain provinces that discriminated in favour of local products. Thus an internal tariff was introduced that was applied not only to an appreciable share of total demand but to a growing one. Pools of industrial capital under various forms were set up by the authorities, not as, in the case of the Industrial Development Bank, as a sort of providence for the small entrepreneur, but as direct interventions of the public sector in large-scale financing of private companies. Quebec has certainly gone further than any other province in setting up new rules, forging new instruments and initiating new policies. But the general principle of provincial responsibility for growth has progressed immensely, through very different channels.

Furthermore, such initiatives have produced measurable results. Provinces have realized that, as economic agencies, they also could be efficient. It took, in fact, surprisingly little time and comparatively little personnel, to achieve results that would have been unthinkable a few years earlier. Indeed, as this process was going on, the federal government tried at last to deal with structural problems on a sectoral or regional basis. Fiscal advantages for new products or designated areas, the establishment of ARDA, loans to municipalities, etc., represent so many initiatives of a kind that were largely unknown before the supplementary budget of 1960 and that have proliferated since.

It would have been too much to expect that so many tools, instruments, and elements of policy could be actively used by several independent agencies without considerable friction with respect to priorities as well as to methods and principles. Some observers hoped that, after a while and after lengthy discussions, a kind of equilibrium would prevail. But this has not been possible. Provinces and, particularly Quebec, were by then too much advanced to relinquish not only their newly acquired techniques but the chances of finding new ones.

Rising demands by provincial governments for more taxation powers,

and the request by Quebec for opting out completely from joint programs thus cutting off any hope of keeping some uniformity in priorities,
sounded the knell of what might have been a grand design of oriented
growth on a federal basis. And finally, in his 1964 spring budget, the
federal Minister of Finance came out with an astonishing statement
regarding the forthcoming negotiations at GATT: negotiators would be
instructed to see to it that any concession given away which could have
an appreciable impact on the economy of a region would be offset by
concessions obtained with respect to another activity of the same region.

This statement did not attract the attention it deserved. It was, in a
way, the end of the line: one of the last important tools of the federal
authorities was being fitted to the new regional pattern. Once more,
the flexibility and autonomy of centralized economic policies was being
sacrificed to a fragmentation of the national economy that the federal
government had been too late to understand and could not stop.

Possibly, this survey of recent developments has been too long, even
though I am aware of numerous oversimplifications. It seemed necessary, however, to emphasize the drastic developments that have occurred
in a federation where the constitutional framework had been remarkably
stable and, yet, had been—irrespective of so many criticisms—flexible
enough to allow what amounts really to a revolution. A new federation
is thus finally emerging, the structure of which is still somewhat hazy
and unsettled. To try to fit to this new federation a detailed set of
economic policies is still in many ways premature. We will have to wait
until the smoke has cleared before we can develop definite notions about
as precise a problem as, say, a joint anti-cyclical policy with respect to
debt management.

Yet, it is already possible to draw a list of relevant questions and
alternatives that are now opened to negotiations. From the answers and
solutions that will finally be reached, one may then be in a position to
reorganize economic policy properly.

Three questions stand out as being particularly relevant. Firstly, how
will financial resources be shared? Secondly, what will happen to joint
programs? And thirdly, can joint decision-making processes be developed? We shall now examine each of these questions in turn.

The sharing of resources is still very fluid, and a prophet rather than
an economist is needed to announce where the dividing line will eventually be set. The BNA Act is of no use at all in this respect. As long
as no agreement is reached as to national priorities, the situation will
remain fluid. For instance, there is no way of knowing whether provinces
should have 25 or 50 per cent of all income taxes as long as we do

not know how much is to be spent for various services. Obviously national defence will always remain under federal jurisdiction, and education will remain under provincial authority. But as long as we have not decided how much of each we want, or worse still, as long as each level of government proceeds on its own to determine the amounts to be spent on each service, sharing resources will remain the result of naked political power. In this respect, no matter how one feels about political agitation in Quebec, it certainly helps the cause of education at the expense of national defence and external affairs. In view of present trends, the limit could be reached when Ottawa would no longer be in a position to carry on as a federal government. Let us eliminate this assumption and imagine that eventually an equilibrium of some sort is reached. Most probably, in the present context, it will be heavily weighted in favour of junior governments. This leads us to our second question.

In effect, because of its relative loss in financial weight, the federal government can only hope to exercise a strong hand in the economy if it uses joint programs as a tool to acquire provincial or municipal resources and, thus, finance projects of national interest or services of uniform quality throughout the country. In other words, the financial logic of joint programs is now exactly opposite to that which prevailed after the war. Then, such shared-cost arrangements helped provinces carry out projects they could not afford. In the future, they may serve the purpose of helping the federal government to find the funds required for national policies. Whichever interpretation is held, joint programs are now more than ever the expression of central government policy.

Under pressure, the federal government may have to allow provinces to opt out. But it must insist that the fiscal resources given to those provinces be used for the same purpose and according to the same standards that were defined in the joint program. Otherwise, the impact of central policies on the economy is bound to shrink further.

For the provinces, or at least some of them, the objective must be exactly the opposite. This is particularly true of provinces engaged in a planning process and particularly of Quebec. To plan properly, a government must spend a great deal, and it must spend as it sees fit. The first condition of operation of a plan is that public expenses be closely tailored to the objectives of that plan. Thus, joint programs which after all are the outcome of other objectives and other priorities can only be a hindrance to provincial planning. Opting out with no strings attached becomes the only logical course to follow.

However, as all provinces have not the same economic policies and, as some are still in a financial position where a cost-sharing arrangement is considered as essential outside help rather than as a hindrance, the solution finally reached can only be a compromise. However, if Quebec opted out of nearly every joint program and was alone to do so, if opting out was not tied to strict agreements with respect to the use of funds; and if, furthermore, the final fiscal arrangements were particularly generous for the provinces, then the scheme according to which Canada could be composed of two associated nations would find its first economic foundation.

Let us again assume that this second question has been solved and let us move to the third. No matter what future constitutions will have to say about fields of exclusive jurisdiction, it is obvious that such rights do not mean much in relation to modern economic policies. Provinces must now be involved in designing, say, commercial policy. Quebec, for instance, cannot build a steel mill without having some idea as to what kind of duties might be applied to steel; and it certainly will not agree for long to be treated in this respect as a private company. Similarly, provincial planners will not accept indefinitely to consider monetary policy as something akin to the weather, without even the help of a weather bureau. On the other hand, the federal government cannot fundamentally accept that the larger part of the public sector be absolutely unconnected to contracyclical policies. And huge public borrowings abroad without any reference to the state of the balance of payments or the exchange rate policy will not always be acceptable.

It will certainly be very difficult to reconcile the requirements of consultation and the exclusive authority of federal and provincial governments. New machinery will have to be set up. It might, to fulfil its role, bring together on a permanent basis official representatives of the parties involved. Anything short of that would be quite inefficient.

On such a basis, one could well envisage, as an example, that the Board of the Bank of Canada be composed not of private individuals who happen to live in different parts of the country, but of appointees of the federal government and of the provinces. In that particular case, it would be logical for the central government to have a majority of seats. For other boards, the opposite might be necessary. But in any case, only through a process of continuous negotiations between governments is there any hope of clearing up the present mess and arriving at working arrangements that will have a certain degree of stability. In practice, it might be helpful not to have each province appoint its negotiators, but to have all the Maritime provinces and the three Prairie provinces appoint regional representatives. In fact, one could go on for some time describing such concrete aspects of the project. But there is no need to do this here: it is enough to recognize the importance of the principle involved.

In any case, even if we do find an answer to the three problems mentioned, could we conclude then that changes in the constitution are likely to help the organization of adequate and co-ordinated economic policies? Personally, I doubt this very much. On the contrary, the constitution as it stands now has helped to narrow the areas of conflict. To attempt, in present circumstances, a full revision or redrafting of the constitution means really that the whole front will be ablaze; any rational solution to urgent problems of economic policies might have to be postponed for a long time. It would seem much more fruitful to find first an empirical equilibrium between the governments and then draft it into a legal text.

Whether the present political situation in the country will allow such a gradual process is, of course, an entirely different problem.

Economic Policy in Our Federal State

WM. C. HOOD

In this centennial year 1964, as we reflect upon the historic conference in Charlottetown at which the proposal for the union of all British colonies in North America was made, Canadians are particularly conscious that the future of their federation could not be guaranteed by the Confederation Fathers and that in each generation we must protect it by remoulding it to conform with our evolving activities and aspirations. In economic, as in political, social, and cultural, affairs this continuous adaptation of institutions and responsibilities must go on if we are to achieve, through union, high and rising standards of living. In this paper I shall be concerned with some (but only some) of the adaptations we have been making recently and may have to make in the near future, if economic policy is to contribute fully to the development of the kind of Canada we want.

I. THE CANADA WE WANT

What kind of Canada do we want? We do not all answer this question with one voice. Many of us do not answer it now as we would have ten years ago, nor as we will ten years hence. There is, however, broad agreement as to several objectives.

The most obvious point on which virtually all Canadians are agreed is that we want Canada to continue as a nation. There are I think three distinguishing *economic* characteristics of a nation. The first is that the component parts are bound in what may best be described as a customs union, having no internal barriers to trade and a common external commercial policy. Canada meets this economic test of nationhood rather well. We have no internal tariffs, and the federal government determines and administers external commercial policy for the country as a whole. Of course, in a federal state differences among levels of provincial taxes, incentives to industry, and social security benefits to individuals do restrict the flows of goods, capital, and persons, to some extent. Such impediments do not detract from the *national* character of the country in the same way as would measures designed deliberately to impede such flows. Government campaigns, of which we have had examples lately in at least Ontario and Quebec, exhorting provincial citizens to buy the products of their native province, or provincial-government purchasing policies that discriminate against goods and services from other provinces do detract seriously from the status of Canada as a nation.

The second economic characteristic of a nation is that it has a national monetary system and policy, adequately supported by other policies. We have had a national monetary system since confederation, in that the BNA Act under section 91 accorded the federal government exclusive legislative authority over "currency and coinage," "banking, incorporation of banks and the issue of paper money," "savings banks," "bills of exchange and promisory notes," "interest," and "legal tender." The establishing of the central bank in 1934 marked an important stage in the evolution of the exercise of federal power in this field. Of course, paper money no longer plays the critical role it did in 1867, its place having very largely been taken by deposits at banking institutions which are transferable on order to third parties. The federal government has not chosen to exercise authority over all institutions whose liabilities include modern money, nor over all savings banks. Indeed, there even exist provincially owned organizations, operating under provincial law, that issue modern money and that are savings banks. Frustrated, to a degree by Supreme Court decisions to the effect that interest, being a matter of contract and hence of property and civil rights, is subject to provincial authority, the federal Parliament has not in fact exercised exclusive authority over interest. Notwithstanding these considerations, Canada meets the test of nationhood rather well in terms of having a national monetary system and policy. The important doubt as to our nationhood, in respect of monetary policy, arises in connection with the supporting policies. If, because of the division of power between the federal and provincial authorities, the federal authority is unable to mount policies in support of monetary policy to achieve national objectives to the fullest extent possible, then we cannot claim to meet the particular test of nationhood we are now discussing.

The third economic criterion of nationhood is that there exist a national dedication to the principle that common minimum standards of welfare and public services shall exist throughout the country and that provincial and federal governments shall co-operate in establishing such minima and in sharing the resources required to meet them. This is the area of the most complex problems of a federal state. The concept of minimum standards of welfare is complicated because it is multi-dimensional and because, with rising living standards, it is subject to incessant upward revision. The problem of sharing resources is complicated because of the variety of techniques available for sharing and because each technique has different implications for the capacities of both federal and provincial governments to meet other obligations and aspirations. Without reviewing now the history of our national development in this regard I feel I shall not be challenged when I assert that in this country there does exist a national dedication to the principle I have stated. Indeed, it is my own feeling, which I shall explain later, that we may very well have been too ambitious in our choice of minimum standards of welfare.

Although we want Canada to continue as a nation with unfettered internal trade, a common commercial policy, an adequately supported monetary policy, and a country-wide commitment to minimum standards of welfare, we share with other nations the goals of rapid economic growth, high employment, and stability of the internal and external value of our currency. These goals have been much discussed in recent years by Canadians and by many others. I have nothing to add to their elucidation on this occasion, but it is important that they be accorded their significant place among the economic characteristics of the Canada we want.

Before leaving this general theme I should like to offer one less positive reflection. It is that Canadians are not doctrinaire on the matter of economic organization. The very nature and history of our federation testify to the pragmatism of our approach to intergovernmental divisions of duties. We sum up our approach nowadays in the phrase "co-operative federalism." We want to retain the flexibility implied in this phrase, and I am sure we shall continue to benefit from this flexibility. Much the same spirit prevails in respect of the relative roles of government and private enterprise. We have characteristically favoured a kind of "co-operative commonwealth" in which the government and private sectors co-operate to promote the common weal. Evidence abounds: in transportation we operate government enterprises in competition with private concerns; the same is true of radio and television, power production, telephone service, the finance of enterprise, and provision of various kinds of insurance. The co-operation of government with private initiative in the realm of education is extensive. Many of our most lucrative farm crops are raised using the results of government research and marketed through government enterprise. There are even some out-standing examples of government operation of purely manufacturing concerns including one with subsidiaries abroad. In common with many countries of the Western world there has been a long-term growth in the share of the national product produced in the government sector and of the national expenditure made by the government sector.

I should have thought the pragmatism and flexibility of our attitudes to intergovernmental organization and to the role of government in the economy were to be counted among the features of the Canada we want.

II. CONSTRAINTS ON POLICY

In developing the Canada we want, we have much to work with. Our endowment of natural resources is liberal, our climate is stimulating, and we are an energetic and well-educated people. We already enjoy an enviable standard of living and we live in a close relationship to the United States' economy which affords us, in many instances, direct access to the technological advances of that economy. But there are constraints upon policy-making in this country and I wish to refer to some of them in this section of the paper.

THE REGIONAL DISPARITIES IN ECONOMIC WELFARE

One of these constraints is imposed by the regional disparities in econo-mic welfare. While almost all parts of Canada share in economic growth as reflected, for example, in real output per head of employed workers, the levels of output per head show wide variation. This fact poses a perennial policy problem of assigning weights to the goal of economic growth, viewed in the aggregate for the nation as a whole, and the goal of reducing regional disparities.

On one view, economic growth in the aggregate should have virtually all of the weight. According to this view it is appropriate that resources should move in response to the incentives provided by the wage and profit differentials that are established through the uninhibited working of the price system. Such a view argues against positive measures to relieve regional disparities on the grounds that such measures inhibit the free flow of resources towards higher returns and, by supporting the *status quo*, impair the aggregate growth of the economy. But this is a harsh view. If it recognizes at all the costs of growth, it assesses the whole of them on the owners of those resources which the changing tides of technology and fashion leave in a condition of excess supply.

It awards the fruits of growth to the owners of the resources more favoured by technology and fashion.

On the other extreme is the view, embracing a rather narrow measure of economic welfare, that all regions of the economy should enjoy the same welfare per head. Often devotees of this view support redistributive and protectionist policies that would impair unduly the capacity of the economy to realize its potential.

Our aim should be, and to a considerable extent has been, more moderate than either of these extremes. We should seek to share both the costs and the gains of economic progress but to do this by measures which retain incentives to adjust to new circumstances and which do not regard national income per head as conventionally calculated as an all-embracing indicator of welfare.

THE CONSTITUTIONAL CONSTRAINT

Another constraint upon policy-making is the constitutional constraint. It was the intention of the framers of the British North America Act that Canada should have a strong central government. The grant to the Parliament of Canada in section 91 of the BNA Act of power "to make laws for the peace, order and good government of Canada" was intended to be a grant of residual power. The specific powers of the federal Parliament enumerated in section 91 were intended as illustrations of the federal power. The specific grants of power to the provinces under section 92 were intended to be just that—specific grants. However, as is well known, the grants to the provinces to legislate in respect of "property and civil rights in the province" and "all matters of a merely local or private nature in the province" have been interpreted by the courts in such a way as virtually to reverse the intention of the Fathers of Confederation and place the residual power with the provinces. Gradually, the scene of the struggle between the provincial and federal authorities is moving from the courts to the political arena, especially the federal-provincial conference. On the whole, I think that is a good thing. It is surely impossible for co-operative federalism to work through the courts. The essential point I am making at this juncture, however, is that the division of powers among governments, and the uncertainty surrounding that division, does act as a constraint upon policy-making. I do not contend that such a constraint is wholly a misfortune. On the contrary, in some respects the sharing of powers between the federal and provincial authorities contributes to administrative efficiency. The quest for autonomy by the provinces, if moderate, may also be constructive, by forcing us continually to re-examine the distribution of power in the light of changing conditions, by contributing to the ferment of ideas and experiment that are essential to economic growth and political maturity, and by broadening the opportunities for training politicians and administrators. Finally, of course, the division of powers acts as a counter to the concentration of power at either the federal or the provincial pole. In the face of the constraint though, large measures of patience, ingenuity, and statesmanship are required for the effective launching and administration of economic policy.

III. *ASPECTS OF RECENT POLICY*

Manifestly the central theme in a discussion of economic policy in a federal state must be the sharing of the task of policy-making between the central and provincial authorities. The accomplishing of the goals we have described is the aim, but these goals are common to unitary and federal states. It is the extent and character of the co-operation among governments that is special in the federal state.

We have worked out our solutions to economic policy problems in recent years against a backdrop characterized by two dominant features: the growth of government and government responsibility taken as a whole, and the ascendency of centrifugal over centripetal forces within government.

The growth of the government sector may be exhibited by any of a number of statistics. Expenditures by all levels of government on goods and services, as a percentage of gross national expenditure have risen from 12 per cent in 1947 to 19 per cent in 1963. If we include government expenditures on transfer payments to the private sector (as defined in the national accounts) the ratio to GNE has risen from 22 per cent to 31 per cent over the same period. This growth of the public sector reflects the increased emphasis upon the goals of high employment, economic growth, and the provision of social services and upon the increased responsibility placed on governments to contribute to achieving these aims.

But while the government sector has been growing in significance, within this sector, the provincial and municipal governments have gained in strength and responsibility relative to the federal government. For example, federal government expenditures on goods and services amounted to 41 per cent of all such government expenditures in 1947 but only 36 per cent in 1963. Federal government expenditures on goods and services *and* direct transfers to the private sector were 58 per cent of all such government expenditures in 1947 and only 43 per cent in 1963. There are many centrifugal forces accounting for the ascendency of the provinces.

The depression of the thirties and the war of the forties strengthened the responsibilities of the federal government. In the war period the doctrine that "the peace, order and good government" clause granted emergency residual powers to the federal authority provided the constitutional basis for the dominance of the federal government. The subsequent rise of the provincial power is in part due to the lapsing of the emergency powers and a reaction to the consequences of their exercise. But there is more to the explanation than that. Of course, the decline in the relative importance of defence expenditures reduced the role of the government sector and of the federal sector in particular. Natural resources discoveries in certain provinces greatly strengthened the financial position of those provinces. More important, the booming exploitation of natural resources in the early fifties brought general prosperity and with it a vastly enlarged demand for highways, education, urban services, and social services generally. Responsibility for programs to meet most of these demands devolve primarily upon the provincial governments. Although the rate of economic growth slowed down in the last years of the fifties, general unemployment did not reach the tragic proportions of the thirties and gradually assumed more of a distinctly local character demanding a more distinctively local response. The federal Parliament, overweighted by rural representation, was not as sensitive to the needs of urban growth or to the later condition of urban unemployment as the local governments. I believe this condition strengthened the position of the provincial and municipal governments, although even in the provincial legislature there is some over-representation of the rural population. At about the time of the slowing down of economic growth, federal politics became more unstable and led to the emergence of minority government which we have now. This condition of federal politics also contributed to the strengthening of the provinces, I believe. Concomitant with all of these developments was the break-up of the old regime in the province of Quebec and the emergence of a dynamic movement in that province to accelerate economic growth and enhance provincial control over it. This movement not only strengthened the position of that province relative to the federal authority, but, I think, led other provinces to increase their demands for power and resources, or forced the federal authority to yield power and resources to them.

There have been centripetal forces operating in the other direction. There was a considerable revival of economic nationalism in the fifties, based in substantial measure upon a reaction against American influence and control over capital and labour in this country. This nationalism, I should have thought, of itself strengthened the power of the centre, although, I think some of the reaction to foreign influence was translated into demand for provincial measures. In addition, many of the forces that lead Canadians to think nationally rather than provincially continued to grow. Among these are the large corporations, for which so many of our people work, national business organizations, trade associations and professional organizations, to mention but a few. But these centralizing forces, in our recent experience, have been rather overpowered by the forces referred to earlier, strengthening the role of the provinces relative to that of the federal government.

While this interplay of forces has been proceeding, we have been evolving a new pattern of federal-provincial financial arrangements. I should like to review this evolution very briefly.

The over-riding aim of federal-provincial financial relations must be:

(*a*) to see that the rates of growth of tax revenue from all sources accruing to the federal government and to the provinces adequately reflect the growth in the total costs of their respective functions;

(*b*) to see that the division of revenues among the provinces permits and induces each province to provide services to a minimum national standard without necessitating punitive disparities in taxation.

(*c*) to divide functions and revenues so as to achieve the most effective administration of functions, the most efficient tax collection procedures, and the least violation of the principle that responsibility for financing expenditure should devolve upon the spender.

We may remark that the net result of the financial arrangements to date has been that, while the outstanding (direct and guaranteed) debt of the federal government is now about 1.1 times larger than it was at the end of 1945, the combined debt of the provinces and municipalities is almost five times larger than it was at the end of the war.

The federal-provincial fiscal arrangements have proceeded from a system of tax rentals with population-related compensation, to a tax-sharing system supplemented by collection agreements and equalization grants. In addition there has been a continuing increase in conditional grants to the provinces as part of "shared-cost" programs. Let us refer first to the tax agreements and the unconditional grants associated with them.

Under the five-year agreements of 1947 and 1952, the signing provinces ceded to the federal government exclusive rights to levy personal income and corporation income taxes and succession duties. In return they received guaranteed minimum payments based on population (or population and the pre-war tax receipts) adjusted annually in accordance with changes in population and GNP. Provinces not signing the agreements did not receive grants. Quebec did not rent any tax fields under the 1947 and 1952 agreements; Ontario did not rent any tax fields under the 1947 agreement but, attracted by a new compensation option, she agreed to rent the personal and corporate income tax fields in 1952. In passing we may note that in the 1947–52 period the federal government repealed taxes on gasoline, amusements, cabarets, pari-mutual betting, and household use of gas and electricity in order to give room to the provinces to obtain tax revenue from these sources.

An important change of principle was made in the 1957 agreements. This was the introduction of tax equalization and tax stabilization payments to be made to a province regardless of whether it rented tax fields to the federal government. Quebec did not rent any tax fields under the 1957 agreements; Ontario agreed to rent only the personal income tax field. Provinces agreeing to rent tax fields to the federal government received: (*a*) 10 per cent of federal personal income tax collections attributable to the province (raised to 13 per cent in 1958); (*b*) 9 per cent of corporate taxable income allocated to the province; and (*c*) 50 per cent of the federal succession duties (later estates tax) allocated to the province. These tax rates are referred to as "standard taxes." In addition, any province, whether party to the agreements or not, received tax equalization payments such that, when added to tax rental payments, they raised the total per caput return in each province to the average per caput return of standard taxes in the two provinces having the highest per caput yield of standard taxes. Moreover, all provinces were accorded the privilege of receiving stabilization payments to bring the level of their revenues from the federal government through tax rentals, tax equalization payments, and revenue stabilization payments up to 95 per cent of the average of such payments in the two preceding years. Taxpayers in provinces not renting any or all tax fields to the federal government enjoyed a reduction of their federal tax liability equal to the standard tax rate in such fields.[1]

A further important change of principle was made in the 1962 agreements. Tax rental agreements in respect of personal and corporate income taxes were replaced with tax-collecting agreements, and all prov-

[1]As of January 1, 1957, the federal tax on insurance premiums was dropped and all provinces moved into this field.

inces became free and indeed were encouraged to impose their own personal and corporate income taxes. In respect of these taxes provinces are free to choose their own tax bases and tax rates; if they use the federal tax bases, they may enter an agreement with the federal government to collect their taxes free of charge. Quebec did not sign the agreement; Ontario signed with respect to personal income taxes only; BC signed the agreement, but set up its own succession duty one year after the new arrangements went into effect; it accepted the federal payment for the first year. All other provinces signed in respect of all three taxes.

The rates of standard taxes, which are the basis of equalization payments and of reductions of taxpayers' liability to the federal government, were fixed as follows:

personal income tax	16 per cent rising to 20 per cent in 1966
corporate income tax	9 per cent of corporate income, except for Quebec it is 10 per cent
estate tax	50 per cent.

The difference in the standard tax rate for corporate income in Quebec was to compensate for an additional 1 per cent tax on corporate income in the province to provide grants to universities.

Equalization payments were continued but on a different basis. The object was again to equalize tax revenues per head, but this time in addition to the yields of the three standard taxes, the revenue to be equalized included 50 per cent of the three-year moving average of natural resources revenue, as defined by the DBS. Moreover, instead of bringing per caput provincial revenues from the four sources up to the average of the two provinces with the highest such revenues, the new formula was designed to equalize such revenues at the national average. The revenue stabilization provisions of the previous agreement were continued and certain other specific guarantees were included.

At the federal-provincial conference in November 1963, modifications of these formulae were agreed upon. The provincial share of the estate tax is now 75 per cent, but for standard tax and equalization purposes the estate tax is still 50 per cent. The average of the two top provinces was restored as the standard of equalization, and the effect of including natural resource revenues among the revenues to be equalized was modified by reducing the equalization payment to any province having a natural resource revenue per head in excess of the national average per head by one half of this excess times the population of the province. Following the conference in Quebec at the end of March of this year, the federal government proposed that the standard personal income tax rates be raised for 1965 from 19 to 21 per cent and for 1966 from 20 to 24 per cent. The effect of this proposal will be to increase the write-off by persons of tax liability to the federal government.

Thus through these arrangements, there has been a considerable restoration to the provinces of revenues from the taxation of incomes and estates, (not to mention other specific tax fields given up by the federal government), all provinces have resumed the levying of personal and corporation income taxes, all are free to levy succesion duties, the principle of equalization payments has been introduced and related to a measure, albeit a political compromise, of fiscal capacity. In the course of the evolution of the arrangements, the isolation of Quebec from the rest of the provinces has been reduced.

Although the present formula for the calculation of equalization grants does not take explicit account of fiscal need as opposed to fiscal capacity, there are certain supplementary unconditional grant programs that do recognize fiscal need. I refer particularly here to special grants paid to the Atlantic Provinces since 1958 known as the Atlantic Provinces Adjustment Grants, now totalling $35 million annually, and the grant now amounting to $8 million paid annually to Newfoundland under the Federal-Provincial Fiscal Arrangements Act, 1961.

In addition to these and other unconditional grants, conditional grants and shared-cost programs have grown in recent years to the point where they cost the federal government upwards of $850 million per year. They divide into two broad categories, capital projects and provision of current services. Among the capital projects, the most important are those relating to provision of facilities for vocational training, highway construction, ARDA projects,[2] and municipal winter works programs. While these programs are long-term in nature, the actual activity under them is somewhat flexible since it is dependent upon the undertaking of specific projects. They have caused some concern in the provinces especially in cases where projects had to be launched or completed within a certain period in order to benefit from federal participation. Among the programs for the provision of specific services the hospital insurance program is the largest. Initiated in 1957, this program provides grants-in-aid to the provinces to help finance the cost of providing hospital services of at least a minimum standard. The federal government pays each province ¼ of the per caput cost of in-patient services

[2]ARDA refers to the Agricultural Rehabilitation and Development Act of 1961 authorizing the federal government to enter into agreements with the provinces for the joint undertaking of projects for improvement of land use, redevelopment of rural areas, and conservation and development of soil and water resources.

in Canada as a whole, together with ¼ of the per caput cost of in-patient services in the provinces, multiplied by the average for the year of the number of insured persons in the province.

These shared-cost programs were introduced in order to provide incentives and means to carry out projects considered to be of importance and to provide services of at least minimum national standards. The providing of the means has become less important as the tax arrangements together with the associated equalization payments, which we discussed earlier, developed. The providing of means will be even less important as the provinces acquire resources under the Canada Pensions Plan to be discussed later. Under pressure from Quebec the federal government has shown a strong disposition to withdraw from such schemes, especially those providing current services. At the federal-provincial conference in Quebec this spring the federal government offered to negotiate terms for contracting out with any province so wishing and to compensate such provinces by further reductions of their residents' federal personal income tax liability provided, in the words of the Prime Minister, "that any contracting out should not prejudice the position of other provinces which remain in the programs" and "that the federal government should do what it could to ensure national standards of services in respect of the shared cost programs."[3] In my view, these shared-cost programs will be of much less importance in the future; such a decline will widen the application in our system of the principle that responsibility for financing of expenditure should be borne by the spender.

We may summarize these recent developments simply as follows. Rapid population growth has combined with relatively high prosperity to create a pattern of demand for capital and services which in our federal state required either a transfer of functions from the provinces to the centre or a transfer of financial resources from the centre to the provinces. Although we started the post-war years on the former course, we have progressively shifted to the second course and that shift has been accelerating in the last year or two. The pressures for decentralized government remain very strong in our federation, especially when the emphasis in government policy is on the provision of educational and welfare services and social capital, and when unemployment is not generally high but concentrated in particular areas. We have, however, adhered to the principle of sharing the fruits and costs of progress and have found some practical means of giving expression to this principle.

[3]Speech of Mr. Pearson to the House of Commons, April 6, 1964, *Debates*, p. 1795.

I think that in making all of these adjustments we have laid up some problems for the future. Before turning to these, however, I must refer to one further recent development which in my opinion may add greatly to our future problems.

This development is the Canada Pension Plan. The Canada Pension Plan has gone through a series of reincarnations and there is no guarantee that the latest version proposed to the provinces and accepted in principle by them in April 1964[4] is the one which ultimately will be adopted. It is this version which we shall discuss here, however. The main features of the plan are the following.

(*a*) Pensions are to be 25 per cent of earnings up to $5,000 a year with benefits available, through constitutional amendment, to widows, orphans, and disabled contributors.

(*b*) This limit of $5,000 will be adjusted in accordance with changes in some long-term average of earnings.

(*c*) Benefits will be adjusted to changes in the cost of living, subject to a maximum increase of 2 per cent in any year.

(*d*) It is to be a compulsory contributory plan with employers and employees each contributing 1.8 per cent of earnings between $600 and $5,000.

(*e*) The details of the plan will be the same in all provinces, though any province will be free to administer the plan within that province or to authorize administration by the federal government.

(*f*) The plan will give rise to a fund, which has been unofficially estimated to reach a level of some $8 billion after the ten-year period before full benefits are available. The fund will be available to the provinces in proportion to the contributions received from each province, and will be invested by the provinces. Provinces which elect federal administration of the plan will guarantee a rate of interest to the fund at least equal to the rate on long-term federal securities.

When all the necessary federal and provincial legislation is passed, the Canada Pension Plan will then comprise a joint government commitment to pay earnings-related pensions to retired citizens and to establish a public development fund of unprecedented proportions. This fund will not cease to grow after the expiry of the ten-year maturity period: it will grow with the size of the working population, it will grow with any increase in the earnings base of the contributions, and it will grow with any subsequent increase in the percentage of earnings con-

[4]*Ibid.*, April 21, 1964, pp. 2332–3 and pp. 2388–9.

tributed. The increase of benefits up to 2 per cent a year in response to increases in the cost of living will of itself, however, be a limit on the increase of the fund.

In my opinion the Canada Pension Plan, by virtue of its funded character, adds a new dimension to economic policy-making in this country and sharpens the policy problems ahead already posed by the other fiscal arrangements we have been making. Let us then, in conclusion, turn to some of these policy problems of the future.

IV. POLICY PROBLEMS AHEAD

In discussing the economic criteria of nationhood earlier in these remarks, I commented upon the importance of a national monetary policy and upon the importance of adequate support for this policy in achieving national objectives of high employment, preservation of the value of the currency, and rising output per head. The doubts generated in my mind by the recent development of economic relations between the federal government and the provinces concern our ability to provide adequate support for monetary policy in pursuing these objectives.

Let me begin by considering our defence posture in relation to general unemployment caused primarily by deficiency of domestic demand. If monetary policy is to receive support from other policies in dealing with a general deficiency of effctive demand, the government sector must bolster such demand through its tax and expenditure policy. In particular, the government sector must be prepared to reduce its taxes and increase its expenditures, in short to reduce its surplus or increase its deficit. Now, in spite of the revolution in economic theory that Keynes brought about, we in Canada have never, apart from war finance, been ardent practitioners of the art of compensatory fiscal policy. There were many reasons for this. By no means all of those who have been in authority have been converts to the Keynesian doctrine, either themselves fearing deficits or fearing others who feared them. In addition fiscal policy at best is not a flexible instrument. It takes time to plan new government works, and get men employed upon them, and most finance ministers prefer to avoid frequent large changes in tax rates in either direction. I cannot parade all the actual and alleged difficulties of fiscal policy here, but I do feel that anti-recessionary fiscal policy is now less capable of providing support for monetary policy than at any time since the war. This feeling derives essentially from the fact that the provinces have so strategic a role in both tax and expenditure policy by virtue of the relative weights of their budgets and from the fact that much of the initiative for changes rests with them. It has been true for some time that by far the bulk of capital expenditures in the government sector is made by provincial governments. This will apparently be increasingly so in the future. The shared-cost capital programs could have been designed so that the timing of their impact could be related to the condition of the economy, but have not been so designed (with the special exception of the municipal winter works programs). I venture to think that these programs will be of diminished importance in the future although in April 1964 the Prime Minister referred to the possible need to use such programs to combat recession.[5] On the tax side, while the federal government is still the biggest tax collector, and will continue to be, there is now no assurance that if the federal government sought to support monetary policy with a cut in the personal income tax, the provinces, who now all have income tax laws of their own, would not render the federal cut nugatory by raising their own rates.

Of course, the decentralizing of fiscal policy does not mean that in principle it cannot be harnessed to serve national objectives. But such co-ordination requires will and machinery. Neither exist in adequate degree at the moment. While I believe that we have to devote ourselves to the devising of means of co-ordinating policies to common ends, we shall not make an adequate effort if we do not recognize the very practical difficulties that will confront us. I shall return to this theme later.

I turn now to the twin objectives of a stable-valued currency and high productivity. I feel that, unless we take special care, we shall find that the added powers of government, combined with their decentralization, will present us with a considerable problem of inflation and one that may, paradoxically, bring with its significant unemployment born of high costs.

We Canadians have joined the twentieth-century quest for security and have increasingly sought this security through government action. But the quest for social security will be illusory unless we maintain growth in productive capacity which is the ultimate guarantor of economic security. Unless the growth in productive capacity is adequate and appropriately distributed, social security benefits will buy more *expensive* goods not more goods.

I should like to illustrate the problems involved by reference to the proposed Canada Pension Plan. I realize that this plan is but one of the

5Opening statement of Prime Minister to Dominion-Provincial Conference in Quebec. *Ibid.*, April 3, 1964, p. 1788.

many forces that will play upon the economy in the next decade or two. But it will be an important new force and it therefore behoves us to study the problems it will raise so that we may cope with them better.

The first point to be made about the Canada Pension Plan is that it will permit retired citizens to lay claim to an increased value of consumers' goods and services. How great will be the increased demand for consumers' goods will depend upon the course of development of private pension plans, and other means of providing for retirement, in response to the government scheme. I find this very difficult to forecast. My own judgment would be that private means of providing for retirement will continue to grow but at a somewhat lesser rate. Certainly it is the hope of supporters of the government plan that the purchasing power of retired persons will show a significant increase per head because of the plan. I have no doubt that this hope will be realized and in significant measure. My only doubt concerns the degree.

The second point, which is intimately related to the first, concerns the effect of the plan upon the supply of saving. Of course the same uncertainty I have just been expressing applies here. The greater is the substitution of saving through the government plan, the less will be the net increase of private saving in response to the plan. I feel that the growth of saving through private channels will be somewhat curtailed, but I would expect the government plan to effect a significant increase of saving.

We come then to the next main point, and that is the application of savings generated through the government plan and through private channels. If we are to meet the commitment to raise the material standard of living of retired persons, it is imperative that the saving be directed to investment in human and physical capital which will yield the requisite increases in productivity. If the saving is not so directed, only two alternatives are open: increased drafts upon the goods and capital of other countries, or inflation. Appropriate allocation of saving to investment is essential whatever is the effect of the government pension plan upon private saving.

The withdrawal of funds from the private sector to the government sector will impair the growth of large aggregations of capital in the private sector. I am not oblivious to the fact that important contributions to productivity may spring from a collection of many small investments. I also believe, however, that there are important projects which require large-scale financing and which have to tap large aggregations of capital funds. I am concerned that the reduction in the growth of saving in the private sector by adversely affecting the accumulation of large blocks of capital may impair the ability of the private sector to undertake large-scale capital projects essential to productivity growth.

I am not propounding the doctrinaire view that what is done by the private sector advances economic growth while anything that is done in the public sector retards it. What I am trying to stress is that the investment by the provincial governments of the very large amounts of capital to be amassed under the Canada Pension Plan must contribute to productivity growth, or else retired persons along with the rest of the residents of this country will not enjoy as high real standards of living as the magnitude of their savings programs would warrant. I do not think provincial governments are yet geared to make the capital investment decisions they are soon going to be faced with under the Canada Pension Plan and under other policies serving to enlarge the role of government in capital formation.

There are some other reasons for being apprehensive about the inflationary potential of the new program. The compulsory contribution rates represent a substantial increase in taxes upon persons and corporations. There is no question that the funds transferred to the provincial governments will be quickly spent on goods and services. Moreover, I would expect that persons will seek to pass on their share of the costs of government pensions to their employers, customers, or clients and that employers, in their turn, will take what steps they may to pass on, through price increases, direct and indirect increases in their burden of pension costs. On the other hand, of course, the pension program will add weight to the existing pressures to economize on the use of labour by adopting labour-saving techniques including automation of processes. For us to institute an old age security program more liberal than the American, with a consequent increase in tax burden, at the time when our major competitor, the United States, is completing a series of major cuts in personal and corporate tax rates, will surely prejudice our competitive position.

If the pension plan, when combined with other forces in the economy issues in a net inflationary effect, the character of the plan itself is such that its scope will be expanded as we have noted. An inflation of prices and costs in Canada, if it is more rapid than in the countries with whom we trade, will result in unemployment of resources in some export and import-competing industries. We may thus experience, as indeed we have before, the very perplexing condition of inflation combined with unemployed resources attached to some industries.

I repeat that I am not predicting that inflation is an inevitable consequence of our present undertakings. I merely draw attention to the fact that we shall have to plan capital investment wisely in the public sector, as well as in the private sector, if the growth in productive capacity, out of which to provide an increased real income for retired persons, is to be forthcoming.

As I have already suggested, the increased role of government and the decentralization of fiscal powers call for changes and improvements in governmental organization in Canada if we are to serve the national employment, growth, and price objectives. Some changes are already taking place or are being actively discussed.

At the provincial level, various organizational developments to facilitate the formulation and conduct of provincial economic policy are taking place. Economic planning is approached in differing ways in the several provinces, but all are now at least conscious that their roles in the provincial economies have expanded to a point which requires deliberate appraisal of and reaction to economic developments within their borders and in other parts of the country. I believe it is essential in modern circumstances that appraisals of economic developments at the provincial level be improved. As I have suggested, it is of very great importance that the provinces gear themselves to channel wisely the very large additions to the investment funds that will be at their disposal.

But while improvements in the machinery for appraising and affecting economic development at the provincial level are necessary, it is equally necessary that the machinery for co-ordinating provincial policies with federal policies be improved. I do not suggest that there is no machinery for co-ordination now. The federal-provincial conference of premiers is essentially a continuing conference. There is a continuing committee of officials keeping a watching brief over matters of concern to that conference. Some very close links have been forged between the spending departments of federal and provincial governments especially in relation to the administration of shared cost programs. There are also some *ad hoc* arrangements such as the present Royal Commission on Taxation and the federal-provincial committee proposed by the premiers at the Quebec conference in late March, 1964.

However, I do not think we have yet found quite the right form of organizing the continuing joint appraisals of economic developments that we shall need. I think the newly formed Economic Council of Canada may play a very useful role, if it establishes appropriate connections with similar arms of the provincial governments. But under its present statute this body is to confine its attention to medium-term and longer-term developments. While these appraisals, especially if actively participated in by the provinces, are of very great importance in warning of problems just as they loom over the horizon, it is also imperative to co-ordinate short-term economic policy measures at all levels of government. Policies to defend the national economy against unemployment, inflation, and inadequate growth must be national policies, having national support and the active co-operation of all governments which have responsibility for their implementation.

What I have been saying in this paper may be put briefly as follows. We Canadians want to maintain a national approach to the economic welfare of our citizens. But we recognize that this will require reallocations of functions and finances among levels of government and between the public and private sectors from time to time. Being essentially pragmatic and non-doctrinaire in respect of economic policy we have made adaptations for one hundred years that have brought us a high measure of prosperity, judged by world standards. Naturally we are never wholly satisfied with our arrangements. Recently we have made a series of further adaptations. It is our hope that they will release new drives for economic development while preserving tested incentives, that they will permit a more equitable sharing of the costs and gains of economic development among our citizens, and that they will render the administration of public services more efficient. I have suggested that in making these recent adaptations we have raised further problems. In particular I think we have weakened our defences against both unemployment and inflation. I feel that important organizational improvements are necessary to ensure appropriate application of the increased flow of saving through the public sector and to provide for concerted fiscal measures to support the national monetary policy.

In short, our next task, as a nation, will be to devise the means of co-ordinating federal and provincial policies so that we may not dissipate the economic gains which we expect from the recent decentralization of responsibility for economic policy.

COMMENTARIES / COMMENTAIRES

G. V. LA FOREST

One point that comes out clearly in both Professor Hood's and Professor Parizeau's papers is that the constitutional provisions affecting economic policy in Canada are so flexible that the centre of gravity can shift from the federal to the provincial governments, and *vice versa*, without constitutional change. This has always seemed a desirable feature of the constitution. It is difficult enough as it is to implement the shifts and adjustments of power between federal and provincial authorities that changing conditions demand. We would only multiply the difficulties of adjustment if we were to enshrine the arrangements required or desired at any particular time into a constitutionally rigid system.

Whenever there is a shift of power from one level of government to another the principal battleground is taxing power. Recently by virtue of the Pearson Accord the federal government has agreed to abandon a substantial part of a number of lucrative tax fields—income, corporation, and estate taxes—to the provinces. I might say that I greeted this decision as an act of statesmanship of a high order, but I am concerned about the further erosion of federal jurisdiction in these fields, not only because of the difficulties raised in Mr. Hood's and Mr. Parizeau's papers, but because they tend to accentuate the already great disparity in the ability of the various provinces to raise an adequate revenue. There is an important point about all these taxes, particularly the corporation tax, that I should like to underline. They tend to be more beneficial—to give a greater yield per capita—to the central provinces where the head offices of the bulk of the national corporations are located. The fortunate position of these provinces in this regard has, as it seems to me, resulted not only from natural advantages but also from federal policies that converted this country from a group of separate economic entities to a country possessing what Mr. Hood calls the economic characteristics of a nation. Because of this, the federal authorities have a strong claim to exercise jurisdiction over a substantial portion of these tax fields and to use the revenues derived from them not only for purely federal ventures but to assist the less fortunate provinces in raising a revenue and, if need be, to promote regional projects in the provinces most detrimentally affected by federal economic policies. In order to demonstrate these points I should like to review briefly a few of the major steps that made this country one economic nation.

The underlying issue that precipitated Confederation in 1867 was political rather than economic. But in order to fulfil this political purpose—the maintenance of the British connection on the northern half of the continent by building a large united nation—it was necessary to weld a number of geographic regions—the area west of the Rockies, British Columbia, looking towards the Pacific, the Maritimes and Newfoundland looking towards the Atlantic, and the vast central region consisting of Ontario, Quebec and the Prairie provinces looking towards the Great Lakes and the outlet afforded by the St. Lawrence—into a single economic unit. The BNA Act itself began this process by providing for a common market—section 121 provides that the produce of each province is to be admitted duty-free to the other provinces—and the construction of the intercolonial railway (section 145). But the process was given powerful impetus by the federal measures made pursuant to its legislative powers over trade and commerce, taxation, and interprovincial transportation that are collectively known as the National Policy.

The main instrument of the National Policy was the tariff. Before Confederation, import duties were the major source of revenue of the various provincial governments. Several results flowed from the transfer of this source of revenue to the federal government. First, the federal authorities had to undertake the payment of subsidies to the provincial governments to reimburse them for the loss of revenue entailed. These subsidies, incidentally, originally amounted to about half the revenues of the provinces, so that from the beginning the principle that responsibility for financing expenditure should devolve on the spending government was not adhered to under Canadian federalism. Secondly, the removal of the provincial tariffs resulted in more competition between the industries of different provinces. Thirdly, the creation of a larger fiscal unit resulted in loss of revenue, interprovincial trade no longer being subject to duty. In order to obtain adequate revenues the federal Parliament had perforce to raise the tariff. A perhaps unintentional effect of this was to erect a higher protective wall for Canadian industry, but, if this result was at first fortuitous, tariffs were later utilized as the key instrument in a deliberate effort to foster industrial development in Canada. (It is interesting that the courts have recognized that, constitutionally, customs duties are not solely a taxing measure but fall under the rubric "trade and commerce" so that the provinces are not exempted from these as they are from other federal taxes by virtue of section 125 of the BNA Act.)

Other factors led to the centralization of Canada's industrial capacity in Ontario and Quebec. The location of industries is largely determined by the interplay of three factors—the market, raw materials, and power. Now the Great Lakes and St. Lawrence river region forms a natural collecting and distributing centre for the central economic division of Canada already described, and at Confederation it was more densely populated than other parts of Canada. Moreover raw material could be gathered more easily, and water power could be produced more cheaply, there than in most other regions of Canada. Given adequate transportation (and this was provided by linking the country by railways from the Atlantic to the Pacific), it was inevitable that the region should become the home of Canada's principal industrial complex. A highly developed economic area naturally attracts other industries, and the attraction is not limited to private capital. Thus the federal government's policy of concentrating wartime industries in Ontario must surely have been owing in part to the industrial "know-how" of the population though the greater political representation of the region is not to be ignored.

The benefit of the federal Parliament's economic policies, then, was to accrue to the central region, Ontario especially and to a lesser extent Quebec. Now no one begrudges the policies that converted Canada from a primary producer into an industrial nation. Yet one must face the fact that the concentration of industrial activity in the central provinces has placed these provinces in a favourable position in raising revenues for the provision of essential services and the development of their own economic policies. This favourable situation, having, to no inconsiderable extent, resulted from federal policies, fairness demands that a substantial portion of taxes from corporate earnings and the consequent higher incomes prevailing in those areas be levied by the federal authorities to be used for viable regional projects. For not only are the large national corporations in great measure dependent for their economic health on the hinterland composed of the outlying provinces, from which they draw a substantial portion of their earnings, thereby draining regional areas, but they are also to a large extent kept alive by the indirect subsidy that is created by the existence of customs duties.

To illustrate this point, I will give one example. When one is forced to buy a car made in Canada because of the high tariff, the additional cost over the price for which one could obtain that car on the world market constitutes in substance a subsidy to the automotive industry of Canada. Because of the centralization of industry effected by other economic forces the outlying areas of Canada pay a subsidy to keep industries alive in central Canada. The central provinces also contribute to this subsidy, of course, but unlike the outlying regions they directly benefit from salaries and wages from these industries and from increased industrial activity.

So far as I am aware the only detailed study of the impact of the tariff on the various provinces was made by Professor N. McL. Rogers appearing before the Jones Royal Commission, the provincial economic inquiry of Nova Scotia, in the early 1930's. The figures he compiled convincingly establish that all the provinces except Ontario and Quebec suffered sizable drains on their economic resources because of the existence of the tariff. The Commission, consisting of Professor John Harry Jones, Dr. Alexander Johnson, and Dr. H. A. Innis, agreed that the effect of the tariffs was highly detrimental to that province. And if this was so of Nova Scotia, whose coal and steel industry derived some advantage from tariff policies, it applies, *a fortiori*, to the other provinces, such as my own, which derive little benefit from the tariff.

Of course the building up of a strong industrial complex may have the effect of lifting the general level of economic activity throughout the country and thereby benefit the whole nation. It can, for example, create a market for the products of the outlying areas. But it does not necessarily work that way; it certainly has not for the Maritime provinces. The important markets for our products are not Canadian; they are the export markets. Our staples, lumber and lumber products, agricultural products, and fish, find their major outlets on the world market and so derive no benefit from Canadian tariff policies. Indeed, the competitive position of our products on the world market is unfavourably affected because of the increased costs of production resulting from the higher prices paid for equipment because of the tariff. As the Special Commission on the Australian tariff stated as long ago as 1927: "The assistance given to Tariff-protected industries is in fact a bounty, but it is paid by the consumers and much of its cost falls ultimately on the export industries." It was considerations of this kind that led the Jones Commission, after careful study, to conclude as follows:

We believe that the industries of Nova Scotia, regarded as a whole, have suffered materially from the high tariff policy pursued by the Confederation during the past fifty years. The compensations offered by the Canadian market have not been sufficient to offset the loss of foreign markets. We believe that the policy has been a factor retarding the economic development of the Province and that if a low tariff policy had been pursued the economic development of the Province would have been more rapid and that the Province would have been able to maintain an increasing population on a higher standard of living than has actually been enjoyed during the last half century.

The foregoing, I hope, establishes that many of our regional problems are national problems. National not only because large geographical regions are affected; national not only because it is no longer acceptable that in a modern industrialized nation there should be vast regions whose inhabitants live at a standard far below the national level; but national because they are often the concommitants of policies implemented to benefit the country as a whole. More than in most countries, regional problems cannot be ignored in a federation like ours; for the resultant discontent can be channelled through the local political units, the provinces. Especially is this so because of the sense of identity of the people within each unit arising from a long separate history. I might add that economic development in the less developed areas would, of course, be beneficial to the whole country. As one example, transportation facilities must be maintained even when there is limited use; this applies with greater force to the railroads which must maintain a large percentage of their resources in fixed equipment. An increased population in these areas would increase the use and consequently the revenues from these necessary transportation facilities.

The provinces which have benefited from national policies and others which may not have received such benefits but are abundantly endowed with natural resources may be both able and willing to put their own houses in order without federal intervention. But that is not true of others; certainly it is not true of the Maritime provinces and Newfoundland. Vigorous federal policies, then, are required to redress the economic disabilities of these provinces. But to do this requires, on the constitutional plane, a federal Parliament that has and exercises for this purpose broad taxing, spending, and lending powers. Though Quebec's Tremblay Commission on Constitutional Problems (whose admirably prepared report merits far more attention in other parts of Canada than it has yet received) questions whether the broad exercise of these powers comes within the letter or the spirit of the constitution, I have little doubt of their legality or their fundamental accord with the basic nature of Canadian federalism. The taxing power is expressed in the broadest terms, and the spending and lending of money (so long as this does not involve the implementation of a scheme that is in substance an exercise of provincial power as occurred in the Unemployment Insurance case) is surely an exercise of the federal Parliament's exclusive legislative power over its public property. Though there has been extra-judicial objection, subsidies have been paid since Confederation and adjustments have been made from time to time without being challenged in the courts.

Lest I be misunderstood I might add, parenthetically, that I have considerable sympathy for the Tremblay Commission's view that the provinces should have considerable control over their economic destinies; particularly is this so of Quebec which has the primary responsibility for maintaining the French-Canadian way of life. I am aware, of course, that this substantially weakens the federal government's ability to promote anti-cyclical measures and other national policies, but the solution under the practical realities of the time would seem to me to lie in attempting to devise adequate machinery for co-ordinating the actions of the various levels of government.

Finally I should like to say a word on the measures taken to assist regional development. For a long period the subsidies were paid on the basis of population, so that they did nothing to redress the balance. Following the Duncan Commission in the late 1920's, payments to the Maritime provinces were increased but it was not until recent years that special grants (notably the Atlantic Provinces Adjustment Grants) were provided for in truly significant amounts. These subsidies assist the provincial governments to provide essential services at a reasonable level, but they do not directly attack the perennial economic problem. Transfer payments, such as old age pensions, family allowances, and the like, probably result in a net gain to regional areas, but these have a tendency to be spent on manufactured goods and be funnelled back into the central Canadian economy. Some of the shared-cost programs also result in net gains for the regional areas, but often the provincial and municipal governments can ill afford to shoulder their share of the costs. Moreover, they tend to channel the available funds towards projects that may be less desirable than the provinces, which have of course more intimate knowledge of the requirements, could devise. At the same time these provinces should be less inclined than the more affluent regions of Canada to take over these projects, not only for financial reasons, but because there is a scarcity of trained personnel owing to the attraction of the affluent regions on the more able segment of the population. Tax incentives may play a useful role, but this has not been as successful as might be expected because they do not always override other economic considerations. One of the most promising steps that has been taken is the establishment of the Atlantic Development Board and through it the making of large capital grants for the over-all improvement of the economic structure of the region. Such policies, I might add, should not be looked upon as largesse by the more fortunate areas of Canada, but as proper steps to redress the inescapable harm resulting to these areas from federal policies for the economic development of the country as a whole.

M. LALONDE

In my part of the country, the most popular game at the present time among intellectuals and politicians, both jurists and non-jurists, is constitution-making—or, should I say, a constitution-unmaking. It was therefore very pleasant to hear this morning two speakers who analysed the problem of economic policy in the federal state without starting from or concluding with the necessity of establishing a wholly new constitutional framework. Indeed, I am in full agreement with Professor Parizeau's remark that to attempt a wholesale revision of the constitution at the present time would probably only delay any rational solution to the urgent problems of Canada.

Secondly, I believe that the extension of local and provincial activities, as shown by the two speakers, does not only bring disorder in traditional economic policies, but also offers a challenge and an opportunity to evolve truly national economic policies, including both federal and provincial governments, by giving more attention than in the past to local and regional problems.

Until 1953, the current income of junior governments amounted to only at most half that of the federal government, but that figure implies a substantial amount of public income and expenditure that remained outside the scope of federal fiscal policy. Nowadays, the income of junior governments is greater by about 15 per cent than that of the federal government. One could say that this does increase the problem; but in a way, it seems to open the door to solutions that were not considered before. Thus while the junior governments had always remained aloof from fiscal policies, the sheer size of their income and expenditure forces them now to open their eyes to these new realities and to assume some responsibilities in this field. I know that hardly anything concrete has been done as yet by the provinces, but the mere fact that the matter is now seriously discussed is certainly a far cry from the situation of, say, fifteen years ago. However cumbersome and inadequate fiscal policy may by itself be, I have not heard yet that it does not matter whether fiscal policy in a country is constantly at loggerheads with monetary policy. The historic evolution explained by the two speakers could progressively contribute to the establishment of more effective fiscal policies than were ever known in the past, provided provincial governments do not define themselves purely in terms of power politics with regards to the central government.

This brings me to another point. I am afraid that, after a period when many believed that the only source of sensible policies could be in Ottawa, we are coming to another period when provincial politicians and their advisers will consider themselves as heads of states, entitled to full powers, if not actually clothed with full powers. What is worrying is that the debate is not firstly taking place in terms of the economic welfare of the individual citizen, but rather in terms of a power struggle between conflicting states.

The dispute between levels of government in Canada, in my opinion, is essentially connected with the power politics of the various groups of people involved and has very little to do with the welfare of the individual citizens of the country. A very close comparative study should be made between the centrifugal forces in Canada and the state's rights movement in the United States. The official reasons for these centrifugal forces will vary between the two countries, but I suspect that strong similarities could be found in both movements.

The struggle between federal and provincial governments in Canada has not caused too much damage up to now, thanks to the beneficial effects upon Canada of the economic conditions in the rest of the world and in the United States in particular. But the two papers we have heard today lead us to believe that this country is more badly equipped than it was twenty years ago to fight either a severe recession or a large dose of inflation. I do not mean that we should set the clock back and return to the type of federal-provincial relations that existed ten or twenty years ago, but while the main aims of economic policies—at least those I was taught at school—are supposed to be a high level of employment, a reasonably stable currency, and an orderly rate of growth—things to which even the overriding aim of federal-provincial relations mentioned by Professor Hood is submitted—the tug-of-war between the central and provincial governments, as well as between the provincial and municipal governments, seems to have taken us farther away from these aims. It is inconceivable that in their fight for a larger share of the taxpayer's shirt the governments should have left on the side of the ring the fundamental aims of economic policies. It is certainly not too late to react, but this is certainly a matter of top priority in the discussions at federal-provincial conference. In that respect, it is rather amusing to see that the provinces insist on controlling and streamlining the operations of local authorities, be they municipal governments or school boards, while at the same time they raise the flag of provincial sovereignty against attempts at streamlining their own policies with those of other provinces or of the central government.

The balkanization of economic policies in this country under the pretence of dealing more adequately with local or regional problems will not improve, but worsen, the lot of all citizens, unless these policies are closely adjusted to one another; this will imply, in my opinion, far more consultation on a continuous basis between all levels of government than has been prevalent in the past. Furthermore, this may even imply a form of binding decision-making process in matters of greater importance. The current concept of planning, to which Mr. Parizeau in particular referred, seems to have been imported directly from a unitary state régime, and no substantial and imaginative effort seems to have been made to elaborate a notion and procedure of planning in a federal state. If this is not done, there will be an inevitable tendency towards autarchy inside each province. This has already started to appear in the form of public encouragement to local buying or even official policies directing public purchases towards local entrepreneurs; and when I hear Mr. Parizeau declare that Quebec, for instance, certainly will not agree for long to be treated as a private company with regard to its steel mill project, either I do not understand what he means, or I fear that such projects will be carried out to the prejudice of Quebec consumers.

In the same line of thought, I fail to share Mr. Parizeau's enthusiasm about current provincial, and particularly Quebec, economic policies. I am little involved in the elaboration and the implementation of these policies and I therefore speak here only as an outside observer without detailed knowledge of the internal activities of the Quebec government. Therefore, I may stand to be corrected on this. But I submit that there is a *non sequitur* when Mr. Parizeau states that the absence of French Canadians from the management of large firms was bound to imply "that policies involved in Quebec would be much more to the left than any of the policies which would emerge from the atmosphere of Ottawa." The factor just mentioned may imply a swing just as well to the right as to the left. Contemporary history is full of examples where xenophobia or mere suspicion of what we consider foreign interests have been the main streams of rightist as well as lefist governments, and I fail to see what is so leftist in Quebec's nationaliza- tion of electricity, for instance, a couple of years after Mr. Bennett had done the same in British Columbia. Or again in the setting up of a "Société générale de financement" where the government holds only a minority interest and where the credit unions and l'Ordre de Jacques-Cartier seem from what I can assess to have a much more effective control of the "société" than the government itself. Or again, in transferring to what is in effect a private corporation, albeit a non-profit one, the responsibility of building a bridge across the St. Lawrence River at Trois-Rivières. Some schemes currently discussed concerning the proposed steel mill bear a strange similarity to the structure of the "Socété générale de financement" and, I should add, imply even less control of the operation by the provincial government. In fact, one could honestly say that the most "left-wing" scheme in operation in Quebec is the ARDA scheme which is a joint plan initiated by the central government. There might be very important projects still in the drawers of the "Conseil d'orientation économique" but I have not any knowledge about these yet.

As to Professor Parizeau's reference to the attitude of Quebec civil servants towards business lobbyists, who might be considered as foreigners, I suggest that at least the largest business corporations have learned a long time ago that they should have good French Canadians to do their lobbying in Quebec City.

I have referred here to Quebec only because this is the province I know best, but I suspect that the situation is not very different in the other provinces.

In another field, I think that Mr. Parizeau's suggestion to assure provin- cial representation on the board of directors of the Bank of Canada is very worthwhile. One could also refer here to the Australian experience whereby the various states have succeeded in co-ordinating their plans of public financing. But by the same token, the central government should also be given a voice in some provincial fields, such as trade and commerce (this implies a voice in provincial planning), and it is well known that the Privy Council has constantly emasculated the trade and commerce clause of section 91 of the BNA Act. If we are not to amend the constitution to give more teeth to that clause, then closer federal and interprovincial co-operation should be considered in that field. Otherwise if, again quoting Mr. Parizeau, "opting out of joint programs with no strings attached becomes the only logical course to follow for the provinces," the country may very well be faced before long with government-planning in eleven different directions. Indeed, I do not believe that Quebec would for purely nationalistic reasons opt out of joint programs if at the same time it was not a reasonably paying proposition; and, if it is so, why should not the other provinces follow suit?

Finally, I raise a point with Mr. Hood's paper. He says that the federal parliament overweighed by rural representation was not as sensitive to the needs of urban growth or to the later condition of urban unemployment as the local governments: Firstly, does he mean to say that over-representation of rural areas was greater in the federal parliament than in the provincial legislatures? Secondly, does he mean that local governments have been more dynamic than the federal government in dealing with the problems of urban growth or urban unemployment? This, truly, I doubt very much.

SCOTT GORDON

I shall be very brief and, I fear, rather haphazard in the small number of comments I want to make. The first point is in connection with Professor Hood's discussion of the implication of pension plans. His argument was that the organization of a governmental pension plan will lead to a reduction in the amount of savings that flows through private channels, will therefore inhibit the growth of large aggregations of capital in the private sector, and will thus impair economic growth. The implication of this argument is, of course, that under current circumstances, the channelling of capital funds to the public sector is not as productive as channelling to the private sector.

I suspect that Mr. Hood may have been writing his address when he was in the midst of reading examination papers: at such a time it is very difficult to believe that social capital investment has very high productivity. But there are many other evidences that social capital investment is grossly deficient in Canada, and that it has very high productivity indeed. The various studies that have been done of the productivity of social capital suggest that the rate of return in general is very high; the places where we seem to apprehend that it may not be very high, or where we seem to be indeterminate on the matter, are usually ascribable to the fact that it is difficult to measure the output of certain types of social capital investments (such as universities, say).

Now there is no particular reason why social capital investment is not done as well, or better, at the provincial level than at the federal level; or

better at the municipal level for certain types of investment than at either
the provincial or federal level. If all that Mr. Hood is saying is that these
large amounts of money must be spent wisely, I do not think there is any-
body who would disagree; but the assumption in his paper that, by channelling them into social channels rather than private, they will not be spent
as wisely is, I think, a very unwarranted assumption indeed.

What has been developing in Canada, and will undoubtedly develop
further if there is not a public pension scheme, is the collection of large
amounts of funds into private pension schemes; such private schemes are
almost guaranteed, by their constitution, to lead to inefficiency in the allocation of capital resources. The pension funds which I contribute, for example,
through the university, to a trust company, are under the control of a trust
contract. The result of that restrictive trust contract is that the trust company does not invest the funds as well as it in fact can, and I do not invest
them as well as I in fact can. This is because of the investment management
rigidity that is always prevalent in trust arrangements of this sort. So I am
not inclined to give much weight to the argument that Mr. Hood built on
this foundation.

But this was perhaps only an auxiliary argument. It seems to me that
perhaps he was more interested in the more general proposition that there
have been certain developments lately (the proposed pension fund being
one, and the general shift of resources to the provincial sectors being
another, and more important) which have decreased the capacity of the
economy to orient itself to economic changes, either through fiscal policy
or through other forms of governmental intervention. In this connection,
he underlined a point which has been made very frequently, and which
I think is perfectly valid: that shifting public resources to the provincial
sectors and away from the federal sector has decreased the capacity of
fiscal policy to act in counter-cyclical fashion. Now this is true. It has
added a rail or two to this particular fence. But if recent experience in
Canada is any measure, the most important thing is that when we try to
jump this fence, we present the right end of the horse to it. I would settle
for an additional rail or two if we could be guaranteed on this essential point.

This brings me to the few very brief comments I want to make on
Professor Parizeau's paper. Mr. Parizeau's paper is a very disturbing but,
if I may say so, a very skilful paper. It is, I think, a stump from which
an agile cat can jump in many directions; which is perhaps a prudent
position for anyone to take these days in Canada, and especially in the
Province of Quebec. I would not want to be accused of being insensitive to
the diplomatic difficulties that people find themselves in from time to time.
Mr. Parizeau's picture, which he drew in the last pages of his paper, of
the emerging federal state in Canada, however, leaves me very unsatisfied
and unenthusiastic. It would seem to me that it marks out a route for our
federal development from which we would emerge as a nation whose degree
of cohesion would be considerably below, say, that of the European
Economic Community as a political organization.

The other point that I want to make (I would not make it at all if I did
not feel so strongly about it, because Professor Lalonde has already discussed it) has to do with the passage to which Mr. Lalonde referred in

discussing whether the prospect that Mr. Parizeau places before us can be construed as measures of the political "left." I think he should have quoted a larger part of that passage in order to give the right and full context. So I shall requote it:

But the situation in Quebec is a much more difficult one. The fact that it is populated by a different ethnic group has well-known repercussions. One of these repercussions, possibly the most important, springs from the fact that French Canadians can control in Quebec nearly all the avenues that lead to power, except large business. They dominate and play an essential role in the government, the civil service, mass media, the labour unions, the academic world, but they are completely absent from the management of large firms. This state of affairs was bound to imply that sooner or later policies evolved in Quebec would be much more to the left than any of the policies which would emerge from the atmosphere of Ottawa.

What I have to say to that is: "Left! Nonsense!" These are interventionist policies sure enough, but the political direction that they have to be interpreted as constituting is very different, and this is very disquieting. I am reminded at this point of the old saw, that people who have not learned the lessons of history will be forced to repeat them. The difficulty, however, is that a lot of the rest of us might be forced to repeat them along with Professor Parizeau.

LEGAL AND POLITICAL ATTITUDES TO THE CONSTITUTION

ATTITUDES JURIDIQUES ET POLITIQUES A L'EGARD DE LA CONSTITUTION

The Balanced Interpretation

of the Federal Distribution

# of Legislative Powers

in Canada

(The Integrity of the Process of Interpretation)

W. R. LEDERMAN

As Canada approaches the centennial of her formation under a federal constitution, the times call for thoughtful consideration of both the past and the future. For almost one hundred years now the distribution of law-making powers made by the BNA Act between the parliament of Canada and the legislatures of the provinces has been under interpretation in the courts. For much the greater part of the period, the final interpretative tribunal was the Judicial Committee of the Privy Council in London, but since 1949 the Supreme Court of Canada has taken the place of the Judicial committee.[1]

While respecting the previous course of interpretation, the Supreme Court of Canada has also shown in some instances that it can and will move along new lines as the basic needs of the country change with changing times.[2] This suggests that it would be profitable to examine closely the system of interpretation itself, if we would discern something of the shape of the future. What are the essential elements of the system of interpretation of the distribution of powers? Where is it flexible and where rigid? What is the nature of its appeal to both reason and authority? Is the traditional superior court essential to the process?

[1] *A.G. for Ontario* v. *A.G. for Canada*, [1947] AC 127 (Privy Council Appeals Case).

[2] For example, respecting the trade and commerce power, see *Murphy* v. *C.P.R. and A.G. for Canada*, [1958] SCR 626.

Certainly the system of interpretation has its purely technical side, but that is not all by any means. Though one starts by looking at a technique or procedure, soon, by travelling this route, one uncovers the detailed and substantive working conceptions of Canadian federalism. In other words, study of the process of interpretation soon reveals essential elements that must be respected if we are to have a balanced federal constitution—one that maintains and develops reasonable equilibrium between centralization and provincial autonomy in subject after subject of public concern. In a brief and preliminary way, I described the process as follows in an earlier essay.[3]

The federal distribution of legislative powers and responsibilities in Canada is one of the facts of life when we concern ourselves with the many important social, political, economic or cultural problems of our country. Over the whole range of actual and potential law-making, our constitution distributes powers and responsibilities by two lists of categories or classes—one list for the federal parliament (primarily section 91 of the BNA Act), the other for each of the provincial legislatures (primarily section 92 of the BNA Act). For instance, the federal list includes regulation of trade and commerce, criminal law, and a general power to make laws in all matters not assigned to the provinces. Examples from the provincial list are property and civil rights in the province, local works and undertakings, and all matters of a merely local or private nature in the province.

These federal and provincial categories of power are expressed, and indeed have to be expressed, in quite general terms. This permits considerable flexibility in constitutional interpretation, but also it brings much overlapping and potential conflict between the various definitions of powers and responsibilities. To put the same point in another way, our community life—social, economic, political, and cultural—is very complex and will not fit neatly into any scheme of categories or classes without considerable overlap and ambiguity occurring. There are inevitable difficulties arising from this that we must live with so long as we have a federal constitution.

Accordingly the courts must continually assess the competing federal and provincial lists of powers against one another in the judicial task of interpreting the constitution. In the course of judicial decisions on the BNA Act, the judges have basically done one of two things. First, they have attempted to define mutually exclusive spheres for federal and provincial powers, with partial success. But, where mutual exclusion did not seem feasible or proper, the courts have implied the existence of concurrent federal and provincial powers in the overlapping area, with the result that either or both authorities have been permitted to legislate provided their statutes did not in some way conflict one with the other in the common area.

The two lists just mentioned, federal and provincial, are collectively

[3]W. R. Lederman, "The Concurrent Operation of Federal and Provincial Laws in Canada," (1962–63) 9 *McGill LJ*, p. 185.

complete (or nearly so) in their enumeration of governmental powers.[4] Accordingly they comprise a classification system for these powers. But, any such classification system brings with it inevitable philosophic dilemmas in logic and valuation for those charged with applying the system to the life of the country. Often our courts have faced these dilemmas in terms of what they call the aspect theory,[5] which is an all-pervasive idea helpful in the solution of such problems. What follows in the balance of this essay is principally an attempt to explain and illustrate the total process of interpretation of the BNA Act on the basis of the aspect theory.

I. *CLASSIFICATION OF LAWS AND THE ASPECT THEORY*

Our legal system consists of a great multitude of rules defining the rights, duties, privileges, powers, and immunities of the people over the whole range of human affairs. Legal relations are specified in everything from crimes to contracts, from torts to taxes, from wills to welfare. It is to this body of the ordinary laws of the land, and to proposed new laws, that the classification system of our federal constitution must be applied.

It seems labouring the obvious to say that only classes or categories of laws can be used to distribute law-making powers, or, putting it the other way around, that only particular laws are appropriate data for the various categories of a system of classification of laws. Nevertheless, there is considerable importance in the point. With respect to both the federal and provincial lists, the BNA Act speaks of power "to make laws in relation to matters coming within the classes of subjects hereinafter enumerated." This is all right provided one realizes that "subjects" and "matters" simply refer to different *aspects* or features of the laws to be classified. It would have been a better and simpler description of the true position if the BNA Act had spoken only of power "to make laws coming within the classes of laws hereafter enumerated," for, as a matter of reason, that is inevitably the position anyway.[6] As Dr. Martin Wolf has put it,[7] "Classification may be compared with the

---

[4]A very few powers are withheld from both legislative bodies. See for examples sections 91(1), 93, 121, and 133 of the *BNA Act*, 30 & 31 Victoria, C. 3 (UK) as amended to date.

[5]"Subjects which in one aspect and for one purpose fall within Sect. 92, may in another aspect and for another purpose fall within Sec. 91." Lord Fitzgerald, in *Hodge* v. *The Queen*, (1883–84) 9 AC 117 at 130.

[6]The writer developed this theme in detail in an earlier essay entitled "Classification of Laws and the British North America Act," in *Legal Essays in Honour of Arthur Moxon* (Toronto, 1953), pp. 183–207.

[7]M. Wolff, *Private International Law* (London, 1945), p. 148.

mathematical process of placing a factor common to several numbers outside the bracket." For instance, the federal category "criminal law" has been defined as including all rules that forbid a specified type of conduct with penal consequences for breach. The prohibitive and penal features are the common denominators here, the aspects that count in this definition of criminal law.

To repeat then, sections 91 and 92 of the BNA Act contain categories of laws, not categories of facts. As Sir Frederick Pollock has said,[8] "The divisions of law, as we are in the habit of elliptically naming them, are in truth not divisions of facts but of rules; or, if we like to say so, of the legal aspect of facts." In other words, when classifying to distribute legislative powers, we approach the facts of life only through their legal aspects, that is, only to the extent that such facts have been incorporated in rules of law as the typical fact-situations contemplated by those rules. For example, one cannot simply look at a particular financial transaction and say, "That is banking within the meaning of section 91(15) of the BNA Act, and hence the federal Parliament and only the federal Parliament can make laws to regulate or affect that transaction in any way." Rather, one must frame the terms of the law whereby one proposes to do something to regulate that type of financial transaction, and then look at that law to see if it is a banking law. What one proposes to *do* by a law about a certain type of fact situation may well have as much bearing on classification of that law as does the nature of the facts alone. Law is normative, not merely descriptive.

The important lesson from this is that, if we would reason our way to precise and meaningful conclusions about the significance for the future of our distribution of law-making powers in Canada, we must be prepared to be specific about the terms of the proposed laws that we hope to have passed in the federal Parliament or the provincial legislatures. On the whole, vague general questions about legislative jurisdiction cannot be answered with any real clarity or precision. The truth of this point can be illustrated from the so-called "reference cases," that is, cases where the judgments are in response to questions put directly to the court by a government. For instance, the federal cabinet is empowered to put questions to the Supreme Court of Canada by order-in-council and the Court is required to answer.[9] If these direct questions take the form of asking the judges to assess the validity of laws that have been enacted, or at least fully drafted, then the judges can and do answer fully and with precision on the issue of legislative

[8]Sir F. Pollock, *A First Book of Jurisprudence* (2nd ed., London, 1904).
[9]The Supreme Court Act, RSC 1952, c. 259, 55.

powers. Reference cases of this type command as much influence in the realm of precedent as do cases originating in actual litigation, in spite of occasional judicial protestations to the contrary.[10] In both types of cases the actual texts of the laws at issue are available. The *Privy Council Appeals Reference* of 1947,[11] which concerned new draft sections for the *Supreme Court Act*,[12] is as influential as the case of *British Coal Corporation* v. *The King*,[13] which was decided in 1935 as the result of actual litigation. The former case expands and adds to the reasoning of the latter, and both are precise and meaningful.

By contrast, nothing much but confusion and talk of competing alternatives comes out of the *Reference respecting Waters and Water Powers*[14] considered by the Supreme Court of Canada in 1929. The questions from the cabinet in that case were very general ones about legislative competence to regulate the use or exploitation of rivers, lakes, and canals. Relevant draft laws were not either suggested or quoted. The reporter for the Canada Law Reports gave up on the headnote. He says plaintively at the start of the report[15]: "In view of the difficulties which the court found in dealing with the questions before it and of the impossibility of giving precise and categorical answers, it was thought best, in order to avoid misleading as to what was decided, to put as a headnote the text of the formal judgment." At one point in the formal judgment, their lordships said of two of the questions, "These questions cannot be answered categorically either in the affirmative or in the negative."[16] The authority to make a reference to the courts is useful, then, only if these questions are properly framed in the light of the process of decision that is involved.

But, even if the Court does have an actual legal text before it, there may still be difficulty similar to that just considered. As Mr. Justice Rand pointed out in the *Saumur Case* in 1953,[17] the law at issue may be so vague and general in its terms that it fails because, given its full meaning, it would exceed the specified powers of either the federal parliament or a provincial legislature. It will be recalled that the Quebec City by-law in that case was as follows: "It is ... forbidden to distribute in the streets of the City of Quebec any book, pamphlet, booklet, circular, tract whatever, without having previously obtained for so doing the

---

[10]See Gerald Rubin, "The Nature, Use and Effect of Reference Cases in Canadian Constitutional Law," (1959–60) 6 *McGill LJ*, p. 168, esp. p. 177.
[11]See n. 1.   [12]See n. (9), 54.
[13][1935] AC 500.   [14][1929] SCR 200.
[15]*Ibid.*   [16]*Ibid.*, p. 201.
[17]*Saumur* v. *Quebec and A.G. for Quebec*, [1953] 2 SCR 299.

written permission of the Chief of Police." In commenting on this, Mr. Justice Rand points out that the laws of a federal country must be specific and detailed enough that they make sense in relation to the categories of the system for the distribution of law-making powers.[18]

> Conceding ... that aspects of the activities of religion and free speech may be affected by provincial legislation, such legislation, as in all other fields, must be sufficiently definite and precise to indicate its subject matter. In our political organization, as in federal structures generally, that is the condition of legislation by any authority within it: the courts must be able from its language and its relevant circumstances, to attribute an enactment to a matter in relation to which the Legislature acting has been empowered to make laws. That principle inheres in the nature of federalism; otherwise, authority, in broad and general terms, could be conferred which would end the division of powers. Where the language is sufficiently specific and can fairly be interpreted as applying only to matter within the enacting jurisdiction, that attribution will be made; and where the requisite elements are present, there is the rule of severability. But to authorize action which may be related indifferently to a variety of incompatible matters by means of the device of a discretionary licence cannot be brought within either of these mechanisms; and the Court is powerless, under general language that overlaps exclusive jurisdictions, to delineate and preserve valid power in a segregated form.

The lesson mentioned earlier may perhaps now be repeated and restated. The most fruitful constitutional discussions are likely to be those that start with specific legal remedies and measures conceived to be useful or necessary to meet our various national and regional problems. With such proposed legal measures in mind, it is then feasible to go on to the special federal issues of whether power to enact this or that measure lies at present with the federal parliament or the provincial legislatures. Also, this approach will raise in specific and useful ways issues of whether power is presently misplaced and needs to be relocated or reformed by amendment of the system for distribution of powers itself.

Nevertheless, even if one does have a specific and simple legal rule to assess for validity, critical dilemmas of classification still arise. Take, for example, the simple proposition, "Marriage revokes a pre-nuptial will of either spouse." Marriage is a federal category of jurisdiction under section 91(26) of the BNA Act while property is a provincial category under section 92(13). Obviously the rule quoted is both marriage law and property law. It has both its matrimonial aspect and its proprietary aspect. Logically it falls within both the federal and provin-

[18]*Ibid.*, p. 333.

cial lists. When the item being classified points both ways in this manner, is it to be characterized as proprietary or matrimonial for purposes of assigning power to enact it?

Consider another example suggested by the recent decision of the Supreme Court of Canada upholding the validity of the Ontario statute, the *Unconscionable Transactions Relief Act*.[19] In that case the law provided that, in respect of money lent, if in all the circumstances the cost of the loan was excessive and the transaction harsh and unconscionable, the judge could reform the contract so as to make its terms fair and reasonable, and order the necesary adjustments at the expense of the lender. Certainly this law has its contractual aspect, and contract is a classic example of civil rights within the provincial category of property and civil rights. But also the same law concerns interest charges, and thus has an aspect or feature pointing logically to the federal category of interest in section 91(19) of the BNA Act. Again one must ask— which aspect is to prevail for purposes of the division of legislative powers?

The point to appreciate is that these simple examples are not exceptional; indeed, they illustrate the usual position. Nearly all laws or legislative schemes have a multiplicity of features, characteristics, or aspects by which they may be classified in a number of different ways, and hence potentialities of cross-classification are ever present. The more complex the statute, the greater the number of logical possibilities in this regard. So, in the case of a particular law challenged for validity, one aspect of it points to a federal category of power with logical plausibility, but, with equal logical plausibility, another aspect points to a provincial category of power. Or, looking at the other side of the coin, one can say the same thing another way. The respective federal and provincial classes of laws often overlap one another as general concepts in many important respects, and thus compete, so to speak, through this partial coincidence of categories, for the allegiance of the statutes to be classified. When one says that the rule, "marriage revokes a pre-nuptial will," is both matrimonial and proprietary, one is necessarily saying that logically the concept of marriage law and the concept of property law overlap one another respecting rules of matrimonial property law. Similarly, in the other example given earlier, the concept of contract law (included in civil rights) and the concept of interest law overlap one another respecting rules regulating unconscionable interest charges. To repeat, this partial but multiple coincidence

---

[19]*A.G. for Ontario* v *Barfried Enterprises Ltd.*, (1964) 42 DLR (2d) 137. *Unconscionable Transactions Relief Act*, RSO 1960, c. 410.

of categories is the usual and not the exceptional situation for a classification system such as that embodied in the BNA Act. Those who make
a federal constitution must generalize in some degree the concepts to be
used to distribute law-making powers. But, once such lists have been
made, those who must interpret the constitution encounter the broad
extensions of meaning and the overlapping of concepts that generalized
thought makes inevitable. At this point it is clear that such generalized
concepts must be used with care if we would preserve the balance of
our federal constitution—preserve, that is, a proper equilibrium between
significant provincial autonomy and adequate central power.

The danger is this, that some of the categories of federal power and
some of those of provincial power are capable of very broadly extended
ranges of meaning. If one of these concepts of federal power should
be given such a broadly extended meaning, *and also priority over any
competing provincial concept*, then federal power would come close to
eliminating provincial power. The converse could happen just as easily,
with the federal power suffering virtual eclipse. Take for example the
federal category of criminal law. If all that is necessary for valid legislation under this head is that the federal Parliament should prohibit
something with penal consequences for breach, then Parliament can
enact any legislative scheme it pleases provided it sprinkles the statute
concerned with a few prohibitions and penalties. There would be very
little left of indepedendent provincial power if the federal Parliament
could really get away with this. And the attempt has been made. In the
Board of Commerce Act and the *Combines and Fair Prices Act* of
1919,[20] the federal Parliament, among other things, enacted a most
elaborate and detailed scheme for the positive control by the Board of
Commerce of supplies and sales of consumer goods at every level, with
penalties for breaches of the regulations. The courts rejected the argument that this could be sustained under the federal criminal law power
at the expense of provincial powers over local industry and commerce
within the province. In the *Margarine Case*[21] the courts reached the

---

[20]*In re: The Board of Commerce Act, 1919, and The Combines & Fair Prices
Act, 1919*, (1921) 1 AC 191.

[21]*Reference re Validity of Section 5(a) of the Dairy Industry Act*, [1949]
SCR 1. Mr. Justice Rand made it clear in the following words that the definition
of "criminal law" for purposes of the BNA Act was not just a matter of prohibition and penalty only. At pages 50–51 he said: "Is the prohibition then enacted
with a view to a public purpose which can support it as being in relation to
criminal law? Public peace, order, security, health, morality: these are the
ordinary though not exclusive ends served by that law, but they do not appear
to be the object of the parliamentary action here. . . . [T]here is nothing of a
general or injurious nature to be abolished or removed: it is a matter of prefer-
ring certain local trade to others."

same result in much the same circumstances concerning attempted federal prohibition of the local manufacture and sale of that one commodity.

In the *Padlock Law Case*,[22] by contrast, the shoe was on the other foot. Briefly, the Quebec legislature had enacted a prohibition on the dissemination of communistic propaganda from any house or building in the province, the penalty being the padlocking of a house so used against any use whatever for up to one year. Counsel for the province argued that this was valid provincial property legislation under section 92(13) because, under this heading, any use whatever of land or buildings could be regulated by a province. The Court rejected the argument, pointing out that there would be no real limit to what a province could do at the expense of federal powers if such an extended conception of the scope of property law were to prevail. In such circumstances, the federal writ would run only in remote air space.

An example of an extreme extension of meaning that has prevailed is afforded by judicial interpretation of the commerce power in the United States. There the Congress was given power by the constitution ". . . to regulate Commerce with foreign Nations, and among the several States. . . ."[23] In the modern period at least, the Supreme Court of the United States has extended the meaning of the commerce power to the furthest limits of which it is capable, so that now there is little or nothing left of the independent power of the respective American states over any economic activities local to a state. For example, the American Supreme Court has held that the commerce power of the Congress extends to regulation of the labour standards of the maintenance employees of the owner of a building (janitors, electricians, window washers, and so on) where the owner has rented the building to a tenant who is principally engaged in the production of goods for inter-state commerce.[24] Now, if a "house-that-Jack-built" chain of relevance like that is to be permitted to extend the meaning of "commerce among the several states," all limits are indeed off. No wonder Professor Alexander Smith, in his recent treatise on the subject, has stated: "[I]t is not extravagant to say that the federal system in the United States exists only on Congressional sufferance."[25]

The Americans may like this sort of result, and indeed it may suit their needs very well. It would never do for Canada. But, if we would maintain a balanced federal system here, there are two dilemmas of

[22]*Switzman* v. *Elbling and A.G. for Quebec*, [1957] SCR 285.
[23]Article 1, s. 8(3).
[24]*Kirschbaum Co.* v. *Walling*, (1942) 316 US 517.
[25]Alexander Smith, *The Commerce Power in Canada and the United States* (Toronto, 1963), p. 371.

classification for the distribution of legislative powers that one must solve. They have been revealed in the foregoing analysis and may be briefly recapitulated as follows.

1. *The categories of legislative power.* No one of the general concepts by which power is given should be allowed to prevail to the extreme limits of its potential meaning, regardless of the competing scope of other concepts. There must be some mutual limitations of definition, and even then much overlapping will remain.

2. *The laws to be classified.* The laws challenged for validity, the particular items to be classified, are almost invariably ambivalent in the logical sense, in that they exhibit both federal and provincial aspects or characteristics. Different aspects of the same particular law point to categories in both the federal and provincial lists respectively, even though no one category in those lists is allowed an extremely extended meaning. So, on this account alone, there must be some further step in the classification process whereby the federal aspect is made to prevail over the provincial one, or *vice versa*, for purposes of decisive classification.

Let us now consider the solutions of these problems.

II. SOLUTIONS OF THE DILEMMAS OF THE DISTRIBUTION OF LEGISLATIVE POWERS

Their lordships of the Privy Council were not long in discovering that they faced the problems of interpretation just outlined. It soon became clear to them that the solutions had to be based on appreciation of the many aspects of meaning involved in the classification process—the range of aspects covered by the definition of a category of laws on the one hand, and the multiplicity of classifiable aspects that a single statutory scheme could exhibit on the other. The process or system is by no means automatic or productive of just one set of "right" answers. It is largely a matter of framing the right questions in the right order, and there are judicial choices to be made about the proper answers at each stage.

In the first place, the courts have indeed tended to avoid extremely extended meanings for categories of federal power at the expense of those of provincial power, and *vice versa*. Definitions have tended to be mutually restrained where the context seems to call for this. Many examples of such mutual modification could be given,[26] but perhaps

[26]See *Citizens Insurance Co. of Canada* v. *Parsons*, (1881–82) 7 AC 96, at 106–7.

one of the best (and most difficult) is afforded by interpretation of
the federal general power. The opening words of section 91 give the
federal parliament power ". . . to make Laws for the Peace, Order and
good Government of Canada, in relation to all Matters not coming
within the Classes of Subjects by this Act assigned exclusively to the
Legislatures of the Provinces; . . ." Classes assigned to the provinces,
however, include "Property and Civil Rights in the Province," and
"Generally all Matters of a merely local or private Nature in the
Province." Obviously there is much logical overlapping of concepts here
with the consequent competition explained earlier. The danger to the
balance of the constitution of overextending the definition of the federal
general power was expressed in 1896 by Lord Watson in the *Local
Prohibition Case.*[27]

. . . [T]he exercise of legislative power by the Parliament of Canada, in
regard to all matters not enumerated in s. 91, ought to be strictly confined
to such matters as are unquestionably of Canadian interest and importance,
and ought not to trench upon provincial legislation with respect to any of
the classes of subjects enumerated in s. 92. To attach any other construction to the general power which, in supplement of its enumerated powers,
is conferred upon the Parliament of Canada by s. 91, would, in their Lordships opinion, not only be contrary to the intendment of the Act, but would
practically destroy the autonomy of the provinces. . . .
. . . Their Lordships do not doubt that some matters, in their origin local
and provincial, might attain such dimensions as to affect the body politic
of the Dominion, and to justify the Canadian Parliament in passing laws
for their regulation or abolition in the interest of the Dominion. But great
caution must be observed in distinguishing between that which is local and
provincial . . . and that which has ceased to be merely local or provincial,
and has become a matter of national concern. . . .

Lord Watson did leave some permanent scope for a federal general
power of permanent significance, particularly as he fully recognized that
there might be some concurrency between that power and competing
heads of section 92. But, restriction of definition no doubt went too far
with Viscount Haldane when, in 1925 in the *Snider Case,*[28] he construed
the federal general power as an emergency power only in any respect
in which it competed logically with one or more of the categories of
section 92. As we have seen, this could be just about every respect
that mattered.

In any event a more reasonable scope for the federal general power
was established by Viscount Simon in the *Canada Temperance Federa-*

[27]*A.G. for Ontario* v. *A.G. for Canada,* [1896] AC 348, at 360–61.
[28]*Toronto Electric Commissions* v. *Snider,* [1925] AC 396.

tion Case of 1946.[29] After rejecting "emergency" as the test, his Lordship said:

> ... [T]he true test must be found in the real subject matter of the legislation: if it is such that it goes beyond local or provincial concern or interests and must from its inherent nature be the concern of the Dominion as a whole (as for example in the *Aeronautics case* . . . and the *Radio case* . . .) then it will fall within the competence of the Dominion Parliament as a matter affecting the peace, order and good government of Canada, though it may in another aspect touch upon matters specially reserved to the Provincial Legislatures. . . . Nor is the validity of the legislation, when due to its inherent nature, affected because there may still be room for enactments by a Provincial Legislature dealing with an aspect of the same subject in so far as it specially affects that Province.

In other words, if a federal statute is challenged and the federal general power is invoked to support it, in competition with the usual provincial powers, then, if the challenged statute proposes to do something that needs to be done at the nation-wide level if it is to be done effectively, or done at all, then this element of necessity causes the statute to fall within the federal general power. It is not enough if one shows that there is some mere convenience or advantage to be obtained by federal legislative action of the type at issue. But, on the other hand, one no longer has to go beyond genuine necessity and establish emergency to invoke the federal general power. So a balanced definition results—some real necessity that is more than just convenience or advantage but less than outright emergency.

Nevertheless, in spite of mutual modification of definitions because of the whole context of the BNA Act, much overlapping of concepts inevitably remains. In other words, the ambivalent character of particular laws or statutes persists. This constitutes the second dilemma of classification. The first step towards solution is to construe the challenged statute itself carefully to be sure of having determined its full meaning, that is, the full range of features by any one of which or by any combination of which it may be classified. A rule of law expresses what should be human action or conduct in a specified factual situation, hence the consequences of observing and enforcing the rule are among its vital aspects of meaning. As Lord Maugham said in the *Alberta Bank Taxation Case* of 1939,[30] in a case of difficulty one must look at the effects of the legislation: "For that purpose the Court must take into account any public general knowledge of which the Court would take judicial notice, and may in a proper case require to be informed by

[29] *A.G. for Ontario* v. *Canada Temperance Federation*, [1946] AC 193, at 205–6.
[30] *A.G. for Alberta* v. *A.G. for Canada*, [1939] AC 117, at 130.

evidence as to what the effect of the legislation will be." Unless this is done, the classification process might well be purely formal or grammatical.

In any event, having thus determined the full range of features of the challenged statute, we find the usual situation, that federal aspects and provincial aspects are both present and compete to control characterization of the statute for purposes of determining the power to enact it. To resolve this competition, the courts must now assess the relative importance of the respective federal and provincial features of the statute in contrast one with the other. Accordingly, criteria of relative value enter the picture. If the judges find a clear contrast, if for instance they deem the federal aspects clearly more important than the provincial ones, then the conclusion is that power to pass the statute is exclusively federal. For the purpose of distributing legislative power then, the challenged statute is decisively classified by its leading feature, by its more important characteristic, by its primary aspects, by its pith and substance. These are synonymous phrases. And if, on the other hand, the provincial features are deemed clearly more important than the federal ones, the power to pass the law in question is exclusively provincial. In this way exclusive power can be assigned to federal parliament or provincial legislature in spite of the purely logical ambivalence of the challenged statute because of its different aspects.

For example, the *Vacant Property Act* of Quebec (1939)[31] provided, to put it briefly, that all financial deposits in credit institutions unclaimed for thirty years became the property of the Crown in right of the Province of Quebec. This would have the sensible effect and object of permitting savings institutions to clear their books of great numbers of small accounts long since forgotten by depositors who could not be traced. But the statute was held *ultra vires* of the province because the Privy Council concluded that this was primarily banking legislation and only secondarily was it property and civil rights legislation.

If that be the main object and effect of the provincial Act it does in their Lordships' view invade the field of banking. It comes in pith and substance within that class and the fact that it may incidentally affect certain other institutions cannot take away its primary object and effect.

In their [Lordships'] view a provincial legislature enters upon the field of banking when it interferes with the right of depositors to receive payment of their deposits, as in their view it would if it confiscated loans made by a bank to its customers. Both are in a sense matters of property and civil rights, but in essence they are included within the category "banking."[32]

---

[31]Statutes of Quebec, 3 George 6 (1939) c. 28.

[32]*A.G. for Canada* v. *A.G. for Quebec*, [1947] AC 33, at pp. 44 and 46.

Further, in the *Alberta Bill of Rights Case* (1947) where there was the same type of problem concerning banking and property and civil rights, the Judicial Committee said: "It is true, of course, that in one aspect provincial legislation on this subject affects property and civil rights, but if, as their Lordships hold to be the case, the pith and substance of the legislation is "Banking" . . . this is the aspect that matters and Part II is beyond the power of the Alberta Legislature to enact."[33]

But, what if the contrast between the federal and provincial features respectively of the challenged law is not so sharp that one can be selected as the leading feature? What if both seem to be leading features? Take, for example, a law making dangerous driving of automobiles an offence with penalties. Because of its power over the civil right to drive and over highways as local works, it is important that a provincial legislature be able to pass such a law in aid of its responsibility for the safe and efficient circulation of traffic on the highways. But likewise it is important that the federal parliament under its general criminal law power should be able to pass such a law in aid of its responsibility to forbid and punish grave and dangerous anti-social conduct of all kinds.

In these circumstances, federal and provincial laws are permitted to operate concurrently, provided they do not conflict in what they prescribe for the persons subject to them. In the words of Lord Dunedin, two propositions are established[34]: "First, that there can be a domain in which provincial and Dominion legislation may overlap, in which case neither legislation will be *ultra vires*, if the field is clear; and secondly, that if the field is not clear, and in such domain the two legislations meet, then the Dominion legislation must prevail."

To sum up, for a concurrent field to be found by interpretation, the following conditions must obtain: (1) the provincial and federal categories of power concerned must overlap logically in their definitions; (2) the challenged law must be caught by the overlap, that is, it must exhibit both provincial and federal aspects of meaning; and (3) the provincial and federal aspects of the challenged law thus manifest must be deemed of equivalent importance or value.

In recent years there seems to be a liberal trend respecting concurrency developing in the Supreme Court of Canada. In the first place, the number of concurrent fields recognized or created by judicial interpretation is increasing. One of the latest examples of this in the Supreme Court of Canada is afforded by the decision there upholding the Ontario

[33]*A.G. for Alberta* v. *A.G. for Canada*, [1947] AC 503, at p. 518.
[34]*G.T. Rlwy. Co. of Canada* v. *A.G. for Canada*, [1907] AC 65 at 68.

Unconscionable Transactions Relief Act as valid provincial legislation.[35]
This means that laws restraining or reforming interest charges that are
harsh or unconscionable fall both ways in our federal system. They may
be enacted by a province as a modification of the contract law of undue
influence, this being a species of civil rights in the province. Or, they
may be enacted by the federal Parliament under the specific federal
power conferred by the word "interest" in section 91(19).

In the second place, given that a concurrent field has been found, the
court is becoming quite liberal about permitting federal and provincial
statutes to live together in that field. In other words the judges seem
reluctant to find conflict fatal to the provincial statute if they can avoid
this result. This seems particularly true of concurrent fields created by
the overlap of the federal and provincial criminal law powers, being
sections 91(27) and 92(15) respectively of the BNA Act. Nevertheless,
if there is conflict between federal and provincial statutes in a concurrent
field, the doctrine of dominion paramountcy is to the effect that the
federal statute prevails and the provincial one is thereby displaced and
suspended. So, in the end, federal power is over-riding in a concurrent
field. One authority must be paramount in the event of conflict in a
concurrent field, for the citizen cannot be subjected to two laws that
contradict one another.

New and specifically defined areas of concurrency no doubt add useful flexibility to the constitution, and often permit the provinces to
legislate in joint fields where the federal Parliament could act but has
not done so. Also, there may be political agreements about what each
legislative body will or will not do in the concurrent area, thus making
possible one form of co-operative federalism. Examples are the federal-
provincial taxation agreements and Sunday observance legislation.[36]
Nevertheless, there is still need to avoid over-extension of the definition
of the scope of federal categories of power if balance is to be main-

[35]See n. 19. Other examples are:
Highways
   P.E.I. v. *Egan,* [1941] SCR 396; *The Queen* v. *Yolles,* (1959) 19 DLR (2d)
19; *O'Grady* v. *Sparling* [1960] SCR 804.
Sale of Securities
   Smith v. *The Queen,* [1960] SCR 776.
Trading Stamps
   The Queen v. *Fleming,* (1962) 35 DLR (2d) 483.
Sunday Observance
   Lord Day Alliance of Canada v. *A.G. for B.C.,* [1959] SCR 497.
Federal Election Propaganda
   Regina v. *McKay & McKay,* (1964) 43 DLR (2d) 401.
[36]See *ibid.*

tained in our constitution. Complete concurrency of federal powers with provincial ones, coupled with the doctrine of dominion paramountcy, would mean the end of a balanced federal system in Canada. The trend to increased concurrency then may have its dangers for the autonomy of the provinces, though so far the main effect of the trend has been to uphold provincial statutes.

Accordingly, federal constitutional interpretation in Canada might be said to call for mutual exclusion of powers if practical, but concurrency if necessary. Moreover, whether one finds mutual exclusion or concurrency, the process requires decisions about the relative values represented by the competing federal and provincial aspects of the challenged statute. Often these are difficult decisions indeed, but they are inescapable. So the question becomes: Is the statutory scheme at issue something that is better done province by province on the basis of provincial autonomy, or is it something better done uniformly over the whole country on a nation-wide basis? What criteria of value move the judges in this respect? In an earlier essay, the writer attempted the following answer to this.[87]

In this inquiry, the judges are beyond the aid of logic, because logic merely displays the many possible classifications; it does not assist in a choice between them. If we assume that the purpose of the constitution is to promote the well-being of the people, then some of the necessary criteria will start to emerge. When a particular rule has features of meaning relevant to both federal and provincial classes of laws, then the question must be asked, Is it better for the people that this thing be done on a national level, or on a provincial level? In other words, is the feature of the challenged law which falls within the federal class more important to the well-being of the country than that which falls within the provincial class of laws? Such considerations as the relative value of uniformity and regional diversity, the relative merit of local *versus* central administration, and the justice of minority claims, would have to be weighed. Inevitably, widely prevailing beliefs in the country about these issues will be influential and presumably the judges should strive to implement such beliefs. Inevitably there will be some tendency for them to identify their own convictions as those which generally prevail or which at least are the right ones. On some matters there will not be an ascertainable general belief anyway. In the making of these very difficult relative-value decisions, all that can rightly be required of judges is straight thinking, industry, good faith, and a capacity to discount their own prejudices. No doubt it is also fair to ask that they be men of high professional attainment, and that they be representative in their thinking of the better standards of their times and their countrymen.

Once again, the importance is apparent of exploring all aspects of the challenged law as a matter of meaning and evidence. A legal system

[87]*Legal Essays in Honour of Arthur Moxon*, pp. 197–8.

must in general be related to the social, economic, and cultural realities, and to the accepted values and beliefs, of the country concerned. Indeed a legal system exists to take account of these realities in a way that advances those values and beliefs as far as laws can do so. In a federal country like Canada this applies to the special issues concerning which legislative body—the central or the provincial—should be responsible for this or that statutory scheme. Professor Bora Laskin seems to have all this in mind when he speaks of "constitutional values" in a special sense. He says[38]:

What the process of constitutional adjudication involves is a distillation of the "constitutional value" represented by challenged legislation (the "matter" in relation to which it is enacted) and its attribution to a head of power (or class of subject). This is not to say that the process is mechanical or that there are logically-discoverable essences which go to make up a class of subject. The distribution of legislative power must surely be envisaged as an instrumental or operating scheme, ample enough to embrace any subject or object of legislation. The classes of subjects must hence be conceived as vehicles through which social or economic or political policy is expressed, and these considerations (however they may be inarticulate or concealed in precedent or logic) cannot be ignored when the courts give content to the classes of subjects and measure the validity of legislation accordingly.

At this point one may well ask: Why all the emphasis on the analytical logic of classification that characterizes the present essay, if in the end logic alone is indecisive? The answer is that such analytical reasoning is necessary to prepare the way for and to reveal the need of the value judgments that *are* in the end decisive. Good analytical jurisprudence isolates issues of form and reveals issues of substance in their true colours. If you can frame the right questions and put them in the right order, you are half way to the answers. In other words, by proper questions and analysis, the issues requiring value decisions are rendered specific and brought into focus one by one in particular terms, so that ordinary mortals of limited wisdom and moral insight can cope with them. This is the reason for insisting that if you would distribute lawmaking powers you must classify laws, and that if you would classify laws you must at least draft the terms of the statute you are talking about and then ascertain all its aspects of meaning as a rule for social action of some kind.

In any event, it ought to be clear that a judge interpreting a federal constitution is no mere automaton—that, on the contrary, he has critical

[38]Bora Laskin, Canadian Constitutional Law (2nd ed., Toronto, 1960), pp. 76–7.

choices to make at different stages of the process. Nevertheless, authoritative precedent does enter the picture in a very important way, and by this factor the guide lines of the distribution of legislative powers are given considerable stability and even rigidity. Writing of this factor elsewhere, I said[39]:

Lest a false impression of complete uncertainty and fluidity be conveyed by the foregoing, the importance of the rules of precedent that obtain in our courts should be remembered. However open logically the classification of a given type of law may have been when first it was considered by the highest court, that decision will in all probability foreclose the question of the correct classification should the same type of law come up again. For instance it was argued that the federal Industrial Disputes Investigation Act of 1907 was within the power of the Canadian Parliament because its provisions regulating the settlement of industrial disputes were classifiable as "regulation of trade and commerce", "criminal law", and rules for "peace, order and good government". Nevertheless the Judicial Committee pointed out that these provisions were also classifiable as laws concerning "property and civil rights in the province" and in effect ruled that such was the important or significant classification for constitutional purposes. Hence the Act was declared *ultra vires* of the Canadian Parliament. Incidentally, in his argument for the validity of the Act, Sir John Simon had pointed to the absence of economic division in Canada on provincial lines; in other words many industries and labour organizations were national or at least interprovincial in scope and hence national regulation of industrial relations was desirable. But the Judicial Committee was not impressed. Tacitly but effectively they decided that provincial autonomy and diversity in the regulation of employer-employee relations were more important when they ruled that the challenged statute "in its pith and substance" interfered with civil rights. Thus the classification of this type of industrial regulation critical for constitutional purposes has been settled by precedent, and in like manner many other classifications are authoritatively settled. It is not clear yet whether the Supreme Court of Canada, supreme now in law as well as name, will assert a right to depart in exceptional circumstances from particular decisions in the accumulation of Privy Council precedents. Certainly it would seem that explicit departures, if any, will be rare. Nevertheless, some new and different scheme of industrial regulation, for example, might well be deemed outside the scope of its precedent just discussed, and then its classification in turn would have to be considered as a matter of first impression with all the problems here explained once more in full bloom.

Moreover, frequently there will be new laws, both federal and provincial, which the precedents on classification will not touch decisively or concerning which indeed there may be conflicting analogies. Thus in spite of the principles of precedent the full-blown problem of classification described earlier is often with us.

In summary then, we can now see that the classification process joins logic with social fact, value decisions and the authority of precedents, to

[39]*Legal Essays in Honour of Arthur Moxon*, pp. 199–200.

define the distribution of law-making powers. The reasoning involved is not automatic or mechanical; rather it makes the highest demands on learning, intellect, and conscience. It permits expression to the real issues of public policy in the country, and indeed brings such issues into focus in many particular ways, thus facilitating their resolution. The point is that, so long as we have a federal constitution, we must be prepared to contend with the real complexity of the interpretative process. In other words, what has been described above is the inevitable operating jurisprudence of the federal form of social order. If we understand the process, we will expect neither too much nor too little of the constitutional distribution of legislative powers as it stands now, or as it may be if certain changes are made. There is much more room for reasonable differences of interpretation than most people realize. These differences then should not be regarded as evidence of bad faith or ignorance; rather, they should be taken as a challenge calling for support of the working of our system of interpretation at its best level. Up to this point, we have assumed that the superior court on the English model is the proper type of tribunal to have the last word on interpretation by the process described. This assumption is correct, but now needs further explanation.

III. *THE NECESSITY FOR INDEPENDENT JUDICIAL REVIEW OF THE FEDERAL DISTRIBUTION OF POWERS*

The need for final judicial review of the federal distribution of legislative powers has roots in the necessities of a federal system. Neither the federal Parliament nor the provincial legislatures could be permitted to act as judges of the extent of their own respective grants of power under the BNA Act. If they were, soon we would have either ten separate countries or a unitary state. Nor are such issues of interpretation suitable for determination by voting in some kind of a special body composed of numerous delegates or representatives assembled for the purpose. In the end this would simply mean majority rule or deadlock through minority veto. Rather, the interpretative process is best carried out in one of our traditional superior courts where, by submission and argument, appeal can be made to the reason, understanding, and sense of values of impartial judges who enjoy secure and permanent tenure during good behaviour.

This is the present position in Canada. Final review of the distribution of legislative powers by superior courts is a principle specially entrenched in the Canadian constitution by necessary implication. As

Mr. Justice McGillivray has expressed it, speaking in the Alberta Court of Appeal[40]:

... consideration of the legislative capacity of Parliament or of the Legislatures cannot be withdrawn from the Courts either by Parliament or Legislature. In my view this statement may rest upon the safe ground that by necessary implication from what has been said in the BNA Act, the Superior Courts whose independence is thereby assured, are just as surely made the arbiters of the constitutional validity of statutory enactments as Parliament and the Legislatures are made law enacting bodies. If, as I think, it is not open to question that neither Parliament nor Legislature may provide as the concluding words of an enactment that it shall be deemed to be *intra vires* by all Courts in the country then neither the one nor the other of these legislative bodies can reach the same end by denying access to the Courts for the determination of constitutional questions.

As the learned justice suggests, certain principles are necessary to ensure the integrity of the interpretative process in the hands of our superior courts, particularly the Supreme Court of Canada. Neither the federal nor provincial legislative bodies can deny access to the courts on constitutional questions, nor can either of them instruct the courts how to determine such issues of validity.[41] The legislative bodies cannot, by statutory recitals, settle the classification of their own statutes for purposes of the distribution of powers. That is, they cannot tell the judges which aspect of the challenged statute is to be considered its leading feature. Selection of the aspect that matters is the exclusive prerogative of the court, and the so-called doctrine of colourability is simply an instance of this rule, meaning that, for example, so far as the court is concerned, a statute cast in the form of a tax law may nevertheless be found to have banking as its leading aspect.[42] Likewise, a statute cast in the form of land law may nevertheless be found to have the crime of sedition as its primary characteristic.[43] Furthermore in this regard, no legislative body is permitted finally to settle the truth of jurisdictional facts by statutory recitals. In the *Fort Frances Case*,[44] Viscount Haldane made it clear that, even on the issue of the existence or continuance of emergency conditions sufficient to invoke the federal emergency power, the court reserved ultimate decision to itself, though normally it would take the word of the federal Parliament or government for this.

---

[40]*I.O.F.* v. *Lethbridge*, [1938] 3 DLR at p. 102–3, affirmed in the Privy Council, [1940] AC 513.

[41]See also note by Laskin, *Canadian Constitutional Law*, pp. 192–3.

[42]See n. 32.

[43]See n. 22.

[44]*Fort Frances Pulp & Power Co. Ltd.* v. *Manitoba Free Press Co. Ltd.*, [1923] AC 695, at 706.

The interpretation of a federal distribution of legislative powers and responsibilities is then a complex process of reasoning, balancing, and deciding that calls for the special qualities of the superior court as that institution was developed in England after the *Act of Settlement* of 1701.[45] This type of tribunal is one of the most important features of our great inheritance in Canada of English public law and institutions. This is not to say that every official working decision about what the federal constitution means should be made in court, for instance in the Supreme Court of Canada. Great numbers of working decisions must, of course, be made at every important level of government by a great variety of officials and their legal advisers. Nevertheless, the relatively few issues taken to the Supreme Court of Canada are critical because this is the final resort in a show-down, and in any event, Supreme Court decisions, being final, are controlling in the field of interpretation, laying down the principles and guide lines to be respected at the other levels of government.

It is necessary that the Supreme Court of Canada should be our final interpretative tribunal rather than the Judicial Committee of the Privy Council in London, though the latter body often served Canada well in earlier times. The point is simply that the judges of the Supreme Court of Canada are Canadians who live all their lives in Canada with the problems and conditions that obtain here under our federal constitution. Because of the discretions inevitably inherent in the process of interpretation, this should bring more wisdom and realism to the process than could be expected of an outside tribunal.

At present the Supreme Court of Canada is constituted by ordinary federal statute, and the judges are appointed by the Governor-General in Council, that is by the federal cabinet. This leads some persons to have misgivings to the effect that the Supreme Court of Canada may not be as truly indepedent of the Parliament and Government of Canada as it should be in a federal country. In this respect the Supreme Court of Canada may seem to compare unfavourably with the Judicial Committee of the Privy Council.

In my view these misgivings are unfounded. The Supreme Court of Canada is pre-eminently a superior court in every sense, and our whole constitutional tradition means that the Canadian Parliament would never change the *Supreme Court Act* in any way prejudicial to the true independence of the Court or its judges. Nevertheless, if it were thought useful to do so, the Statute of the Court could be specially and formally entrenched in appropriate clauses of the Canadian constitution.

As for the power of appointing Supreme Court judges, I consider this

[45]12 & 13 William III, (1701) UK c. 2, s. 3.

should remain with the prime minister of Canada and his cabinet, responsible as they are to the Parliament of Canada representing all parts of the country. The main point is that, once a highly qualified person has been appointed to the security and independence of the Supreme Court Bench, he must simply be trusted to rise to the challenge of the office with integrity and intelligence. This applies both to constitutional interpretation and to the disposal of ordinary appeals. The presence of judges learned in the French civil law of Quebec is ensured by the provision of the present statute of the court that requires one-third of the judges to be selected from the bar of Quebec. In the result, the two great legal traditions of the Western world come together in the Supreme Court of Canada. The French civil law of Quebec traces its roots back two thousand years to the finest period of the Roman law. The English common law tradition of the other provinces is the distinguished inheritance of one thousand years of English history. Drawing as it does on these two sources, the Supreme Court of Canada should be able to serve the country well. Judges and lawyers of the civil law and the common law have found that they can communicate sympathetically with one another—that they can understand one another. I believe this is because the appeals to reason and justice in both systems of law are basically the same.

My position is then that the Supreme Court of Canada should be continued in its present function and power of final interpretation of the distribution of legislative powers. No institution is perfect, but an independent superior court manned by Canadian judges provides the best tribunal available for balanced interpretation of law-making powers of Canada and the provinces in relation to one another.

Les Attitudes changeantes du Québec à l'endroit de la Constitution de 1867

JEAN BEETZ

Les Québecois se considèrent, au Canada, comme une collectivité minoritaire. Une minorité culturellement homogène, concentrée dans un territoire, qui veut assurer la sauvegarde de son identité collective, doit se prémunir contre plusieurs sortes de périls. L'un de ces périls est extérieur. Il provient de la majorité. Il consiste à se voir imposer par la majorité un cadre de pensée dont la forme, le style, la tradition sont étrangers à la minorité et dont il peut même arriver que le fond lui soit contraire. Il résulte de ce que la majorité est différente de la minorité, de ce qu'elle est plus forte qu'elle, de ce qu'elle peut la transformer sans même le souhaiter. Un second péril est intérieur; il résulte de l'inaction de la minorité. Il consiste à manquer de dynamisme, à ne pas profiter de tous les moyens où il est possible à cette minorité d'avoir une activité distincte.

Le péril qui vient de l'intérieur est le plus grave : une collectivité dynamique, sûre d'elle-même et de ses moyens, a moins à craindre de ses voisins, en quelque domaine que ce soit. Contre le premier péril, qui vient de l'extérieur, de la majorité, il est parfois possible de se garder, dans une certaine mesure, par des moyens juridiques. Le second péril en est un que le Québec peut vaincre, dans le contexte actuel, par des moyens surtout politiques.

Mon propos est de tenter d'expliquer les attitudes changeantes du Québec à l'égard de la constitution, ou encore les sens variables que la constitution a pris pour la collectivité québecoise à diverses époques. Est-il besoin de le dire ou de s'en excuser ? Une entreprise aussi audacieuse n'apporte qu'un témoignage subjectif et ne compromet que celui qui l'exprime.

I. *L'ATTITUDE PASSIVE: LA CONSTITUTION, PROTECTRICE DE LA MINORITÉ*

1. L'ÉLABORATION DE LA CONSTITUTION

Les auteurs de la Confédération ont estimé nécessaire de préserver les traits culturels de la minorité en organisant la protection juridique de certains secteurs stratégiques ou jugés tels par la minorité et la majorité, soit parce que ces secteurs sont caractéristiques de la minorité, soit parce que la minorité s'est identifiée à eux et qu'ils ont acquis une valeur symbolique. Ces secteurs sont ceux de la religion, de la langue, et des lois. C'est aussi celui de l'éducation, parce qu'il commande les deux premiers, et même le troisième.

L'organisation constitutionnelle de cette protection est connue : elle consiste à conférer une compétence pratiquement exclusive sur certains aspects de ces domaines aux organes politiques que la minorité contrôle. Il importe toutefois que cette minorité, devenue majorité dans des secteurs donnés, ne se serve point de sa juridiction nouvelle pour réduire les avantages dont bénéficie chez elle la minorité anglophone. Pour atteindre cet autre but, l'on met en place des mécanismes de sûreté comme la réserve et le désaveu des lois provinciales, la compétence conditionnelle et supplétive du pouvoir fédéral en matière d'éducation. Cette deuxième technique, employée aussi à l'extérieur du Québec, pourra servir du même coup à rassurer la diaspora québecoise qui a pu se regrouper en d'autres lieux du territoire canadien. Enfin, l'adoption d'une règle fondamentale, mise à l'abri d'une simple modification législative, assure un statut particulier aux deux langues officielles, dans certaines institutions publiques. Cependant, l'aspect capital de cette protection constitutionnelle, d'un point de vue québecois, reste l'exclusion de principe du pouvoir fédéral, contrôlé par la majorité en matière d'éducation et de lois civiles : l'éducation, parce que c'est d'elle que dépendait en grande partie, croyait-on, la tradition de la religion, de la langue, et de la culture ; les lois civiles — sauf le mariage et le divorce — parce qu'elles affectent intimement la personne dans son état et sa capacité, parce qu'elles organisent la famille, parce qu'elles règlementent la propriété conçue comme un moyen d'action nécessaire à l'individu.

2. L'INTERPRETATION DE LA CONSTITUTION

Une fois désignés par la constitution ces domaines que l'on voulait en partie protéger contre l'action, même bien intentionnée, de la majorité, il importait encore, d'un point de vue québecois, que la constitution soit interprétée d'une manière favorable à la compétence de la province.

Cette interprétation dépendait à son tour, d'une part, de la méthode que l'on allait suivre pour harmoniser les articles 91 et 92 l'un avec l'autre, et d'autre part, de la définition, empirique ou à prioriste, que la jurisprudence allait donner des compétences législatives nommées dans ces dispositions.

La méthode. L'on pourra discuter jusqu'à la fin des temps de la méthode qu'il convenait de choisir pour interpréter la constitution de 1867 ; dans cette matière, il n'est pas d'autre arbitre autorisé que les cours de justice, mais leur jugement est rarement final, car il n'est pas à l'abri de la critique doctrinale et des renversements, avoués ou non, de la jurisprudence.

Les lois écrites s'interprètent de manière variable, selon leur nature et selon la méthode employée pour les rédiger. Ainsi les lois civiles, qui sont le verbe du droit commun, bénéficient d'une interprétation libérale parce qu'elles expriment l'ordre établi, les valeurs traditionnelles ; en étendre l'application par des procédés d'analogie, c'est se montrer favorable à l'extension de l'ordre établi ; c'est aussi permettre l'évolution nécessaire à la conservation de ces lois, car une interprétation fixative risque de les détruire en les rendant insupportables.

En revanche, l'on interprète littéralement et restrictivement les lois fiscales parce qu'elles sont défavorables à la propriété ; elles décrètent une espèce d'expropriation calculée suivant des critères à tout le moins discutables et elles ne comportent pas d'indemnité autre que les services que l'Etat est appelé à rendre au contribuable. L'on interprète restrictivement les lois pénales parce qu'elles sont directement prohibitives dans leur forme et répressives dans leurs sanctions et que la société ressent une prédilection pour la liberté ; elle permet donc tout ce qu'elle ne défend pas expressément. L'on interprète restrictivement les lois statutaires parce qu'elles font exception à la liberté des contrats, à l'état des personnes, ou à quelqu'autre principe du droit commun, que l'interprète leur préfère.

En réalité, cette méthode d'interprétation, bien loin d'élaborer des règles neutres, objectives, désintéressées qui permettraient uniquement de trouver la signification d'un texte et l'intention de son auteur, dicte à l'interprète des maximes d'ordre public qui mettent en oeuvre des critères fondamentaux auxquels l'on veut accorder la priorité même à l'encontre, dans certains cas, de la volonté expresse du législateur[1].

[1]L'on trouvera un exemple de cette mise en échec de la volonté du législateur

Mais ce n'est pas seulement la nature de la loi écrite qui dicte son attitude à l'interprète ; c'est aussi le style particulier de rédaction employé par le législateur. Il arrive que celui-ci confesse ses principes dans la loi elle-même[2], et qu'il utilise, pour les mettre en oeuvre, une réglementation très générale et forcément imprécise[3], des termes abstraits et difficiles à définir[4], des standards de la plus grande relativité[5]. Ce style législatif laisse à l'interprète sa liberté, et il facilite l'évolution des lois sans qu'il soit nécessaire d'avoir recours à la modification législative.

Au contraire, il se peut que le législateur taise ses principes, évite l'emploi de standards relatifs, et règlemente longuement les situations sur lesquelles il veut exercer son empire au moyen de préceptes minutieux, de catégories rigides, et de concepts aisément définissables[6]. L'interprète, devenu le prisonnier d'un texte précis mais sans fécondité, doit généralement se contenter de lui faire produire des effets prévus. Il y a risque que la loi se démode rapidement et requière l'intervention fréquente du législateur.

Le choix de l'une ou de l'autre de ces méthodes de rédaction est le dilemme constant du juriste, qui recherche et la sécurité de la précision et la durabilité des lois.

La constitution de 1867 est un document paradoxal. Son caractère de loi fondamentale, la difficulté que l'on éprouve à la modifier, devrait normalement commander l'usage d'une méthode d'interprétation large, libérale, analogique. Par ailleurs, son style est caractéristique des statuts d'interprétation restrictive. Le législateur y cache pudiquement ses principes : c'est ainsi, par exemple, que le principe de l'indépendance des juges, pourtant fondamental en droit britannique et doublement important dans une constitution de type fédéral, n'y est nulle part exprimé[7]. Il n'y est pas non plus expressément question du contrôle de légalité constitutionnelle exercé par le pouvoir judiciaire, des libertés

dans l'insuccès relatif des dispositions exclusives de la juridiction des tribunaux judiciaires sur les organes de l'administration.

[2]Par exemple, une déclaration des droits de l'homme.

[3]Par exemple, l'article 1053 du Code civil de Québec.

[4]Par exemple, la faute, l'exécution des fonctions, la propriété et les droits civils, la réglementation du commerce.

[5]Par exemple, l'ordre public et les bonnes moeurs, le bon père de famille ou l'homme raisonnable, l'obscénité.

[6]Les exemples de ce genre de lois abondent : mentionnons les règlements douaniers, les lois sur l'hygiène, les aliments et les drogues, certaines lois de procédure, les lois concernant la forme des documents, etc.

[7]On doit l'induire de l'article 99 qui pourvoit au mécanisme de la destitution des juges des cours supérieures provinciales. Il en résulte une conséquence inattendue : selon la lettre de la Constitution, sinon selon son esprit, l'indépendance des juges de la Cour Suprême du Canada, relativement à leur destitution, ne semble garantie que par une simple loi, tandis que celle de magistrats de juridiction inférieure l'est par la Constitution.

individuelles, de la suprématie de la constitution, de la souveraineté du Parlement et des législatures, du principe de légalité — « rule of law » . Par ailleurs, la constitution de 1867, à l'exception peut-être des dispositions qui partagent la compétence législative entre le pouvoir central et les provinces, est rédigée dans un jargon d'hommes de loi besogneux mais totalement insensibles à l'esthétique, celle-ci fût-elle juridique ; c'est un document hautement technique et par conséquent hermétique, trompeur pour le juriste qui n'est pas familier avec nos lois, interdit au profane, inaccessible pour le commun. Ce style de rédaction entraîne normalement une interprétation purement exégétique et littérale, la seule à laquelle croyaient probablement les juristes victoriens qui ont donné une expression statutaire aux résolutions de Londres.

Ce divorce entre la nature de la constitution de 1867 et sa forme explique peut-être en partie les fluctuations de la jurisprudence relativement à la méthode d'interprétation qu'il sied d'employer pour l'appliquer[8]. Cependant, rien n'indique, *a priori,* qu'une interprétation littérale de la constitution, ait pour effet d'étendre la compétence des provinces, et qu'une interprétation analogique ait pour résultat de la restreindre ou *vice versa,* sauf, peut-être, en ce qui concerne les droits des minorités en matière d'école, où le littéralisme semble avoir généralement pour effet d'accroître la liberté d'action des législatures provinciales.

Application de la méthode à la structure des articles 91 et 92. Une certaine école doctrinale[9] tient que le Comité judiciaire du Conseil privé a ignoré la lettre et trahit l'esprit de la constitution distinguant entre les compétences nommées du pouvoir fédéral et sa compétence résiduelle ou innommée, et en conférant à celles-là seulement la suprématie sur les compétences provinciales. Une autre école de pensée[10] est au contraire d'avis que le Comité judiciaire du Conseil privé a fidèlement interprété le texte des articles 91 et 92 en ne donnant la primauté qu'aux compétences nommées du pouvoir fédéral. Ainsi donc, ces deux écoles, en se fondant d'abord sur la même méthode, la pure exégèse des textes, en arrivent à des résultats opposés[11].

[8]*Bank of Toronto* v. *Lambe,* (1887) 12 AC 575; *Henrietta Muir Edwards* v. *A. G. Can.,* (1930) AC 124.

[9]Cf. Wm. F. O'Connor, *Report to the Senate of Canada on the B.N.A. Act* (Ottawa, 1939); W. P. M. Kennedy, "Interpretation of the British North America Act," (1943) 8 *Camb. L. J.,* p. 146; Vincent C. MacDonald, "The Constitution in a Changing World," (1948) 26 *Can. Bar Rev.,* p. 21.

[10]Cf. Louis-Philippe Pigeon, "The Meaning of Provincial Autonomy," (1951) 29 *Can. Bar Rev.,* p. 1126; "French Canada's Attitude to the Canadian Constitution," *Canadian Jurisprudence,* E. McWhinney, ed. (Toronto, 1958); Gray V. Evan, "The O'Connor Report on the B.N.A. Act," (1939) *17 Can. Bar Rev.,* p. 309.

[11]Je suis personnellement d'avis le Conseil privé a correctement interprété les articles 91 et 92 à ce point de vue, compte tenu des imperfections et même

118 *Attitudes à l'égard de la constitution*

Quoiqu'il en soit de cette controverse, il faut reconnaître que l'interprétation du Conseil privé relativement à la structure des articles 91 et 92 a été généralement favorable aux provinces. Mais ce tribunal n'a pas eu, dans ce domaine, autant de discrétion qu'on l'a prétendu. *Application de la méthode à la définition des compétences.* Là cependant où le Conseil privé a pu jouir d'une liberté infiniment plus grande, c'est dans la définition des compétences législatives énumérées dans les articles 91 et 92, ainsi que dans la qualification des lois dont on contestait devant lui la constitutionnalité. L'on pourrait penser, à première vue, que les articles 91 et 92 se prêtent surtout à la méthode d'interpréfédéral, une mesure exceptionnelle à l'époque dans les constitutions de concepts qui, pour être vagues, restent théoriquement susceptibles d'analyse et de définition ; ils ne mentionnent aucun standard relatif ; les seuls standards relatifs qui semblent avoir été employés dans l'interprétation de ces dispositions sont celui de l' « état d'urgence » et celui des « dimensions nationales », tous deux d'invention jurisprudentielle, et entre lesquels les cours ne semblent pas avoir finalement opté[12]. Enfin, l'on a pris la précaution singulière de rédiger deux listes de compétences nommées, en sus de l'attribution de la compétence résiduelle au pouvoir fédéral, une mesure exceptionnelle à l'époque dans les constitutions fédérales. Les personnes qui ont rédigé les articles 91 et 92 pouvaient difficilement se montrer plus explicites même si elles mettaient surtout leur confiance dans la lettre de la loi.

Pourtant, les articles 91 et 92 aménagent les compétences législatives

---

des contradictions du texte, que l'interprète ne peut supprimer, et dont il ne peut que s'accommoder. Ainsi, les droits d'auteur sont sûrement des droits civils qui seraient tombés dans le champ de la compétence provinciale, s'ils n'en étaient exclus par leur mention dans l'article 91. Cette mention était donc nécessaire et, en soustrayant à la compétence provinciale sur la propriété et les droits civils, elle « ajoute » en ce sens à la compétence innommée du pouvoir fédéral, non pas tant à cause de la clause « non obstante » de l'article 91 mais selon la règle d'interprétation qui veut que les dispositions particulières l'emportent sur les générales. Par ailleurs, et paradoxalement, il semble que certaines compétences, innommées en 1867, la radiodiffusion, l'aéronautique, aient été effectivement « nommées » depuis par la jurisprudence, et soient pratiquement équivalentes aux autres compétences énumérées dans l'article 91, l'emportant sur la propriété et les droits civils du fait de leur particularité.

[12]Voir par exemple, pour la théorie de l' « état d'urgence », les arrêts suivants : *Fort Frances Pulp and Power Co.* v. *Manitoba Free Press*, (1923) AC 695; *Cooperative Committee on Japanese Canadians* v. *A. G. Canada*, (1947) AC 87; *Reference re Validity of Wartime Leasehold Regulations*, (1950) RCS 124; *Canadian Federation of Agriculture* v. *A. G. Québec*, (1951) AC 179. La théorie des « dimensions nationales » semble avoir été esquissée pour la première fois dans l'arrêt des prohibitions régionales ((1896) AC 348) et avoir été appliquée dans l'arrêt *A. G. Ont.* v. *Canada Temperance Federation*, (1946) AC 193.

en termes si généraux qu'ils laissent à l'interprète une marge consi-dérable de discrétion. Et surtout, ce sont eux qui mettent d'abord en oeuvre le principe le plus fondamental de la constitution, le principe fédéral. La constitution de 1867, nous l'avons vu, est généralement inexpressive quant à la promulgation de critères de valeur. Mais le principe fédéral, le seul que la constitution exprime, et encore, seule-ment dans son préambule, n'est point neutre. Il propose le dilemme de la centralisation et de la décentralisation.

Le Conseil privé a donné à la compétence provinciale relative à la propriété et aux droits civils une extension si grande qu'il a presque transformé cette compétence nommée en une compétence innommée à laquelle font exception les compétences nommées par l'article 91[18]. Le Conseil privé déplaçait ainsi, en grande partie, le site du pouvoir résiduel. Il est à noter que, pour déterminer l'étendue de cette com-pétence provinciale, le Conseil Privé a utilisé, entre autres critères, le Code civil de la Province de Québec, qui constituait un système juridique complet adopté avant la Confédération par la législature d'une colonie à constitution unitaire[14]. Les arguments juridiques invoqués dans cet arrêt, pour bons qu'ils soient, auraient pu être d'une portée moins générale. En revanche le Conseil privé a réduit considérablement l'éten-due de certaines compétences fédérales, particulièrement celle relative à la réglementation de l'industrie et du commerce, allant jusqu'à com-pléter, et peut-être jusqu'à trahir, la lettre de l'article 91[15]. Il est difficile de contester que plusieurs de ces décisions auraient pu être différentes de ce qu'elles ont été, sinon à l'effet inverse, et que la discrétion dont jouissait le tribunal a servi l'intérêt des provinces plutôt que celui du pouvoir fédéral.

3. L'IMMUTABILITE DE LA CONSTITUTION

D'un point de vue québecois, la compétence de la majorité et celle de la minorité ayant été déterminées de manière aussi favorable à la minorité qu'il était possible de l'espérer, il importait à cette minorité, en premier lieu, que cette interprétation restât inchangée le plus long-temps possible. Il lui aurait importé, en deuxième lieu, d'exploiter pleinement la compétence qui lui avait été reconnue.

Pour que l'interprétation de la constitution restât immuable, il était nécessaire que le Conseil privé respectât la règle du *stare decisis*. Les

[18]*Affaire Parsons*, (1881–82) 7 AC 96; *affaire des prohibitions régionales*, (1896) AC 348; *A. G. Can.* v. *A. G. Alta.*, (1916) 1 AC 588; *affaire Snider*, (1925) AC 396; *affaire du Traité de Versailles*, (1937) AC 326; etc.
[14]*Affaire Parsons*, (1881–82) 7 AC 96.
[15]*Affaire Snider*, (1925) AC 396.

Québecois ont été assez bien servis à ce point de vue par le Conseil privé, qui a généralement obéi à cette règle, sauf dans certains arrêts comme l'arrêt Russell, l'arrêt des prohibitions régionales, l'arrêt Canada Temperance Federation[16], où il semble bien s'être contredit sur la structure générale des articles 91 et 92, et la portée du pouvoir résiduel.

Il était utile aussi que les appels au Conseil privé fussent maintenus longtemps et c'est sans enthousiasme que beaucoup de Québecois ont accueilli leur abolition : la Cour suprême du Canada, à ses débuts, avait manifesté des tendances nettement plus favorables au pouvoir central ; il était de plus à craindre que cette cour locale ne se montrât plus sensible qu'une juridiction éloignée, à des considérations d'ordre fonctionnel et d'efficacité administrative ; il était aussi à redouter que l'abolition des appels au Conseil privé ne remît en question la règle du *stare decisis*.

L'immutabilité de l'interprétation constitutionnelle supposait enfin un certain rejet des notions purement relatives, des données quantitatives, de l'innommé, de la jurisprudence dite « réaliste » et purement descriptive, des considérations d'ordre surtout fonctionnel ; elle supposait au contraire que l'on mette l'accent sur le qualitatif, l'approfondissement et la précision des concepts, la jurisprudence analytique.

C'est ainsi, par exemple, qu'entre la notion d' « état d'urgence »[17], qui est relative mais qui est susceptible d'une appréciation assez précise, et celle des « dimensions nationales »[18] d'un problème, qui est purement relative et d'application toujours discutable, les Québecois auront une tendance à préférer celle d'état d'urgence à celle des dimensions nationales, tout simplement parce que la première se rationalise comme une suspension provisoire de la constitution, tandis que l'autre risque de se solder par une modification permanente, au profit du pouvoir fédéral, de l'aménagement des compétences. C'est ainsi que le juriste québecois ne peut se montrer que méfiant à l'endroit de la thèse selon laquelle, par exemple, la compétence législative doit être à la mesure du problème à résoudre[19]. Il lui semble d'abord que ce n'est pas un argument juridique mais une raison politique et fonctionnelle de modifier, s'il y a lieu, la constitution. Il lui paraît ensuite, d'un point de vue politique, que c'est là un argument permanent, favorable à la concentration fédérale des compétences, car il est évident que les problèmes à résoudre ne cesseront de croître en intensité, en complexité, et par leurs ramifications.

[16](1881–82) 7 AC 829; (1896) AC 348; (1946) AC 193.
[17]*Fort Frances Pulp and Power Co.* v. *Manitoba Free Press*, (1923) AC 695.
[18]*A. G. Ont.* v. *Canada Temperance Federation*, (1946) AC 193.
[19]F. R. Scott, "Federal Jurisdiction over Labour Relations: A New Look," (1960) 6 *McGill Law Journal*, 153, p. 161.

De même le juriste québecois sera porté à s'inquiéter de la tendance si justement décrite par le doyen Lederman[20] vers une extension des compétences communes : il lui semble que l'adoption de deux lois, l'une fédérale, l'autre provinciale, toutes deux destinées à régir la même activité matérielle, toutes deux adoptées dans le même but et sous le même aspect, est clairement exclue par la constitution sauf en matière d'agriculture, d'immigration, et de pension de vieillesse ; mais surtout, cette tendance a pour effet d'étendre la zone de suprématie des lois fédérales ; elle est nettement centralisatrice.

Enfin le juriste québecois ne peut que se troubler devant l'attitude de certains juristes canadiens qui ou bien se contentent de critères surtout quantitatifs pour déterminer la validité des lois dont la constitutionnalité est mise en doute[21] ou bien prennent plaisir à souligner le degré considérable d'intuition qui entre en jeu dans l'interprétation judiciaire de la constitution[22]. L'attitude de ces juristes constitue peut-être une description fidèle du processus d'interprétation constitutionnelle, mais lorsque l'on s'y complaît, elle peut provoquer une confusion entre la science politique et le droit, et entraîner une démission de l'esprit d'analyse et une renonciation à la conceptualisation, tous deux indispensables à la fécondité du droit. Or, d'un point de vue québecois, le droit, toujours selon la logique de cette phase passive, est indispensable à la sauvegarde de l'identité collective du Québec.

4. LE NON-USAGE DE LA CONSTITUTION

Une fois déterminée par la constitution l'étendue de leur compétence, une fois réservées par la règle de droit certaines zones de compétence identifiées à des caractères ethniques — l'éducation, à cause de la confession religieuse et de la langue, et les lois civiles — une fois cristallisée l'interprétation judiciaire de cette règle de droit, il aurait été nécessaire que les Québecois occupent et exploitent à fond le champ qui leur était assigné, et même qu'ils cherchent à en étendre les bornes.

Mais les Québecois craignaient l'Etat. C'est ainsi, par exemple, que pendant de nombreuses années après la Confédération, la Province de Québec s'est montrée bien moins autonomiste que la Nouvelle-Ecosse et l'Ontario. Celles-ci étaient autonomistes à cause du dynamisme initial

---

[20]W. R. Lederman, "Balanced Interpretation of the Federal Distribution of Legislative Powers in Canada," ci-dessus.

[21]Celle du doyen Lederman, par exemple, dans la communication citée plus haut.

[22]Celle du professeur Bora Laskin, par exemple, dans "Tests for the Validity of Legislation: What's the 'Matter' ", (1955) 11 *U. of Toronto Law Journal*, p. 114.

et interne dont elles avaient pu jouir avant la Confédération, et pour des motifs qui n'étaient pas nécessairement reliés au maintien de traits ethniques distinctifs. Le Québec, qui en était à sa première autonomie depuis la conquête, faisait craintivement l'expérience politique. S'il revendiquait une compétence, c'était moins pour s'en servir que pour empêcher le pouvoir fédéral, la majorité, de le meurtrir par son usage.

L'on peut discuter longtemps des causes de cet anti-étatisme initial des Québecois. Pendant cent ans après la Conquête, les Québecois avaient complètement désappris à se servir de l'Etat ou même à y participer selon un style qui leur fut propre, et c'est là une tradition dont les secrets peuvent se perdre irrémédiablement. Le « self-government » ne fut accordé au Canada qu'au moment précis où les Canadiens francophones cessèrent d'y constituer la majorité. Cet Etat, qu'ils n'avaient point façonné eux-mêmes selon leur génie propre, et qu'ils ne pouvaient influencer, dans la mesure où ils y participaient, que selon des modalités et des cadres qu'ils n'avaient point choisis, finit par être considéré comme une institution au mieux étrangère, au pis hostile. Les Canadiens français ressentaient, à l'égard de l'Etat, un sentiment d'aliénation. C'est là aussi, à mon sens, qu'il faut chercher la source de cette réputation de corruption politique des Canadiens français. La corruption politique est, profondément, une trahison de l'Etat. Or on ne trahit vraiment que ce qui nous appartient et vis-à-vis de quoi l'on ressent une loyauté. Il n'est donc pas contradictoire de soutenir qu'on achetait les Canadiens français sans qu'eux-mêmes aient l'impression de se vendre. C'est d'ailleurs Lord Sydenham, gouverneur général, qui, l'un des premiers, leur a enseigné la corruption, et ils ne s'y montrèrent point mauvais élèves. Quand plus tard ils apprirent l'histoire, particulièrement celle d'Angleterre, ils se rendirent compte que la vertu politique de leurs concitoyens anglo-saxons était bien trop fraîche pour qu'elle puisse sérieusement leur être proposée en exemple.

Lorsque les Québecois acquirent, en 1867, un embryon d'Etat qu'ils contrôlaient seuls, ils reportèrent sur lui, non pas logiquement, mais par habitude, la méfiance qu'ils avaient si longtemps ressentie à l'endroit de l'autre. Quand même d'ailleurs ils n'auraient point ressenti cette méfiance, ils ignoraient comment se servir d'un Etat moderne. Ils furent confirmés dans ces sentiments anti-étatiques par une influence cléricale qui atteignit son apogée à la fin du siècle dernier et au début du présent : le clergé français, ayant eu à souffrir du laïcisme de la troisième république française, réussit à faire croire aux Canadiens français, soit directement, par l'émigration de certains de ses prêtres, soit indirectement, par une littérature qu'il inspirait largement, que l'Histoire, ou plus précisément la Providence, avait protégé les Canadiens français en leur épargnant la révolution française, le jacobinisme, le républicanisme, et le laïcisme. Les Canadiens français, comme bien des gens méfiants, sont aussi des gens crédules. Ils crurent cette sottise pendant au moins cinquante ans.

Les Canadiens français du Québec n'ayant point de grandes richesses, ne sachant ou n'osant utiliser, pour les augmenter, le seul levier puissant qu'ils commandaient, finirent par s'imaginer que leurs classes les plus modestes avaient une vocation agricole et que les classes plus instruites étaient destinées aux professions libérales. L'industrie, le commerce, les finances — par exemple, à cette époque, les chemins de fer, le transport maritime, la banque — activités matérielles plus ou moins viles, et dont le contact risquait toujours, pensaient-ils, d'engendrer quelque turpitude, étaient réservés, généralement, au contrôle des institutions fédérales et à la possession des Anglo-Saxons. L'histoire et la constitution leur avaient réservé à eux l'éducation, le droit des personnes, l'humanisme, et les choses de l'esprit. Comme ils n'en étaient pas à une crédulité près, ils se convainquirent qu'ils avaient eu la bonne **part**.

CONCLUSIONS

La protection de l'identité québecoise est d'abord d'une nature juridique plutôt que politique. Elle a pour but et partiellement pour effet d'empêcher l'action de la majorité anglophone dans des domaines considérés comme reliés directement aux caractères ethniques de la minorité. Sans doute est-elle politique dans un certain sens et jusqu'à un certain point puisqu'elle permet à la minorité d'agir comme elle l'entend dans ces domaines, mais c'est là surtout un effet indirect du partage des compétences. Ce n'en est point l'objet. L'objet est négatif. L'objet consiste à réduire les zones de contact entre une majorité trop forte et une minorité trop faible, dans les domaines considérés comme d'importance vitale, parce que l'on semble croire, à cette époque, qu'un tel contact avec l'autre en ces domaines risquerait de détruire l'identité collective de la minorité. La minorité est donc considérée et elle se considère elle-même comme fragile et ayant besoin du secours des lois pour survivre ; l'on croit que son dynamisme propre ne suffit pas à garantir sa survivance. Il est d'ailleurs question de survivance, et non point de vie, et encore moins de développement, de croissance, d'épanouissement. De la même façon que la collectivité québecoise est concentrée sur un territoire, de même, certains champs de l'activité politique lui sont-ils « réservés » ; en d'autres termes, elle est, pour ces domaines, considérée comme devant vivre dans une « réserve » constitutionnelle. Elle doit rester repliée sur elle-même car l'on craint que le contact avec l'autre ne la tue lentement. Enfin, la détermination de ces zones où le contact ne doit pas avoir lieu reflète une mentalité libérale, individualiste, rurale, et mercantile qui tardait déjà sur son époque — l'industrialisation étant déjà commencée — et qui, à plus forte raison, nous semble dépassée aujourd'hui : la religion, la langue, les lois civiles sont des domaines qui maintenant prennent parfois, si l'on insiste pour en parler avec un certain accent, allure de folklore ; mais le fait que l'on ait cantonné la collectivité québecoise à ces domaines en 1867, et qu'elle ait été écartée des grandes compétences politiques d'un état du dix-neuvième siècle manifeste que l'on se faisait d'elle et qu'elle avait d'elle-même une image bucolique, pittoresque peut-être mais déjà surannée, sûrement retardataire et légèrement mélancolique comme tout ce qui est visiblement menacé de disparition.

Ainsi, la constitution de 1867 prend dans cette première phase, vis-à-vis la collectivité québecoise, un sens surtout juridique, statique, négatif, et protecteur, et enfin folklorique, pour ne pas dire qu'il confine à la conservation anthropologique.

II. *L'ATTITUDE ACTIVE: LA CONSTITUTION, UN FREIN AU DYNAMISME DU QUEBEC ET UNE LACUNE JURIDIQUE*

L'idée que les Québecois se font maintenant de la constitution n'est plus celle que je viens de décrire. Il est difficile et il n'est pas indispensable de retracer les étapes et d'identifier toutes les causes du changement. Le rythme de celui-ci s'est récemment précipité, mais il y a déjà bien des années que l'Etat québecois a manifesté des velléités d'augmenter son influence en subventionnant, par exemple, des institutions d'éducation ou même en créant celles-ci de toutes pièces — comme l'Ecole des Hautes Etudes commerciales ou les écoles techniques — et non sans rencontrer une opposition locale suffisamment vigoureuse pour l'empêcher d'être audacieux en ces matières, ou encore, en découvrant, apparemment pour la première fois dans son histoire, l'importance de la fiscalité. La crise économique des années trente, la guerre, l'industrialisation, les progrès scientifiques, l'augmentation des standards de vie, le chômage, la transformation de la scène internationale, la décolonisation et la naissance de multiples Etats moins développés que le Québec, le déclin relatif ou du moins le ralentissement du Canada anglophone depuis qu'il a rompu ses liens avec la métropole britannique, qu'il a fini de réaliser la plénitude territoriale — l'un des buts de la Confédération — les incertitudes du gouvernement d'Ottawa balançant entre l'expansion économique et l'indépendance vis-à-vis les Etats-Unis, sont autant de facteurs complexes qui ont produit, dans le Québec comme ailleurs, des effets considérables conditionnés par la situation particulière de la population qui s'y trouvait soumise. Ces causes et leurs effets, répartis sur plusieurs décennies, sont diversement perçus et interprétés à diverses époques, et à la même époque par diverses personnes.

Il n'en résulte pas que la conception que les Québecois avaient de la constitution autrefois, tant au point de vue des valeurs qu'elle défend que des techniques qu'elle prescrit pour les défendre, soit entièrement disparue dans la mentalité québecoise. Celle-ci, cependant, il ne paraît pas exagéré de le prétendre, s'est substantiellement transformée sur ce sujet.

1. LE RENVERSEMENT DES VALEURS

Les Québecois, individuellement et collectivement, convoitent les richesses matérielles et ce qu'elles procurent dans cette civilisation, le pouvoir, l'influence, le prestige, l'efficacité technique, le confort, le luxe, et la sécurité. Ils sont devenus ou sont en passe de devenir un peuple nord-américain. Eux qui avaient réussi à croire qu'ils s'étaient vu attribuer la meilleure part avec les valeurs culturelles, la tradition humaniste, et la vie de l'esprit, ou bien ont fini par leur en préférer d'autres qui sont plus concrètes, ou bien, et plus justement, ont appris que les valeurs culturelles devaient s'incarner et qu'elles étaient condamnées à s'étioler si elles n'étaient stimulées, appuyées, par des ressources abondantes. Ils se sont rendu compte qu'il est impossible que la collectivité, comme les individus, progresse dans les arts et les sciences et périclite dans l'industrie, le commerce, les finances et la politique, et qu'il était tout aussi impossible qu'une société réussisse dans ses entreprises matérielles sans que son activité spirituelle en profite. Observant autour d'eux, ils ont appris une leçon pourtant élémentaire savoir, qu'avec de l'argent l'on peut acheter des oeuvres d'art et constituer un musée, qu'avec de l'argent l'on peut faire vivre un orchestre symphonique, qu'avec de l'argent l'on peut subventionner le théâtre, qu'avec de l'argent l'on peut activer la recherche scientifique, qu'avec de l'argent l'on peut développer une université, qu'avec de l'argent l'on peut importer des talents. Ils commencent d'admettre que les arts, les sciences, et les lettres se nourrissent aussi de nourriture terrestres. Comparant leurs propres institutions culturelles, scientifiques, ou éducatives avec les institutions de la même nature qui appartenaient à la majorité hors du

Québec et dans le Québec, ils ont constaté qu'elles étaient inférieures à ces dernières, et qu'ils étaient vaincus sur le terrain même où ils avaient pu espérer garder des avantages.

Ils ont appris bien d'autres choses encore. Par exemple, qu'avec de l'argent, en Amérique, l'on peut décrotter une famille en moins de trois générations et en faire accéder les membres à la classe dirigeante. Par exemple, qu'il y a des chances que l'on fasse de la meilleure politique avec beaucoup d'argent qu'avec peu, mais surtout que même un gouvernement doit être responsable du prélèvement et de la perception de l'argent qu'il dépense, s'il ne veut pas prendre des habitudes de femme entretenue.

Ils croient que les richesses proviennent de la croissance de l'économie, qu'elle réside dans l'industrie, le commerce, et le capital. Mais ils possèdent peu de capitaux, et ils ne détiennent que partiellement les moyens de règlementer l'industrie et le commerce et de contrôler le rythme de la croissance économique.

Leur compétence en matière d'éducation signifiait autrefois, nous l'avons vu, et elle n'a pas totalement cessé de signifier la protection de la confession religieuse et de la tradition linguistique et culturelle— quoique la constitution ne mentionne point cette dernière. Elle prend aujourd'hui une autre proportion : c'est d'elle que dépend en nombre et en qualité, la satisfaction des besoins de l'industrie, du commerce, du gouvernement en personnel techniquement qualifié. Les institutions d'enseignement québecoises étaient autrefois pauvres et elles manifestaient une préférence pour les humanités. Le Québec accorde aujourd'hui la priorité à l'éducation, et l'accent y est mis, comme dans le reste de l'Amérique, avec plus d'enthousiasme peut-être que de discernement, sur les sciences et la technique, même dans les humanités.

La compétence constitutionnelle du Québec sur la propriété et les droits civils signifiaient autrefois la sauvegarde de la Coutume de Paris telle qu'adoptée au Québec, la protection du droit de la famille et des personnes, de l'autonomie de la volonté et de la propriété privée. Mais l'on revise maintenant le Code civil sans que ce projet réchauffe le coeur des Québecois sauf quelques juristes, et celui qui prétendrait aujourd'hui que le Code, à l'image de la foi et de la langue, est l'objet des affections passionnées d'un peuple ferait sourire comme tout orateur s'exprimant dans le style du dix-neuvième siècle. La compétence du Québec sur les droits civils lui permet encore, bien sûr, de veiller à l'intégrité de ses lois civiles, mais elle l'habilite surtout, et c'est ce qui lui importe davantage actuellement, à règlementer les conditions de travail, à prévoir l'arbitrage et la solution des conflits industriels, à établir un salaire minimum, à gouverner le commerce des valeurs mobilières, à déterminer les conditions de mise en marché des produits agricoles ou de tout autre produit s'il lui plait, à intervenir dans les contrats pour en modifier au besoin les clauses les plus importantes malgré la volonté initiale des parties, à régir les loyers et le transport interne, à fixer les prix, à prohiber la fabrication, la circulation, la vente et la consommation de certains produits, et à règlementer le commerce intérieur en général.

Sans doute, grâce à l'interprétation du Conseil privé, cette extension de la compétence civile a-t-elle été reconnue pour toutes les provinces et non seulement pour le Québec, mais elle a pris, au Québec, une saveur particulière. Elle a démystifié, ou si l'on veut, désacralisé un domaine législatif étroitement associé à l'identité collective des Québecois et auquel la constitution elle-même, par ses articles 94, 97, et 98 avait fait un sort à part. Elle a de plus procuré à la collectivité québecoise des moyens de contrôler en partie ce domaine qui avait été pratiquement interdit à ses membres, à l'époque du libéralisme économique, la grande industrie, la haute finance. Elle lui a donné prise sur l'une de ces valeurs nouvelles pour elle, et qu'elle convoite d'autant plus âprement qu'elle en a été longtemps sevrée, les richesses matérielles.

Deux valeurs d'importance capitale demeurent pour les Québecois, le nationalisme et la démocratie. La première de ces valeurs s'est fortement accentuée. La seconde subsiste.

Il n'est point besoin, je pense, de longue démonstration pour établir que les Canadiens français du Québec sont demeurés profondément nationalistes et que leur nationalisme s'identifie aux institutions qu'ils contrôlent, les institutions provinciales. Il suffit de rappeler que les revendications du gouvernement Duplessis vis-à-vis le gouvernement fédéral ont été entièrement reprises, quoiqu'avec un style différent, par le gouvernement Lesage. Peu de gouvernements peuvent se maintenir longtemps au Québec s'ils ont une réputation de mollesse vis-à-vis les autorités fédérales, et les partis au pouvoir peuvent difficilement se permettre d'être dépassés, sur ce point, en zèle et en vigilance, par l'opposition. Il suffit de souligner l'unanimité du parti ministériel et de l'opposition sur une question aussi importante que l'établissement du comité parlementaire de la constitution. Il suffit de mentionner que plusieurs parlementaires québecois, y compris des ministres, se sont prononcés en faveur du droit du Québec à l'autodétermination. Il suffit de constater la naissance de partis indépendantistes dont certains veulent contester les prochaines élections provinciales. Le style du nationalisme québecois a pu se modifier, mais son intensité s'est accrue.

Quant aux valeurs démocratiques, elles subsistent pour le moment dans le Québec, mais la lucidité commande que l'on s'interroge sur la profondeur de leurs racines. Les Québecois vivent dans un régime démocratique dont on leur a, bon gré mal gré, fait le cadeau. Au fond, ils n'ont jamais été libres d'être libres. Si la liberté individuelle y est protégée, c'est en partie parce que les Québecois ont été conquis par un peuple démocratique. L'asservissement collectif des Canadiens français québecois peut bien être considéré comme l'un des facteurs de leur liberté personnelle. La disparition partielle ou totale de ce facteur ne compromet pas nécessairement le principe de la liberté individuelle, mais elle remet en question au moins son organisation juridique particulière. Le principe lui-même, cependant, peut être mis en cause. La liberté, l'individuelle comme la collective, se gagne, se mérite et c'est une expérience qui peut être longue et pénible. La liberté s'apprend mais elle s'enseigne mal. Les Canadiens français ont reçu bien des leçons mais ils ont eu peu d'occasions d'apprendre.

2. LE DYNAMISME DU QUEBEC

Les valeurs anciennes dans lesquelles la collectivité québecoise croyait, elle en attendait surtout la protection de la constitution et des lois. Celles qu'elle poursuit maintenant, elle sait qu'elle devra se les procurer elle-même.

Sans doute, le gouvernement de Québec n'occupe pas, quantitativement, tout le champ de sa compétence. S'il le faisait, nous serions fort près de l'état totalitaire. Sans doute peut-on lui reprocher, et depuis des années, de ne pas mieux administrer les domaines qu'il a décidé d'occuper : d'une part, l'amélioration est toujours possible, et d'autre part elle dépend, en partie, de ressources qui manquent à la province.

Mais les actes que la province de Québec a posés depuis trente ou quarante ans témoignent d'un dynamisme progressif qui n'est pas nécessairement plus vigoureux que celui d'autres provinces, mais qui obéit à d'autres impératifs et qui fait contraste avec l'attitude timorée de la période précédente.

Elle a d'abord occupé par sa législation et son administration à peu près toute la compétence qui lui avait été reconnue en matière civile et en matière de sécurité sociale, compte tenu de ses ressources. Elle a revendiqué contre le pouvoir fédéral les ressources nécessaires à l'expansion de ses services et seule, contre l'opinion publique de tout le reste du Canada, elle a voulu assumer la responsabilité du prélèvement des impôts nécessaires, allant jusqu'à imposer à ses citoyens la double taxation. Elle souffrait, par comparaison avec d'autres pays, de certains

retards qu'elle cherche à rattraper ; elle tente, par exemple, par la créa-
tion d'un ministère de l'éducation, d'exorciser le vieux démon de
l'étatisme québecois, et de construire un appareil administratif efficace.
Elle a institué, non sans difficultés considérables, l'assurance-hospitalisation. Elle est désireuse de mieux exploiter ses ressources et les problèmes
actuellement à résoudre avec le pouvoir fédéral relativement aux esqui-
maux ou avec Terre-Neuve relativement aux frontières du Labrador ne
sont que des incidents relatifs à une politique d'aménagement et de mise
en valeur de son territoire. Elle tâche d'équilibrer l'industrie d'extraction
par l'établissement dans la province d'une industrie de transformation.
Seule encore, contre le pouvoir fédéral et une bonne partie du Canada,
elle a insisté pour établir sa propre caisse de retraite dans un but de
sécurité sociale mais aussi pour constituer une masse monétaire avec
laquelle elle pourra influencer l'économie.

Si le péril qui menace une minorité vient non seulement de l'extérieur,
mais aussi de l'intérieur, de la passivité même de cette minorité, c'en
est un que la minorité québecoise tente vigoureusement de surmonter.

Certains gestes, cependant, dictés par cette attitude nouvelle, sont
parfois mal interprétés par le reste du Canada, parce qu'on les croit à
tort inspirés par l'ancienne conception de la constitution. Ainsi, autrefois,
les subsides fédéraux aux universités et à l'enseignement technique, les
bourses du Conseil des Arts, le projet de bourses fédérales aux étudiants
auraient d'abord été regardés, par les Québecois, comme un péril extérieur, c'est-à-dire comme un danger de transformation et de corruption,
par la majorité, d'institutions vitales du Canada français. L'on a donc
vu les apologistes de ces mesures s'évertuer à démontrer que ces subventions n'étaient point conditionnelles et qu'elles ne portaient point
atteinte à l'intégrité des institutions. Or non seulement ce raisonnement
pêchait-il contre la logique puisqu'un subside même non-conditionnel
implique au moins l'identification du bénéficiare et par conséquent un
choix politique délibéré de la part du pouvoir fédéral dans une matière
provinciale[28], mais encore il démontrait, chez ceux qui tenaient ce raisonnement, une incompréhension profonde du point de vue québecois :
c'est doublement que le pouvoir fédéral portait atteinte à l'autonomie
du Québec, d'abord en agissant dans un domaine réservé à la province,
mais surtout parce qu'en faisant cette dépense il privait la province des

[28]Il s'agit d'ailleurs de fonds publics, que le bailleur a acquis grâce à la force
coercitive de ses lois fiscales ou grâce aux profits du domaine public, lui-même
obtenu, aménagé ou développé grâce aux ressources fiscales, ce qui, dans tous les
cas, exclut toute espèce d'analogie avec la philantropie privée et tout concept de
« générosité » , à moins que l'on ne retombe dans des confusions désuètes entre le
trésor public et la cassette privée du prince.

ressources nécessaires pour agir elle-même de la même manière ou de tout autre manière dans ce domaine ou dans un autre, au moment de son choix, selon son bon plaisir.

La compétence du Québec en matière d'éducation a donc non seulement, en pratique, un contenu matériel différent de celui qui était le sien lors de la confédération, mais encore, l'attribution de cette compétence qui avait d'abord un but négatif, l'exclusion du pouvoir fédéral, acquiert un sens dynamique, l'exploitation par le Québec de sa compétence, la revendication des ressources nécessaires pour l'exploiter et de la responsabilité du prélèvement de ces ressources.

Ainsi encore, lors des conférences fédérale-provinciales sur le rapatriement de la constitution, plusieurs parties aux conférences commenceront souvent les discussions par l'assurance d'une sauvegarde constitutionnelle de quelque sujet auquel elles croient le Québec fondamentalement attaché, par exemple le « status » des langues officielles. Ayant l'air d'avoir fait les premiers pas, elles procèdent ensuite à demander des concessions du Québec, par exemple en matière de propriété et de droits civils. Elles ne se méprennent point sur l'attachement vital du Québec à la langue française. Mais ce que le Québec ne peut point facilement leur dire, c'est qu'il a plus confiance en sa propre force politique qu'aux garanties légales pour assurer le « status » actuel du français. Faute cependant de pouvoir facilement en convenir, le Québec voit ainsi diminué son pouvoir de marchandage. L'on serait sans doute étonné si le Québec offrait au reste du pays des garanties concernant l'usage de la langue anglaise dans les institutions fédérales, en échange de quelque compétence fédérale importante.

3. L'OBSTACLE DE LA CONSTITUTION

La vitalité que le Québec a manifestée dupuis quelques années ne l'empêche point de rester une minorité. Cette vitalité d'ailleurs s'est exprimée beaucoup plus dans les institutions provinciales que dans les fédérales, dans la recherche de moyens d'action provinciaux, dans l'exploitation, l'expansion ou la défense des compétences provinciales. L'action du Québec, à longue échéance, est infiniment moins perceptible dans le domaine fédéral. Ses fonctionnaires fédéraux, ses députés, ses ministres même, peuvent à peine infléchir la politique fédérale, à brève échéance, et encore leur influence grandit, surtout quand le gouvernement central est faible et qu'il redoute le pire. Pour les domaines qu'il partage avec la majorité, le Québec ne peut que surnager péniblement dans une mer anglo-saxonne, canadienne, et même nord-américaine, où il risque à chaque instant de se noyer. En d'autres termes, le Québec ne ressent une certaine force que dans les domaines pour lesquels la constitution l'a séparé de la majorité et dans lesquels elle lui permet d'avoir une action autonome. Il n'est donc pas étonnant que le Québec ressente le désir d'étendre ces domaines et qu'*a fortiori* il s'oppose à leur contraction.

Or l'examen critique du contexte constitutionnel et de la constitution elle-même ne peuvent que le rendre pessimiste sur ce point.

La loi de centralisation. Ceux qui ont étudié les constitutions fédérales ont remarqué la tendance qu'elles avaient toutes à concentrer graduellement la puissance de l'Etat sur les institutions centrales. Ils en ont même déduit un principe, la loi de centralisation, à laquelle seraient soumises toutes les fédérations.

Il peut sembler, à première vue, que cette loi de centralisation se soit appliquée au Canada avec moins de vigueur qu'à d'autres fédérations parce qu'entre autres raisons les diverses régions du Canada ont été soumises à une autre force d'attraction, celle des Etats-Unis. Il peut aussi sembler intempestif, pour ne pas dire inexact, de parler centralisation au moment précis où les institutions provinciales se font accorder des budgets dont la somme dépasse les dépenses fédérales, et où les gouvernements provinciaux, politiquement puissants, affrontent un gouvernement fédéral politiquement vulnérable. Ce ne peuvent être là pourtant que des épisodes qui aient pour effet de retarder provisoirement l'application d'une loi inexorable. Et il est fort possible que les fédérations n'aient le choix qu'entre une centralisation graduelle et l'éclatement.

L'examen attentif de la constitution démontre que celle-ci est juridiquement capable de la plus grande centralisation sans modification constitutionnelle, tandis qu'il semble juridiquement difficile de la décentraliser davantage autrement que par des modifications constitutionnelles.

Les modifications formelles à la constitution sont difficiles à obtenir, et celles qui ont été acceptées ont toutes un effet ou bien neutre ou bien centralisateur ; il n'en fut jamais décrété qui ait eu pour conséquence d'augmenter la compétence des provinces au détriment de la compétence fédérale.[24]

D'un autre côté la constitution de 1867 est susceptible de se prêter à une expansion presque indéfinie de la compétence fédérale, soit à cause de renversements jurisprudentiels toujours concevables, soit par suite de l'exploration par la jurisprudence de domaines qu'elle a laissés jusqu'ici intouchés, soit enfin par la pratique ou l'usage plus abondant par le pouvoir fédéral de compétences qui lui sont déjà reconnues.

Les techniques selon lesquelles l'on a diminué la compétence rési-

---

[24]Sauf peut être, si l'on veut les inclure dans cette catégorie, celles relatives au transfert des richesses naturelles et à la modification des frontières.

duelle du pouvoir fédéral ainsi que sa compétence relative à la règle-
mentation du commerce et de l'industrie sont susceptibles d'être remises
en question par la jurisprudence, comme l'y invite d'ailleurs presque
continuellement une partie substantielle de la littérature juridique canadienne d'expression anglaise. Dans certains cas, il serait à peine besoin
de renverser la jurisprudence, il suffirait de mettre l'accent sur certains
arrêts plutôt que sur d'autres, par exemple sur l'arrêt Russel[25] et sur
l'arrêt *A. G. Ont.* v. *Canada Temperance Federation*[26] plutôt que sur
l'arrêt relatif aux prohibitions régionales[27]. Il suffirait de revenir à la
lettre de l'alinéa 2 de l'article 91 pour donner au pouvoir fédéral une
puissance infiniment accrue, excédant même celle du pouvoir central
aux Etats-Unis, sur le commerce interne et l'industrie. Il suffirait de
mieux explorer le concept de citoyenneté, comme l'a fait le juge Rand[28]
ou celui de défense du pays, pour donner à la compétence fédérale des
ramifications insoupçonnées. Quant à la compétence du pouvoir fédéral
sur le droit criminel, elle est susceptible d'une expansion presque illimitée, parce que les cours peuvent difficilement en contrôler l'exercice
sans porter un jugement d'opportunité. Il suffirait, comme l'a noté le
doyen Lederman, d'étendre le champ de la compétence commune pour
augmenter du même coup la suprématie fédérale. Il suffirait de donner
aux relations ouvrières ou industrielles qui recoupent les frontières provinciales un aspect ou une dimension dite nationale pour les soumettre
à l'empire des lois fédérales.

Il y a peu de limites connues à la faculté que possède le pouvoir
fédéral d'augmenter unilatéralement sa compétence en déclarant que
certains travaux profitent au Canada ou à deux provinces. Le pouvoir
fédéral peut aussi constituer des sociétés qui poursuivent des buts provinciaux à travers le Canada, et il règlemente ainsi, par leur constitution,
une partie substantielle de leur activité.

Que dire enfin du pouvoir financier des institutions fédérales? Malgré
un caveat inefficace de la jurisprudence[29] l'on a réussi à créer une
nouvelle espèce de législation qui permet au pouvoir fédéral d'influencer
les domaines provinciaux en y dispensant ses largesses selon la politique
de son choix.

Il faut en dernier lieu faire mention du pouvoir fédéral de réserve
et de désaveu des lois provinciales. Son usage est aujourd'hui malaisé

[25](1881–82) 7 AC 829.
[26](1946) AC 193.
[27](1896) AC 348.
[28]*Affaire Winner*, (1951) SCR 887, partiellement infirmée, et partiellement
confirmée par le Conseil privé, (1954) AC 541.
[29]*A. G. Can.* v. *A. G. Ont.*, (1937) AC 355.

et pourrait équivaloir à un suicide politique. Mais il n'est pas inimaginable que l'on songe à le ressusciter dans des circonstances favorables ; or il confère au gouvernement fédéral une compétence législative négative qui est quasi illimitée en matière provinciale.

Si la compétence fédérale semble presque indéfiniment expansible sans qu'il soit nécessaire de recourir à la modification constitutionnelle, celle des provinces, en revanche, semble avoir atteint sa limite.

Le Comité judiciaire a élargi autant qu'il était humainement possible l'extension de l'article 92. Une province ne peut, sans modification constitutionnelle, espérer voir sa compétence augmenter. Elle ne peut qu'accroître ses moyens d'action, soit en trouvant de nouvelles ressources fiscales, soit en ajoutant au domaine public. Mais pour ajouter au domaine public, cette province doit procéder à des expropriations ou à des nationalisations, ou organiser et dispenser elle-même de nouveaux services publics : la liberté dans le choix de ces procédés est en pratique limitée parce que ces mesures s'avèrent souvent dispendieuses, ou parce qu'elles sont considérées comme trop radicales et qu'elles risquent de décourager les investissements nécessaires à la croissance économique.

Juridiquement, la constitution peut donc se prêter à toutes les centralisations, mais ce n'est qu'avec difficulté qu'elle pourra se décentraliser plus qu'elle ne l'est, abstraction faite des modifications constitutionnelles. D'un point de vue québécois, cette situation signifie que le nombre des domaines dans lesquels la minorité peut agir comme une majorité n'est pas susceptible d'augmentation tandis que celui des domaines où elle ne peut exercer que la pâle influence des minorités peut, parfaitement, lui, se multiplier. Potentiellement, la constitution actuelle menace donc de placer les Québecois en minorité sur un nombre de plus en plus grand de domaines.

Mais ce n'est pas uniquement dans le droit de la constitution que l'on trouve des causes de centralisation. Hors le point de vue purement juridique, les forces d'intégration qui produisent leurs effets sur le Canada, et qui, par conséquent, pourront l'inciter à vouloir consolider le pouvoir de l'Etat, et singulièrement, celui de l'Etat central, sont nombreuses et puissantes. Ces forces d'intégration cependant n'influencent pas également les Québecois et les autres Canadiens, et, surtout, elles ne produisent pas les mêmes effets chez les uns et les autres.

La crainte d'une domination économique et culturelle des Etats-Unis, en un certain sens, affecte plus les Canadiens anglophones que les Québecois ; ceux-ci ne souhaitent point cette domination pour eux-mêmes ; mais, assimilation pour assimilation, celle-ci ne serait point pire qu'une autre : la proie se demande rarement par quel carnassier il est préferable d'être dévoré. Bien des Canadiens plaident que la permanence de la Confédération protège le Québec contre une assimilation par les Etats-Unis. Ce n'est point prouvé. L'on pourrait aussi logiquement soutenir que la Confédération entraîne le Québec vers l'assimilation par les Etats-Unis.

Une autre force d'intégration, c'est le développement d'une vie canadienne, industrielle, commerciale, financière, politique, professionnelle, syndicale, scientifique, qui multiplie les relations et qui facilite et accentue l'interchangeabilité et la mobilité des individus. Le Québecois participe infiniment moins à cette force. Un Québecois est toujours étonné de constater qu'un Canadien a été éduqué à Dalhousie, qu'il a fait carrière de haut fonctionaire à Ottawa, qu'il est passé à l'industrie torontoise, et qu'il prend sa retraite à Victoria. Peu de Québecois, en auraient-ils le goût, peuvent se permettre une telle mobilité sans risquer de se « déculturaliser » eux-mêmes et sans que leur famille ne s'assimile. D'un point de vue ethnique, les membres d'une collectivité minoritaire ne quittent point la réserve sans courir les plus grands dangers.

D'autres forces d'intégration, enfin, ont agi ou agissent également sur les Québecois et les autres Canadiens, mais produisent des effets divers et même divergents. La dépression économique, la participation à deux guerres mondiales, la guerre froide, l'acquisition d'un status international pour le Canada, l'expansion de l'industrie, du commerce, des transports, l'augmentation des besoins et des désirs de la population et le développement de la sécurité sociale, la diminution des ressources naturelles non renouvelables, l'amenuisement des ressources renouvelables ont créé et créent encore des problèmes majeurs dont la solution implique une énorme augmentation de la puissance de l'Etat, la planification et le contrôle de l'économie, la concentration des ressources fiscales, la conscription des énergies.

Soit pour des considérations d'ordre fonctionnel, soit pour des motifs sentimentaux, l'Etat fédéral est celui sur lequel les Canadiens anglophones ont tout naturellement songé à concentrer la puissance requise, même lorsqu'il s'agissait d'assumer des responsabilités provinciales. Pendant des années, l'on a prétendu, dans la littérature politique anglocanadienne, que la constitution, telle qu'interprétée par le Conseil Privé, était mal faite, à refaire dans le sens d'une centralisation devenue fonctionnellement indispensable. La doctrine juridique et politique anglocanadienne, écrite dans les périodiques scientifiques, a reçu de manière acerbe et parfois avec férocité les décisions du Conseil privé concernant, par exemple, l'invalidation du New Deal de Bennett. Le principe même du partage des compétences était battu en brèche, comme hostile à l'Etat et paralysant son intervention efficace. L'on imputait aux juges du Conseil privé des motifs inspirés du libéralisme le plus sinistre.

Les commissions royales comme la Commission Rowell-Sirois ou la Commission Massey recommandaient l'accroissement de la compétence, de l'action, ou de l'influence du pouvoir fédéral. Presque tous réclamaient un assouplissement de la constitution qui signifiait surtout la centralisation et proposaient, pour l'accomplir, des mesures comme par exemple la délégation de pouvoirs entre les provinces et le pouvoir fédéral. On a d'ailleurs continué de réclamer cette délégation, comme une panacée, jusqu'aux conférences constitutionnelles de 1960 et de 1961[30]. Les Canadiens concentrent aujourd'hui sur les provinces une plus grande partie qu'autrefois de la puissance de l'Etat. Mais, sauf au Québec, les Canadiens anglophones sont en majorité dans les provinces et ils sont en mesure de faire le choix qu'ils estiment le plus fonctionnel. Cette alternative fonctionnelle est interdite aux Québecois. Ils ne contrôlent que le Québec.

Au début de la même période, les Québecois ont commencé par ignorer les problèmes matériels et fonctionnels auxquels la Confédération a eu à faire face. Pouvaient-ils d'ailleurs seulement les percevoir, éloignés qu'ils étaient, sauf de rares exceptions, des grandes affaires de l'Etat, de l'industrie, du commerce et des finances, ignorants de la haute administration, peu frottés à l'économique. S'ils les abordaient, c'était à travers les données et les schèmes de pensée de la majorité. Ensuite, la vieille tradition anti-étatique des Québecois les a incités à regarder cette littérature juridico-politique comme une élucubration d'intellectuels socialistes, dangereux dans la mesure où ils pouvaient exercer quelque influence. Enfin, le nationalisme québecois répugnait à l'ensemble des solutions proposées parce qu'elles étaient centralisatrices.

Or, la plus grande partie des problèmes fonctionnels soulevés par le partage des pouvoirs est aujourd'hui perçue au Québec. Ces problèmes ont plus d'acuité encore qu'autrefois. La vieille méfiance éprouvée à l'endroit des interventions de l'Etat disparaît rapidement. La nécessité de renforcer le pouvoir des institutions politiques est plus facilement admise. Mais le nationalisme, lui, est resté. L'Etat dans lequel il est nécessaire de concentrer des pouvoirs n'est pas le même, c'est l'Etat québecois. La constitution de 1867 apparaît donc à beaucoup de Québecois aujourd'hui, exactement comme il y a trente ans à bien des jeunes intellectuels anglophones, comme un obstacle à l'action justifiée de l'Etat ; mais il ne s'agit plus du même Etat.

[30]Et si le Québec admet finalement l'interdélégation de pouvoirs, ce sera, pour consommer la méprise, dans une perspective de décentralisation.

Poursuivant des valeurs nouvelles pour lui, la richesse matérielle et la supériorité qu'elle symbolise en Amérique et qu'elle est susceptible de procurer à ceux qui la possèdent, le Québecois constate d'abord que le seul instrument fort qui soit à sa discrétion est l'Etat provincial. (L'Etat fédéral n'est pas à sa discrétion parce qu'il le partage, mais comme dans ce partage il se trouve en minorité, cet Etat n'agit point nécessairement pour lui et jamais par lui.) Or, cet unique instrument de puissance, l'Etat provincial, il est porté à le considérer comme encore trop faible : il ne peut agir sur la monnaie, sur les banques, sur le tarif douanier, sur le budget de la défense, sur la conduite des affaires extérieures, domaines fort importants dans la poursuite de ces fins. Quoi de plus normal que de songer à en augmenter la puissance par l'adjonction d'une partie et même de la totalité de ce qui lui manque? Le Québecois hésitait autrefois à user de la compétence qu'il avait. Il commence d'en convoiter qu'il ne possède pas.

Le partage fédéral des compétences a déjà pu être considéré par le Québecois comme la dévolution d'un pouvoir qui était conféré aux institutions politiques québecoises. Il est maintenant vu comme la privation, pour ces institutions provinciales, du pouvoir conféré aux institutions fédérales.

Le Québecois peut lire dans des douzaines d'articles du *Canadian Bar Review* ou du *Canadian Journal of Economics and Political Science* que le fédéralisme canadien a eu pour effet d'aider à conserver les richesses là où elles se trouvaient, mais il n'a qu'à regarder autour de lui, dans sa propre province, pour se rendre compte que c'est généralement exact, et pour admettre aussi que si le fédéralisme canadien et la philosophie libérale qui l'a inspiré se sont avérés favorables au développement des capitaux, ce n'était pas les siens.

Les lacunes du fédéralisme. Le principe même du fédéralisme, dans ses assises fondamentales, devient contestable, théoriquement et pratiquement. Le fédéralisme, en un certain sens, c'est l'absence de droit, c'est le vide politique au niveau le plus élevé. Dans une constitution fédérale comme celle du Canada, il n'y a aucun corps, aucune personne, parlements, gouvernements, électeurs, juges, qui ait le pouvoir par son arrêt, son vote, son décret, ou sa loi, d'établir une priorité, un choix par exemple entre le budget de la défense et celui de l'éducation, entre l'amélioration des conditions de la navigation et l'administration de la justice, entre la construction d'un pénitencier et l'ouverture d'une route, entre la recherche atomique et l'établissement d'un hôpital. Il n'est personne qui puisse vraiment décider de la coordination entre l'immigration et l'aménagement d'un territoire donné. Il n'est personne qui puisse décider de la plupart des conditions relatives aux multiples emprunts d'une puissance publique également multiple. Une constitution fédérale interdit que ce choix soit fait par des institutions déterminées. Or gouverner c'est choisir. La constitution interdit donc que l'on gouverne, elle décrète, pour certaines fins, le manque de gouvernement. Elle s'en remet, pour ces fins, à la force, et consacre la faillite de la règle de droit.

Sans doute est-ce là une lacune théorique dans un Etat libéral, dont l'idéologie, par hypothèse, désire le moins de gouvernement possible, dont les ressources paraissent inépuisables, dont la population clairsemée éprouve des besoins limités que l'on peut satisfaire à prix modique. Mais le Canada n'est plus cet Etat, s'il l'a jamais été. Les lacunes politiques que suppose le fédéralisme commencent de le faire souffrir et il est à prévoir que la douleur deviendra de plus en plus cuisante.

CONCLUSIONS

Comment combler ces lacunes juridico-politiques ? L'on a parlé de fédéralisme coopératif. Il est possible que ce soit là une diète pour gouvernements minoritaires. Quoiqu'il en soit, la coopération est toujours souhaitable mais elle ne se commande point, surtout du plus faible au plus fort. Les conférences fédérale-provinciales, les conférences interprovinciales, les commissions inter-ministérielles ne sont pas institutionnalisées et ne disposent point de la faculté de prendre des décisions exécutoires. Ce sont des conférences diplomatiques où des gens bien élevés font poliment l'inventaire de leurs désaccords. Si elles réussissent, leur succès implique souvent une nouvelle concession à la majorité, une nouvelle centralisation, c'est-à-dire une négation, dans un certain sens, du fédéralisme que le fédéralisme coopératif est censé sauvegarder. Le fédéralisme coopératif, c'est du fédéralisme tempéré par un début d'intégration. C'est l'admission implicite des lacunes du fédéralisme.

Si j'ai raison de soutenir que le principe fédéral comporte des lacunes théoriques qui sont en train de produire des conséquences pratiques au Canada, il faut combler ces lacunes par une atténuation ou une suppression du principe fédéral. Or l'atténuation ou la suppression du principe fédéral ne peut signifier que l'éclatement ou la centralisation du Canada. Et la centralisation veut dire pour le Québec l'assimilation. Je veux bien que la centralisation soit affaire de degré et non de nature, mais je doute que le Québec soit dans les dispositions requises pour transiger, même en termes de degrés, de ce qui peut signifier son assimilation.

Si le reste du Canada écarte certaines formes de centralisation, l'on peut douter qu'il subsiste indéfiniment comme état indépendant. Alors il est à craindre qu'il n'entraîne avec lui le Québec, et devant cette perspective, il est à prévoir que le Québec se sépare graduellement d'avec la Confédération. Il est plutôt normal que le reste du Canada veuille subsister et qu'il optera pour la centralisation. Dans ce cas, il est douteux que le Québec puisse résister bien longtemps à un processus accéléré d'assimilation et subsister comme collectivité distincte, et il paraît probable qu'il songe à quitter la Confédération de façon moins graduelle.

Reste la possibilité d'une centralisation du reste du Canada, qui ne s'appliquerait point au Québec, dont, au contraire, l'on étendrait la compétence. C'est la thèse du status spécial du Québec. Au point de vue de la technique juridique et politique, elle est d'une réalisation fort complexe, mais non pas d'une difficulté insurmontable. C'est l'opinion publique qui lui fera surtout obstacle, non pas tant celle du Québec, pour l'instant, que celle des autres provinces.

Enfin, si l'on veut être lucide, l'on ne doit pas écarter une dernière hypothèse, celle selon laquelle, abstraction faite de la centralisation, de la décentralisation, ou du maintien du *statu quo* pour le reste du Canada, le Québec serait désireux d'obtenir son indépendance de toutes façons.

Dans cette étude, trop longue et malgré tout incomplète, où j'ai tenté de donner une interprétation personnelle de l'attitude du Québec vis-à-vis la Confédération, j'ai dû ignorer des facteurs fort importants, mais qui ne se rattachent pas nécessairement à la Constitution, particulièrement le problème démographique, l'état croissant de minorité où se trouve le Québec dans le Canada, le manque de puissance assimilatrice du Québec à l'intérieur même de son territoire vis-à-vis l'immigration, particulièrement dans les régions urbaines et développées, le dilemme où il se trouverait placé si l'accroissement de son économie rendait nécessaire une importation massive de main-d'oeuvre étrangère.

A des non-Québecois, cette étude pourra de plus sembler outrageusement centrée sur le Québec : et il serait absurde d'expliquer la Confédération par une seule province quelle qu'elle soit. Mon but cependant n'a pas été d'expliquer la Confédération mais l'attitude du Québec par rapport à la Confédération. Je ne regrette donc point cet égocentrisme car je crois qu'il reflète bien la mentalité qui sera l'attitude du Québec devant les choix qui se présentent à lui ; il sera guidé uniquement par ce qu'il considérera être de son intérêt.

A REVISION OF THE CONSTITUTION?

VERS UNE NOUVELLE CONSTITUTION?

Vers un nouvel équilibre
constitutionnel au Canada

JACQUES-YVAN MORIN

Depuis quelques années, le Canada se trouve engagé dans une véritable crise de l'état. On entend parfois affirmer, particulièrement au Canada anglais, que cette crise est née en 1957 ou en 1960, années certes marquantes dans l'histoire du Québec, mais qui ne sauraient néanmoins rendre compte de la profondeur du malaise. En réalité, le conflit des cultures et des nationalismes apparut dès 1760, comme le constata Lord Durham à la suite de la Rébellion de 1837, pour resurgir plus d'une fois à la surface depuis lors. L'intervention croissante de l'état dans la vie socio-économique, au cours des dernières décennies, a ravivé le feu qui couvait sous la cendre et, dans un contexte international qui favorise « le droit des peuples à disposer d'eux-mêmes », a contribué largement à précipiter la crise. Pour comprendre cette dimension nouvelle d'une très ancienne lutte, reportons-nous à ces deux documents capitaux de l'histoire canadienne, datés respectivement de 1940 et 1956, que sont les rapports soumis par la Commission fédérale chargée d'enquêter sur les relations entre le *dominion* et les provinces (présidée par MM. Rowell et Sirois) et la Commission provinciale créée par le premier ministre Duplessis dans le but préciser l'attitude du Québec face à l'évolution constitutionnelle du pays (connue sous le nom de Commission Tremblay). Les deux conceptions opposées du fédéralisme qui y sont proposées serviront de point de départ à notre exposé.

La Commission Rowell-Sirois vit le jour dans le sillage de la dépression économique et dans le premier enthousiasme suscité par le *New Deal* américain et les théories interventionnistes de Keynes. Elle avait été créée par le gouvernement fédéral dans le but de trouver des solutions à des problèmes financiers et fiscaux ; ses méthodes furent essentiellement empiriques et ses conclusions pratiques. Il ne faut pas chercher dans le volumineux rapport des commissaires une théorie de l'état fédéral, mais plutôt une apologie de l'efficacité administrative et de la centralisation.

Les provinces, pensaient les commissaires fédéraux, avaient des revenus trop restreints et trop inégaux ; dans plusieurs domaines, leur administration défectueuse n'avait entraîné que gaspillage et accumulation de dettes. Seul le gouvernement central, doté de pouvoirs de taxation illimités, était en mesure d'assurer le partage équitable des finances publiques et la stabilité économique. La commission invitait donc les provinces à renoncer à leurs sources de revenus indépendantes et à remettre tous les impôts directs au pouvoir central ; en contre-partie, elles recevraient de généreuses subventions qui leur assureraient « le revenu nécessaire pour dispenser les services exigés par la norme nationale ». Implicitement, la commission effaçait ainsi toute l'évolution constitutionnelle qui, depuis 1883, avait été favorable à la décentralisation.

Bien au contraire, la Commission Tremblay, créée en 1956 par le gouvernment québecois, conçoit avant tout le fédéralisme comme une solution au problème de la coexistence de deux collectivités d'origine et de culture différentes ; ces deux groupes ethniques entendant conserver leur identité, c'est dans ce phénomène irréductible qu'il importe de chercher la raison d'être de la forme fédérative de l'Etat canadien. Dans cette perspective, on ne doit pas se soucier uniquement de construire un état techniquement efficace, mais s'efforcer de répartir les fonctions et compétences étatiques de manière que soit assuré le développement parallèle des deux collectivités et que chacune s'administre selon les modes les plus conformes à ses propres caractéristiques, tant intellectuelles que sociologiques.

Or, ajoutent les commissaires dans leur rapport, le Québec est devenu le véritable foyer de la nation canadienne-française et se voit de la sorte investi d'une mission particulière. Pour accomplir ce rôle, la province ne saurait se passer d'autonomie ; toute intervention fédérale dans les domaines qui touchent à la culture, notamment, risque d'imposer des façons de penser et d'agir qui sont étrangères au Canada français. On le voit, cette conception du fédéralisme est essentiellement différente de celle qu'avait proposée le rapport Rowell-Sirois.

Aussi ne faut-il pas être surpris outre mesure de constater que les conclusions pratiques de la Commission Tremblay soient aux antipodes des recommandations de la commission fédérale. Il faut, disent en substance les commissaires, réadapter le régime de l'impôt selon l'esprit du fédéralisme, c'est-à-dire partager les champs de taxation suivant un système qui permettra à chaque échelon de gouvernement de se procurer, de sa propre autorité, les ressources fiscales nécessaires au libre exercice de ses fonctions. Aux provinces, à qui incombe la responsabilité en matière culturelle et sociale, devraient donc être réservés les impôts directs et les redevances sur les ressources naturelles. Par ailleurs, le gouvernement central, étant investi des responsabilités économiques générales, devrait avoir accès aux impôts portant sur la circulation des biens.

Les deux commissions ne s'entendaient, en somme, que sur un seul point : l'état est appelé à jouer un rôle plus important dans la vie de la collectivité. Toutefois, les commissaires fédéraux et provinciaux n'étaient plus d'accord dès qu'il s'agissait de déterminer quel serait l'état dont le rôle s'accroîtrait ; pour les uns, c'était sans conteste l'Etat fédéral, tandis que les autres voyaient tout naturellement dans l'Etat québécois le représentant légitime du peuple canadien-français.

A l'heure actuelle, la grande question n'est pas de savoir s'il est souhaitable où non d'attribuer à l'état des compétences nouvelles dans les domaines culturel et socio-économique ; nous savons que le développement du pays exige une intervention croissante des organes gouvernementaux. Etant donné que la planification économique et le *welfare state* sont déjà amorcés et que l'anti-étatisme traditionnel du Canada français est en voie de recul, les deux problèmes importants dont la solution s'impose d'urgence sont, en premier lieu, de décider si le destin de la collectivité canadienne-française devra être confié à l'Etat central ou à l'Etat provincial et, en second lieu, si l'Etat québécois pourra véritablement être un agent de progrès social ou simplement devenir la chasse gardée des classes privilégiées. Plus que jamais, le problème national canadien-français et la question sociale sont intimement liés, au point qu'il devient difficile de concevoir la solution de l'un sans le règlement de l'autre. Cela étant, existe-t-il un régime de gouvernement qui permette de réconcilier les thèses de plus en plus opposées dont les commissions Rowell-Sirois et Tremblay furent les porte-parole ?

I. *UN NOUVEAU CONCEPT DE L'ETAT PROVINCIAL*

Le moment est venu de bâtir au Québec un état moderne qui soit le serviteur de la collectivité, en même temps que l'un de ses moteurs. Les citoyens acceptent de plus en plus cette orientation progressiste et le gouvernement provincial actuel s'est senti suffisamment soutenu pour créer le Conseil d'orientation économique et la Société générale de financement et pour instituer l'assurance-hospitalisation.

Ce n'est là, il faut l'espérer, qu'un début ; on a parlé d'une « révolution tranquille » , alors qu'il s'agit plutôt d'une modernisation. Certes, il convient de se féliciter des progrès accomplis par la pensée politique canadienne-française, mais ces progrès sont encore peu de chose au prix de ceux susceptibles d'être réalisés. Les étudiants, qui sont l'image de nos lendemains, l'ont bien compris : ils sont allés dire au gouvernement que sans une politique sociale radicale, l'autonomie économique risquait de ne servir que les seuls possédants. Et, de fait, les besoins à satisfaire restent extrêmement chargés : domestiquer, planifier l'économie au profit du peuple, ouvrir les portes de l'enseignement secondaire et de l'université à tous ceux qui, dépourvus de moyens, ont le talent nécessaire pour servir la collectivité, construire une société fondée sur la justice, l'engagement des citoyens et la liberté, qui soit en même l'héritière des traditions les plus fécondes et le reflet de la culture du Canada français.

Le nouveau concept de l'état provincial que nous venons de décrire heurte de front l'idéal anglo-canadien d'un Etat fédéral dynamique et puissant. Venus avant le Canada français à la notion de l'état moderne, nos compatriotes s'imaginent volontiers que le progrès s'identifie immanquablement avec la centralisation et confondent souvent l'attitude canadienne-française avec un conservatisme réactionnaire.

Depuis quelques années, on parle beaucoup à Ottawa de « fédéralisme coopératif » , expression subtilisée au Nouveau Parti Démocratique, qui l'avait lui-même empruntée aux théoriciens américains. Cet appel à la coopération entre le pouvoir central et les provinces est certainement très louable, mais que signifie-t-il au juste ? Pour les uns, il se définit par l'existence de « zones grises » dans le partage des compétences : la planification économique, la politique d'utilisation des ressources naturelles, la sécurité sociale et même l'éducation constitueraient des exemples de cette pénombre constitutionnelle. Pour les autres, la coopération signifie plutôt que le gouvernement fédéral devrait abandonner sa tentative de centralisation et que les provinces devraient avoir leur mot à dire dans l'élaboration des politiques tarifaire et monétaire du pouvoir central ; telle est la position officielle du gouvernement du Québec. Bien entendu, ces deux façons de concevoir la coopération sont tout aussi incompatibles que l'autonomie et la centralisation elles-mêmes. Il reste en effet à savoir si la pénombre s'étendra sur les compétences provinciales ou sur les pouvoirs fédéraux.

Rien ne saurait mieux illustrer le dilemme dans lequel se débattent actuellement nos hommes d'état que les deux dernières conférences fédérale-provinciales (novembre 1963 et avril 1964). Le premier ministre du Québec y exprima l'avis que le premier pas en matière de fédéralisme coopératif devrait être de rendre aux provinces les impôts directs qu'Ottawa s'était appropriés pour payer des frais de la guerre ; M. Lesage insista également pour que le Québec perçoive lui-même ces impôts. Le pouvoir central, de son côté, n'est pas prêt de renoncer à sa politique, résultat de vingt années d'efforts ; en cela, il bénéficie de l'appui de la population des autres provinces. Le gouvernement fédéral croit qu'il est de son devoir d'étendre son intervention : ne vient-il pas de proposer une nouvelle loi sur les prêts aux étudiants ainsi qu'une hausse des allocations familiales au bénéfice des jeunes gens qui poursuivent leurs études ? Rappelons qu'au début d'avril, à Québec, M. Pearson a laissé entendre que son gouvernement n'écartait pas le principe d'une diminution des programmes conjoints de type permanent, comme l'assurance-hospitalisation, mais qu'il s'agissait dans ce cas d'une entreprise difficile ; par ailleurs, en ce qui concerne certains programmes de construction, il faudrait même attendre que les provinces financièrement défavorisées fussent en mesure de faire face par elles-mêmes à ces dépenses.

Il se révèle donc presque impossible pour le pouvoir fédéral, soumis aux pressions de la majorité anglo-canadienne, de satisfaire aux exigences fondamentales du Québec. Quelques premiers ministres provinciaux appuient en principe certaines attitudes de M. Lesage, particulièrement en ce qui concerne la détermination des priorités dans les dépenses par les gouvernements locaux, mais les déclarations du premier ministre de l'Ontario, lors de la dernière conférence, constituent à la fois un rappel à la réalité et un avertissement. Le fédéralisme coopératif, a-t-il dit en substance, ne doit pas conduire à l'instauration de régimes particuliers à l'intérieur de la Confédération ; il importe que toutes les provinces soient placées sur le même pied et si le Québec, par exemple, doit se retirer systématiquement des plans conjoints, on ne voit pas pourquoi l'Ontario n'en pourrait faire autant. Il n'était point nécessaire pour M. Robarts d'être plus explicite : tous les hommes politiques présents savaient que le système des programmes conjoints ne saurait exister sans la participation de la province la plus prospère du pays.

Les relations entre le Québec et le reste du Canada s'engagent donc dans une dangereuse impasse. D'une part, le Québec, par sa seule présence, risque plus que jamais de constituer une hypothèque pour le fédéralisme anglo-canadien ; l'affaire de la caisse de retraite fédérale en témoigne avec éloquence. D'autre part, le Canada anglais, en voulant imposer à la population québecoise les solutions qu'il croit les meilleures, est amené à nier implicitement le *self-government* plus étendu qu'elle réclame. A l'heure actuelle, l'affrontement des deux nationalismes atteint les dimensions d'une crise : l'équilibre de 1867 est définitivement rompu. Sans doute, pourra-t-on allévier la crise par une série de compromis savamment dosés, notamment en matière fiscale. Toutefois, ce ne seront là que des « cataplasmes » qui n'atteindront pas les causes profondes du malaise. La tâche qui s'impose à nos hommes d'état paraît donc être l'établissement d'un nouvel équilibre, qui permette aux deux Canadas d'atteindre leurs objectifs socio-économiques et culturels respectifs, sans se brider mutuellement. La solution la plus plausible est celle qui donnerait au Québec un statut constitutionnel particulier, au sein d'une confédération rénovée.

II. *UN STATUT PARTICULIER POUR LE QUEBEC*

Quel serait le contenu de ce statut particulier et de quelle nature seraient les liens du Québec avec la Confédération ? L'idée n'en est pas neuve ; il existe en effet des exemples tant historiques que contemporains, de statuts particuliers attachés à des territoires ou à des collectivités minoritaires. On peut fort bien concevoir, par exemple, une système hybride entre l'état fédéral et la confédération, c'est-à-dire tenant du premier quant au partage des compétences, mais de la seconde à l'égard des garanties données à l'autonomie de certains états-membres et à leur participation privilégiée aux activités fédérales.

Il convient de préciser quelles pourraient être les modalités d'application d'un tel régime au Canada. Nous ferons les quelques suggestions suivantes en ce qui concerne (1) un nouveau partage des compétences ; (2) de nouvelles institutions fédérales ; (3) un système de protection des droits collectifs et individuels ; enfin, (4) un mode d'amendement de la constitution nouvelle dont nous anticipons l'élaboration.

1. UN NOUVEAU PARTAGE DES COMPÉTENCES

La tâche à accomplir consiste, à notre avis, en la réconciliation de deux objectifs en apparence incompatibles : le *self-government* le plus complet possible pour le Québec et une intégration croissante pour les autres provinces. Sur le plan économique en particulier, le Québec se considère de plus en plus comme le centre des décisions portant sur son propre développement, jouissant de tous les pouvoirs nécessaires à la planification régionale et à la mise en valeur de ses ressources naturelles. En outre, comme la véritable planification ne peut exister qu'en fonction d'objectifs sociaux, le Québec tend à devenir un état social (*welfare state*) autonome, possédant la plupart des compétences en matière de sécurité sociale et voulant établir lui-même les priorités dans ce domaine.

En ce qui concerne les autres provinces, la constitution pourrait faciliter le processus de centralisation, soit en attribuant au pouvoir fédéral des compétences plus étendues, soit en autorisant les législatures provinciales à déléguer leurs pouvoirs au Parlement central. La nécessité s'imposera évidemment tôt ou tard de planifier l'économie au niveau fédéral, mais le Québec ne serait alors associé aux décisions qui l'engagent qu'après discussion avec le gouvernment central ; l'accent porterait sur la coordination plutôt que sur la subordination.

En ce qui concerne la réglementation du commerce, la portée de la compétence fédérale a été limitée considérablement par le Conseil privé depuis l'arrêt *Citizens Insurance co. v. Parsons* (1881). Il serait possible d'envisager une disposition constitutionnelle modifiant cette jurisprudence de manière à rendre au Parlement la prépondérance que pensaient lui donner les Pères de la Confédération dans ce domaine, mais seulement à l'égard des provinces anglophones. Quant au Québec, la compétence fédérale y serait restreinte au commerce inter-provincial.

Abordons rapidement la question des compétences internationales. Les provinces canadiennes se trouvent enfermées dans un véritable dilemme à l'égard des traités : elles sont dans l'impossibilité d'en conclure, alors qu'elles sont compétentes dans un vaste domaine interne qui intéresse de plus en plus le droit international (régime du travail, droits de l'homme, développement culturel). Il n'existe que deux moyens de mettre fin à ces difficultés : soit attribuer aux organes centraux le pouvoir exclusif de mettre en œuvre tous les traités, même si la compétence locale se trouve de la sorte supplantée, soit reconnaître aux provinces le pouvoir de conclure des traités dans les domaines qui relèvent de leur compétence législative, à l'instar des *Länder* allemands. Le premier système pourrait être appliqué aux provinces anglophones et le second au Québec. Les accords conclus par celui-ci ne seraient sujets à aucun contrôle de la part de l'état central, mais pourraient être soumis aux tribunaux quant à leur légalité au regard du partage des pouvoirs.

Il y aurait également lieu de prévoir une disposition en vertu de laquelle le Québec nommerait la moitié des représentants du Canada aux assemblées des organisations internationales. En outre, au sein du ministère québecois des affaires fédérales-provinciales pourrait être créé un service chargé de l'administration des compétences internationales que nous venons de décrire.

Il convient maintenant d'examiner brièvement la question des pouvoirs de taxation. Il va sans dire que tout réaménagement dans la répartition des pouvoirs doit entraîner des ajustements concomitants dans le partage des revenus. Le gouvernement fédéral devrait cependant conserver dans le Québec l'accès à certains impôts, dont la constitution déterminerait la nature et le rendement, proportionnellement aux besoins réels du pouvoir central (dans le but notamment de maintenir le système de péréquation financière entre provinces riches et provinces sous-développées).

2. NOUVELLES INSTITUTIONS FEDERALES

La nouvelle répartition des pouvoirs, dont nous venons de donner un aperçu, laisserait aux organes fédéraux un certain nombre de compétences qui sont de la plus haute importance pour les intérêts canadiens-français : les affaires étrangères (sauf les aspects décrits ci-dessus), la défense, le commerce et les transports internationaux et inter-provinciaux, la politique douanière et monétaire, la péréquation financière, et la planification économique à grandes mailles. Le principe qui doit nous guider dans l'élaboration de nouvelles structures fédératives est donc celui d'une participation intensive des Canadiens français à tous les paliers du processus législatif, juridictionnel, exécutif, et administratif. Toutes les institutions devraient refléter le caractère bi-national du pays. *(a) Un nouveau rôle pour le Sénat.* Il est reconnu que le rôle historique des chambres hautes a consisté à mettre un frein aux incartades des assemblées populaires ; sous cet aspect, elles demeurent dans certains pays un relent de l'époque pré-démocratique. Ailleurs, on les conserve pour le décor, comme les clavecins hors d'usage. D'autres pays, enfin, s'en sont débarrassés. D'aucuns disent que l'abolition de la Chambre haute constitue l'aboutissement normal du processus démocratique.

John A. Macdonald déclara en 1865 que le Parlement central serait composé « du roi, des lords et des communes » . La Chambre haute, qu'on appelait à cette époque le Conseil législatif, devait occuper, par rapport à la Chambre basse, « la même position que la Chambre des lords occupe vis-à-vis des communes en Angleterre » . Son rôle, ajouta Macdonald, devait être de « modérer et contrôler » la législation. De fait, le Sénat s'est montré plutôt conservateur, surtout en matière de législation sociale, mais il a rarement osé tenir tête à l'opinion publique.

En 1926, il apposa son veto au premier projet de loi sur les pensions de vieillesse, mais il se fit plus docile par la suite. Depuis 1940, en particulier, il ne s'est guère opposé à l'extension du *welfare state* fédéral, bien que de nombreux sénateurs se soient élevés contre les tendances socialistes qu'ils croyaient déceler dans plus d'une loi. Le fait que le parti au pouvoir contrôlait entièrement le Sénat entre 1944 et 1957 n'est sans doute étranger à ce bel esprit de coopération.

Quoi qu'il en soit, la critique la plus sévère susceptible d'être formulée contre la Chambre haute ne tient pas tant à son conservatisme en matière sociale qu'à son inutilité croissante. C'est ainsi qu'au cours des sept ans qui suivirent l'établissement de la fédération, le Sénat modifia 25,2 pour cent des lois qui lui furent présentées et en fit échouer 7,9 pour cent. Entre 1944 et 1957, la proportion des lois amendées par les sénateurs n'atteignait plus que 13,1 pour cent et aucun projet émané des communes n'échouait entièrement. Enfin, entre 1957 et 1960, durant le séjour du parti conservateur au pouvoir, le Sénat libéral ne modifia que 6,4 pour cent des projets de lois.

Par ailleurs, le rôle de modérateur n'est pas le seul que le Sénat canadien ait été appelé à jouer en 1867. Dans le Bas-Canada et les colonies du littoral atlantique, on craignait l'influence du Haut-Canada au sein de la Chambre basse ; si les Anglo-Canadiens avaient voulu se défaire du régime de 1840, c'était en grande partie pour obtenir le *rep. by pop.*, la représentation proportionnelle, de manière à échapper à ce que George Brown appelait la *French domination*. A l'instar des Etats-Unis, les nouvelles provinces voulurent donc se protéger en se faisant représenter au sein de la Chambre haute. En effet, depuis que la Convention de Philadelphie confia au Sénat américain la tâche de représenter les Etats-membres de l'Union au sein des organes centraux, les chambres hautes ont trouvé une nouvelle raison d'être et le bicaméralisme est devenu un trait commun à toutes les fédérations.

A la Conférence de Québec (1864), les délégués des colonies passèrent six jours sur quatorze, paraît-il, à chercher un terrain d'entente sur la question de la répartition des sièges du futur Sénat. En fin de compte, il fut décidé d'attribuer 24 représentants à chacune des trois divisions constituées par l'Ontario, le Québec, et les Provinces maritimes. Macdonald lui-même admit la nécessité de protéger les intérêts locaux, d'autant qu'il se faisait, par ailleurs, l'avocat d'un gouvernement central fort. Le Sénat pourrait fort bien s'acquitter de cette tâche, à condition qu'il ne devienne pas trop puissant. L'année suivante, au cours des débats sur la Confédération, il s'exprima en ces termes : « A la Chambre haute sera confié le soin de protéger les intérêts locaux *(sectional interests*) ; il en résulte que les trois grandes divisions seront également représentées pour défendre leurs propres intérêts contre toutes combinaisons de majorités dans l'Assemblée » . Cependant, le gouvernement central se réservait le soin de nommer les sénateurs. Macdonald, une fois devenu premier ministre de la nouvelle fédération, eut grand soin de ne nommer que des partisans conservateurs à la Chambre haute ; en vingt ans, il ne dérogea à cette pratique qu'a deux reprises. Laurier, pour contre-balancer l'influence conservatrice, se crut à son tour obligé de n'appeler que des libéraux. C'est ainsi que se forgent les traditions : aucun premier ministre n'y a échappé depuis.

La composition du Sénat s'est profondément ressentie de ces procédés, d'autant plus qu'une fois installés à leur poste, les sénateurs y demeurent leur vie durant. Que de vieux routiers de la politique, que de militants chevronnés ont ainsi trouvé leur récompense dans le Walhalla de Bytown ! Mais on y cherchera en vain d'anciens hauts fonctionnaires ou des diplomates, encore moins des socialistes ou des intellectuels ; ces gens ne savent en effet qu'inventer des problèmes. L'âge moyen des sénateurs était de 64 ans en 1920 et de 68 ans en 1940; il est aujourd'hui d'environ 70 ans, tandis que seize membres atteignent plus de 80 ans.

Les constituants de 1867 voulurent donc imiter à la fois la Chambre des lords et le Sénat américain, dont les fonctions sont essentiellement différentes. Ils ne réussirent guère qu'à créer une Chambre des lords au petit pied, si peu soucieuse de protéger l'autonomie des provinces qu'elle « représente » et si mal préparée, au demeurant, pour le faire, qu'il est permis d'affirmer que cet aspect de l'ordre constitutionnel canadien n'est qu'un simulacre de fédéralisme. Paralysé au départ, l'évolution constitutionnelle du Sénat ne fit qu'accentuer la superfluité de l'institution. Si les hommes d'état de 1864 avaient eu sérieusement l'intention de protéger les intérêts provinciaux, ils se seraient inspirés des constitutions américaine (1787) et helvétique (1848), lesquelles prévoyaient la désignation des membres de la Chambre haute par les cantons ou les états-membres, de manière que les sénateurs devinssent les authentiques représentants des provinces.

Il faut aujourd'hui revenir au bicaméralisme en tant que moyen de maintenir l'équilibre entre les forces centripètes et les forces centrifuges qui s'affrontent au sein de la Confédération. Le Sénat n'a plus aucun rôle utile à jouer sous son aspect de Chambre des lords ; il serait préférable de l'abolir que de le voir subsister indéfiniment sous cette forme. Mais la véritable solution est autre : à notre avis, elle ne réside

pas dans la suppression du Sénat—laquelle équivaudrait à une renonciation définitive au fédéralisme—mais plutôt dans la transformation de
son rôle et la réforme de sa structure.

Les politologues du Canada anglais s'ingénient, depuis deux générations déjà, à revaloriser le Sénat. L'ouvrage le plus remarquable traitant
du sujet est *The Unreformed Senate of Canada* du professeur R. A.
Mackay, paru pour la première fois en 1926. Tous les auteurs sont
d'accord sur le choix d'un certain nombre de remèdes qui auraient pu
être appliqués au Sénat depuis de longues années : par exemple,
l'imposition d'une limite d'âge, comme il a été décidé récemment pour
les juges des cours supérieures. Cette mesure bénéficia de l'appui d'un
grand nombre de députés lors du débat de 1951 sur le Sénat et le gouvernement présenta même en 1962 un projet de loi en ce sens, lequel
disparut mystérieusement en cours de route. Il convient cependant de
mentionner qu'il a été aussi proposé quelques remèdes d'une efficacité
plus grande, partant plus difficiles à faire accepter. Par exemple : désignation des membres de la Chambre haute limitée à des périodes
restreintes, allant de six à dix ans ; extension de leur choix à tous les
partis politiques, et peut-être même jusqu'au sein des associations professionnelles, des syndicats et des groupes culturels, comme il est
procédé dans certains pays européens. Certes, ce sont certainement là
des suggestions très aptes à insuffler un peu de vie au Sénat ; toutefois,
déplorons qu'elles ne s'attaquent pas réellement à la racine du mal. Que
servirait-il, en effet, de posséder une Chambre des lords rajeunie, si l'on
ne lui donne pas un véritable rôle à remplir ?

Pour que la Chambre haute puisse remplir efficacement les fonctions
qui lui incombent dans un régime fédéral, la désignation de ses membres
doit relever exclusivement des entités constituantes de la fédération.
Rappelons qu'en 1951 quelques sénateurs opinèrent qu'il était opportun
de confier aux gouvernements provinciaux la nomination d'un quart, ou
d'un tiers, des membres de la Chambre. R. A. Mackay approuve le
principe de cette réforme, mais craint qu'une trop grande proportion de
représentants provinciaux ne nuise au fonctionnement du régime parlementaire ; un Sénat trop dynamique aurait tendance, selon lui, à imiter
les communes et voudrait sans doute contrôler les agissements du cabinet.

On peut, en effet, s'interroger sur l'effet qu'un Sénat plus représentatif
et doté de pouvoirs réels produirait sur le système parlementaire canadien. La prépondérance du cabinet et l'influence de l'*establishment*
seraient sans doute contrecarrées par la présence d'une chambre haute
plus forte ; on pourrait également craindre que cette chambre et les

communes n'entrent en conflit à tout propos, engendrant une instabilité chronique. En outre, un Sénat doté du pouvoir de provoquer une dissolution du Parlement placerait le gouvernement devant la nécessité de se garer de deux côtés à la fois, facteur encore plus grave d'instabilité. Or, la raison d'être d'une chambre haute rénovée ne serait pas, à notre avis, de faire concurrence aux communes, mais de sauvegarder les droits des collectivités-membres dans les domaines qui touchent celles-ci de près. Aussi serait-il préférable d'instituer une certaine spécialisation dans les attributions des deux chambres. La compétence du Sénat pourrait s'étendre, par exemple, aux droits des minorités, à l'approbation et à la mise en oeuvre des traités conclus par le gouvernement fédéral, à l'approbation des nominations d'envoyés diplomatiques ou de juges fédéraux, à la radiodiffusion, et aux amendements constitutionnels. Dans tous ces domaines, la Chambre haute serait en mesure de tenir le gouvernement en échec, sans pour autant provoquer sa chute. De ce qui précède, il ressort qu'il n'est pas impossible de réconcilier un fédéralisme plus authentique avec le parlementarisme.

Une fois admis que les sénateurs doivent représenter directement les entités constituantes, surgit une question plus épineuse : le Sénat devrait-il émaner des dix provinces ou des deux groupes ethniques qui ont posé les fondements du pays et du régime actuel ? Dans le premier cas, il est évident que le Québec demeurerait une minorité au sein de la Chambre ; il ne pourrait guère, dès lors, réclamer une plus grande proportion des sièges que celle qui lui est dévolue à l'heure actuelle, soit environ 21 pour cent ; encore ce pourcentage n'est-il pas fondé sur le principe de l'égalité des états-membres de la fédération. Néanmoins, si le Québec obtenait le droit de désigner lui-même ses représentants, ce système constituerait déjà, à notre avis, un progrès sensible par rapport à la situation actuelle.

La réalité canadienne, cependant, devient de plus en plus celle de deux nations coexistant au sein d'un même état ; les provinces elles-mêmes ont perdu une part de leur importance, du moins dans la mentalité anglo-canadienne, au profit du pouvoir central. Aussi serait-il préférable que le Sénat réformé reflétât ce caractère foncièrement binational du Canada, en accordant une représentation égale aux anglophones et aux francophones, sans tenir compte des frontières provinciales. En d'autres termes, les sièges seraient répartis dans tout le pays, solution qui permettrait aux groupes minoritaires de toutes les provinces d'être représentés à la Chambre haute. Le nombre des sénateurs pourrait de la sorte demeurer sensiblement le même qu'à l'heure actuelle, tandis que le représentation au sein des communes continuerait d'être fondée sur la *rep. by pop.*

Cette nouvelle structure du Sénat supposerait l'élection des membres, procédé qui assurerait une représentation directe du peuple, et, sans doute, une plus grande souplesse dans les délibérations ; elle permettrait également aux partis provinciaux, notamment aux partis d'opposition, de se faire représenter.

(b) Les tribunaux. Passons maintenant au pouvoir judiciaire. La Cour suprême est l'arbitre ultime, à l'heure actuelle, dans tous les litiges d'ordre constitutionnel, civil ou pénal. Le contrôle juridictionnel des compétences peut-il vraiment être exercé de façon impartiale lorsqu'il est confié à un tribunal dont les membres sont nommés par la gouvernement central ? La position officielle du Québec sur ce point est connue : dans le mémoire qu'il soumit à la conférence fédérale-provinciale de 1960, M. Lesage déclara en toutes lettres qu'il faudrait prévoir l'organisation d'un tribunal constitutionnel conforme aux principes essentiels du fédéralisme. Il précisa sa pensée en ces termes : « Le principe fondamental de ce régime exige que ni l'un ni l'autre des deux ordres de gouvernement ne puissent toucher au partage des pouvoirs établi par la constitution. Il s'ensuit que l'arbitre des conflits ne doit pas relever exclusivement de l'un d'eux. » Si cette attitude trahit une conception intransigeante de l'autonomie, elle est cependant la seule susceptible de protéger le Québec du « rôle dynamique » que plusieurs juristes anglo-canadiens voudraient faire jouer à la Cour suprême.

La solution idéale consisterait à créer un tribunal constitutionnel spécial composé d'un nombre égal de juristes du Canada anglais et du Canada français. Tous les problèmes d'ordre constitutionnel qui surgiraient devant l'une quelconque des cours de justice seraient immédiatement renvoyés au tribunal sous forme de questions préjudicielles. Quant à l'établissement des critères qui, en principe, devraient orienter le choix des membres, on pourrait s'inspirer de la constitution fédérale autrichienne, qui institue un tribunal analogue à celui que nous proposons ; il serait également possible de prévoir la présentation des candidats par les provinces et leur élection par le Sénat.

La Cour suprême demeurerait compétente à l'égard des affaires civiles et pénales, mais il conviendrait de faire en sorte que cessât l'érosion à laquelle le droit civil a été soumis de la part du Conseil privé et de la Cour. Comme l'a fait remarquer le Pr. Baudouin, l'interprétation judiciaire anglaise se situe aux antipodes de l'interprétation française, et même de l'interprétation canadienne-française ; en réalité, ce n'est pas toujours la pensée française qui l'a emporté et la pensée propre à la *common law* s'est insinuée dans plus d'un recoin du code civil. S'il était jugé opportun de mettre fin à cette hybridation, on pourrait suggérer comme solution de diviser la Cour en deux chambres distinctes, l'une composée de *common lawyers* et l'autre de civilistes ; la chambre civile ayant juridiction exclusive sur les appels émanant du Québec. Une solution plus radicale encore consisterait à faire de la Cour d'appel du Québec l'arbitre ultime en matière de droit civil.

Pour ce qui a trait aux appels relevant du droit pénal et des litiges intéressant les libertés publiques, les juges pourraient être choisis en nombre égal dans les deux chambres de la nouvelle Cour suprême.

3. LA PROTECTION DES DROITS COLLECTIFS ET INDIVIDUELS

Toute nouvelle constitution devra protéger les droits scolaires des Anglo-canadiens et des Canadiens français d'un océan à l'autre. Il existe plusieurs façons d'obtenir ce résultat. En premier lieu, l'instruction publique continuerait à relever exclusivement des provinces, mais celles-ci seraient tenues d'accorder à toutes les commissions scolaires, quelles qu'elles soient, françaises ou anglaises, catholiques, protestantes, ou neutres, les mêmes droits et pouvoirs fiscaux, ainsi que les mêmes subventions. En second lieu, on pourrait transférer au Parlement fédéral (et plus particulièrement au Sénat) la compétence législative en ce qui concerne les établissements d'enseignement de la minorité anglophone du Québec et des minorités françaises des autres provinces : voilà certes un moyen efficace d'assurer l'égalité des droits, mais les provinces y perdraient évidemment un fragment de leur autonomie.

L'usage des deux langues officielles dans l'ensemble du pays présentera plus de difficultés. Il serait souhaitable que chacun pût, dans toutes les législatures provinciales et devant tous les tribunaux, se faire entendre dans sa langue, suivant la règle suivie au Parlement fédéral et à la Législature du Québec. Mais il semble qu'il serait plus facile d'obtenir ce droit au Nouveau-Brunswick qu'en Colombie-Britannique. . . . Le problème qui se pose est de trouver une règle qui soit à la fois réaliste et d'application générale. Toutes les provinces dont la minorité francophone atteint cinq pour cent de leur population ne devraient-elles pas reconnaître à cette minorité de droits semblables à ceux que le Québec accorde aux anglophones ? La solution alternative consisterait à établir l'unilinguisme dans Québec, tel qu'il est pratiqué dans les autres provinces.

Traitons maintenant brièvement de la question des droits de l'individu. Notons d'abord que ces droits doivent être distingués des droits collectifs, dont les particuliers ne bénéficient qu'en tant que membres d'un groupe ; les droits individuels appartiennent en effet à tous les citoyens, quelles que soient leur langue, leur race, ou leurs croyances. Au Canada, la constitution actuelle comporte, selon la jurisprudence de la Cour suprême, des garanties implicites contre l'abolition des libertés publiques par le Parlement ou les législatures. En outre, le Code criminel protège certaines libertés personnelles des individus qui sont aux prises avec la police ou avec la justice, tandis que la « Déclaration canadienne des droits » , votée en 1960, garantit le droit de la personne à la vie, à la liberté, à la sécurité, à la jouissance de ses biens, ainsi que les libertés de religion, de parole, de réunion, et de presse.

Cependant, cette protection ne couvre qu'une partie restreinte des droits de l'homme tels qu'ils sont définis à notre époque dans les grandes conventions internationales. C'est ainsi, par exemple, qu'elle ne défend pas l'individu contre la discrimination raciale, ni ne lui garantit ses droits en matière économique et sociale ; en effet, ces aspects des droits de l'homme relèvent, au Canada, de la compétence des provinces. Il importe donc que celles-ci prennent leurs responsabilités et adoptent une législation destinée à faire respecter des droits individuels. A l'heure où prend forme, dans le Québec, un état moderne appelé à remplir de multiples fonctions dans le domaine socio-économique, il paraît urgent que la collectivité définisse ses buts sociaux et que le pouvoir donne des garanties contre les abus qui pourraient éventuellement se commettre. Point n'est même besoin d'attendre la moindre modification constitutionnelle pour accomplir cette tâche.

De toute façon, aucune nouvelle constitution ne devrait ni ne pourra être adoptée, sans qu'une large place ne soit faite à la protection des droits collectifs et individuels.

4. LA MODIFICATION DE LA CONSTITUTION

Si nos hommes d'état trouvent le moyen, au cours des prochaines années, de s'entendre pour reconnaître au Québec un statut spécial au sein de la Confédération, rien ne s'opposera plus à ce que le pouvoir d'amendement soit entièrement et définitivement transféré du Parlement de Westminster à l'organe constituant canadien.

Toutefois, une fois ce « rapatriement » effectué, il se pourrait que le travail d'érosion des compétences du Québec recommençât de plus belle. Aussi convient-il de découvrir une méthode de révision de la nouvelle constitution qui permette à la fois aux provinces anglophones d'évoluer vers une plus grande centralisation, si telle est leur volonté, et au Québec de décider librement de son avenir. On devrait envisager l'adoption de deux modes d'amendement distincts, le premier applicable aux provinces anglophones (*v.g.*, majorité des deux tiers des provinces et majorité simple au Sénat) et le second permettant au Québec de modifier son statut constitutionnel par le moyen d'un accord avec le gouvernement central, entériné par le Sénat. Cependant, la partie de la constitution fédérale protégeant les droits collectifs ne pourrait être amendée sans le consentement unanime des provinces.

La complexité des solutions que nous venons d'esquisser, sans y voir autre chose, d'ailleurs, que de simples indications sur la nature du *modus vivendi* qui permettrait aux deux Canadas de coexister au sein d'un même état, choquera sans doute les esprits absolus et passionnés d'uniformité ; d'autres opineront que la majorité n'acceptera jamais d'accorder à la minorité canadienne-française toutes les garanties que comporterait un statut particulier pour le Québec.

Pourtant, il est bien évident que nous sommes à la croisée des chemins. S'il n'obtient le *self-government* accru qu'il réclame et auquel il a droit, le Canada français sera sans doute enclin à rechercher un dénouement plus radical à la crise actuelle. Malheureusement, la solution de ses problèmes sociaux en pourrait être retardée. Dans l'avenir prévisible, le seul régime qui permettrait, d'une part, de réconcilier les thèses Rowell-Sirois et Tremblay et, d'autre part, de favoriser le progrès social, demeurera, à notre avis, un statut particulier du Québec au sein d'une nouvelle confédération.

Federalism, Constitutionalism, and Legal Change: Legal Implications of the "Revolution" in Quebec

EDWARD McWHINNEY

I take it that I am writing as a more or less representative common-law member of what is, in effect, a "legal establishment"—the law professors, judges, practitioners, civil service lawyers, and related legal groups. These presumably constitute, in our own society, what Max Weber calls the "honoratiores"[1] or dignitaries of the law, whose opinions are supposed to be authoritative in shaping representative public attitudes. I certainly would make no claim to represent English-speaking Canada as a whole; any more than our Quebec academic constitutional lawyers would, I am sure, fairly claim to speak on behalf of French-speaking Canada as a whole. The Tremblay Report[2] which remains today perhaps the most authoritative, and certainly the most comprehensive, statement of the legal-institutional implications of biculturalism, essays a basic distinction between the culture of the élite and popular culture. For example, what my friend Jacques-Yvan Morin is proposing may properly be taken as a sophisticated *élitist* attempt at a projection of what would be the constitutional aspirations of the people of Quebec

---

[1] See generally Max Weber, *Law in Economy and Society*, ed. M. Rheinstein, (Cambridge, Mass., 1954).

[2] *Report of the Royal Commission of Inquiry on Constitutional Problems, Province of Quebec*, 4 vols. (Montreal, 1956), Hereafter referred to as the *Tremblay Report*.

if they were all legally trained. The distinction between *élitist* and popular aspirations may lead us to the fundamental question of which group constitutes the legal *élite* and just how representative it can really claim to be. This important point will be discussed below.

So far as the common-law legal establishment is concerned, and in spite of the popular clamour and the occasional strong newspaper editorials to the contrary, it can be said that there is no real or sustained opposition to change as such. The British North America Act is, we are told, the second oldest written constitutional instrument, exceeded in age only by the US Constitution. Yet we recognize and concede that there is no especial legal merit in an argument from age alone. It may indicate no more than that Canada has so far been fortunate enough to have been spared the cataclysm of popular revolution or military defeat which overwhelmed constitutions like the Austro-Hungarian dual monarchy or *Ausgleich*, adopted in the same year as the BNA Act; or, for that matter, the federal constitution of Imperial Germany, of 1871; or even the unsatisfactory compromise constitution of theThird French Republic which endured, it must be admitted, until the military disaster of 1940.

For it is, as Mr. Justice Oliver Wendell Holmes has reminded us, revolting to have no more substantial justification for a claimed legal rule than that it was laid down in the time of Henry IV. No one of us is inclined, therefore, to try to counter any Quebec demands for fundamental revision or rewriting of the BNA Act with the prestige argument that because the BNA Act has lasted so long it deserves to remain as it is. What we would suggest, as common lawyers, is that the fact that the BNA Act does seem to have worked fairly well over a period of years carries with it a certain *prima facie* presumption of utility and rationality. The onus, I suggest, is fairly upon the proponents of any particular constitutional change to demonstrate just how existing sections of the BNA Act fail to satisfy present-day needs, and also to demonstrate clearly the reasonableness of their own concrete proposals for change—meaning, here, reasonableness not merely in terms of their own special interest group but reasonableness in terms of the country as a whole.

The life of the common law, to quote Holmes once again, has not been logic but experience. The spirit of the common law, and not less of common law constitutionalism, is change—of a continuing adjustment of positive law rules to new societal conditions and expectations. The BNA Act, as such (meaning here its text, as written), has hardly experienced major constitutional rewriting since its adoption in 1867. The procedures for formal amendment of the Act, simple as they have been in positive law terms with the recourse to Westminster for a plain statute of the British Parliament, have rested nevertheless on a complex series of informal consultations and discussions between the Dominion and the various provincial governments, which have had some of the elements of rigidity and inflexibility of old constitutional custom as classically limned by Dicey.[3] The Founding Fathers did not have the foresight to include within it, as the Swiss did with their constitution, formal procedures allowing for its total revision from time to time.[4] Yet it would be a grave error to assume from this that the Canadian constitution has remained unchanged in substance since 1867. Direct amendment of a constitution, through use of formal amending machinery that is included within the constitution itself, is only one method—and merely the most obvious method at that—of effecting constitutional change. The history of the Canadian constitution in action, not less than that of the American constitution in action, has been one of continuing development and growth, achieved through informal, indirect agencies of change. Words do not have an absolute meaning through time. The constitution itself may remain graven on stone tablets, but its words have a lapidarian quality of generality that enables new content and meaning continually to be given to the constitution. The record of judicial interpretation of the Canadian constitution, on the part of the Privy Council and of the Canadian Supreme Court, is one of pendulum-like swings from an original Founding Fathers' conception of centralization, on through the decentralized, pluralistic federalism of the Watson-Haldane era of judicial interpretation, to the modern era when, I suggest, a strong centripetal trend in federalism is to be observed once again.[5] It is, as our best Canadian constitutional jurists have pointed out, only by the exercise of the most considerable judicial ingenuity and dexterity that these dramatically differing interpretations could possibly be reconciled with the one, unchanging constitutional text.[6] But although we might have wished

[3]A. V. Dicey, *The Law of the Constitution* (London, 1885).

[4]On constitutional amending machinery in federal constitutions generally, see R. R. Bowie and C. J. Friedrich, eds., *Studies in Federalism* (Boston, 1954), pp. 790–815.

[5]For the changing patterns of judicial interpretation of the BNA Act, consult, for example, E. McWhinney, *Judicial Review in the English-Speaking World*, 3rd ed. (Toronto, 1965), pp. 61–75.

[6]See, for example, Frank R. Scott, "The Consequences of the Privy Council Decisions," 15 *Canadian Bar Review* 485 (1937); Vincent MacDonald, "The Canadian Constitution Seventy Years After," 15 *Canadian Bar Review* 401 (1937); Vincent MacDonald, "The Constitution in a Changing World," 26 *Canadian Bar Review* 21 (1948); Bora Laskin, " 'Peace, Order and Good Government' Reexamined," 25 *Canadian Bar Review* 1054 (1947).

for some greater display of public candour on the part of the judges as to the free-law-finding, judicially legislative role that they were in fact exercising, no one can reasonably complain that these dramatically changing judicial interpretations were out of touch with the temper and mood and expectations of Canadian society in the particular periods concerned.

The Canadian constitution has also been modified vastly since 1867, under another, informal, and publicly almost unremarked agency of change: namely, executive and administrative practice, manifesting itself through affirmative governmental action and sometimes through conscious governmental inaction. The latter amounts almost to a species of law-making through constitutional attrition or desuetude. One may speak in this latter respect, for example, of the practical disappearance, as a matter of constitutional law-in-action, of the erstwhile prerogative powers as to reservation or disallowance of legislative measures, or the erstwhile prerogative powers as to acceptance of the advice of a prime minister on the dissolution of Parliament. One might go further and suggest that the really substantial constitutional innovations and changes, of the postwar years at least, manifested in the constitutional *law-in-action* as distinct from the *law-in-books* (or constitutional text of 1867), have occurred in the closed sessions of the various dominion-provincial conferences and in the even more informal and confidential discussions between dominion prime ministers and their various provincial spokesmen of the day, especially those from Quebec. Until the closed proceedings of the various dominion-provincial conferences become available, or until some of our political leaders develop the habit of publishing their indiscreet public reminiscences, we may have largely to indulge in informed guesses at the trends in Canadian constitutionalism initiated and developed through these means. I will suggest, however, that since the war, and parallel to the renewed centripetalism in Canadian federalism initiated through judicial activism, there has been manifest another and distinct trend in Canadian federalism in favour of what I have elsewhere called *dualistic* federalism.[7] This looks almost to a principle of "concurrent majorities," French-speaking and English-speaking, on issues of political, social, and economic policy, a principle going, in the viewpoint of Quebec's political *élite*, to the fundamentals of Quebec's culture and special way of life. If one looks for the evidence in support of such a federalism of dual sovereignty—in national, ethnic-cultural terms—one might find it in such matters as the compro-

---

[7]E. McWhinney, *Comparative Federalism: States' Rights and National Power* 2nd ed. Toronto, 1965), p. 17 *et seq.*

mise resolution by the dominion government of the military conscription issue during the Second World War; the substantial dominion
acquiescence, over the past decade and a half, in the practical stale-
mating of the attempts at securing autonomous, self-operating, direct
constitutional amending procedures for Canada; even the decision on,
and method of handling of, the issue of the adoption of a new and distinctive Canadian national flag and a new and distinctive Canadian
national anthem. Sometimes the principle of "concurrent majorities"
has seemed to operate by way of a practical Quebec veto on dominion
action that would otherwise have been initiated; sometimes it has
seemed to operate to spur on the dominion government in areas where,
in the past, it has been overly timorous about acting. My point would
be, simply, that to a considerable, and, I believe, an increasing extent,
biculturalism as a constitutional phenomenon having concrete substantive legal and institutional consequences, is already part of the constitutional law-in-action in Canada. If asked to define its character in
formal constitutional terms, I would say that it operates by way of a
gloss on the constitution as written, a species of developing constitutional
convention or custom. I believe that it has been accepted, by Canadians
generally up to date, partly because it has been a quiet constitutional
revolution or innovation, achieved without all the fuss and bother and
inevitable ill-feeling attendant on any public attempts at securing direct
amendment of the constitutional system through recourse to the formal
agencies of constitutional change. But I would further say that it has
been accepted by English-speaking Canadians, to the extent that the
legal establishment has taken note of this development, because of the
innate reasonableness, good sense, and modesty inherent in the particular concrete demands that have come from Quebec governmental
spokesmen, in the past, in the name of biculturalism.

My next point is almost an inevitable one. If, in fact, there exists
today a practical constitutional requirement of concurrent majorities as
to policy issues really affecting the fundamentals of Quebec's culture,
what need is there of any more formalized and institutionalized protec-
tions for Quebec's special interests? I say this more particularly in view
of a noticeable feeling of hostility, in English-speaking areas of the
country, over what are widely felt to be currently quite unreasonable
demands on the part of Quebec spokesmen—demands that are only
remotely, if at all, related to the conceded need to protect Quebec's
special interests. For our criteria of what is constitutionally reasonable
may tend to differ, as between French-speaking Canada and English-
speaking Canada. The advantage of constitutional change through the

informal agencies of developing custom and convention is that the very process of balancing competing, and possibly quite opposing, community interests can make an ally of time and allow compromise to emerge gradually on a basis of reciprocity and mutual give-and-take. Pressure, on the other hand, for acceptance of direct amendment of the BNA Act and related constitutional instruments seems to compel a taking of black-and-white positions in public if only for tactical or defensive reasons, and so obscures and impedes that business of reconciliation of conflicting social interests which is at the core of democratic constitutionalism in general and of federalism in particular. In a word, are our Quebec friends straining too much at the present time for purely abstract, verbal recitations in rationalized constitutionalism at the expense of the substance of a French-speaking/English-speaking accord that is already emerging as constitutional law-in-action and which will clearly continue in the future?

I had promised some further remarks on the importance of the distinction between the *élitist* and popular aspirations in Quebec regarding biculturalism; and these comments relate specifically to the concrete proposals for direct constitutional change now sponsored by our Quebec friends. It is suggested, for example, in the Tremblay Report that the Supreme Court of Canada, as at present constituted, does not "enjoy the complete confidence of the people"[8]; and various suggestions are advanced for its reform or reorganization, the Federal Constitutional Court of West Germany and the International Court of Justice being invoked as sources of analogies for changes in structure and in personnel. Professor Morin has been even more specific in calling for the creation of a "special constitutional tribunal" composed of an equal number of jurists from each of English-speaking and French-speaking Canada. Those of you who know my earlier published studies in the constitutionalism of civil-law as well as of common-law countries will know that, in the context of Continental Europe, I have a special sympathy for the role of such specialist final appellate tribunals. It is, indeed, my conclusion that, in the case of post-war Germany, the Federal Constitutional Court, drawing as it did in such considerable measure on American Supreme Court experience and general jurisprudence as well as on indigenous, German civil-law sources, has proved not merely a viable political-legal institution but in fact the prime safeguard for a continuance of democratic constitutionalism in Germany under the Bonn constitution.[9] But post-war Germany started, in effect, in a constitutional

---

[8]*Tremblay Report*, III, p. 296.
[9]E. McWhinney, *Constitutionalism in Germany and the Federal Constitutional Court* (Leyden, 1962).

vacuum, and it was therefore both possible and necessary to start completely afresh. In the case of a supreme court that is already a going concern, like the Supreme Court of Canada, we are entitled to ask in just what the Court has proven itself to be "unsatisfactory," as the Tremblay Report suggests.[10] If it is a matter that the Court has too much business today to discharge its work efficiently—as some in English-speaking Canada might also feel, for example—then a simpler remedy might be to strengthen and extend the Exchequer Court so that it could serve as a general federal court of first instance, thereby reducing the work load of the Supreme Court of Canada, which presumably would then function almost exclusively as a final appellate tribunal. If it is a matter that the Court has far too wide a general jurisdictional competence for its individual members to develop either specialist expertise in several different fields or else intellectual breadth generally in relation to the whole field, then there may indeed be a case for court specialization on the Continental European model; though an intermediate step might be simply to divide the Supreme Court as at present constituted into specialist *bancs* for certain purposes—for example, appeals on the Quebec Civil Code—without trying to transform the over-all structure of the Court.

If, however, the over-all complaint against the Court is really in terms of voting powers on the Court, based on a notion that the individual judges should be, in effect, representatives of the respective ethnic-cultural groups from which they stem and on the further notion that the three civil-law judges—in effect "French-Canadian spokesmen" on the Court—have been wilfully outvoted by what the Tremblay Report would identify as an "Anglo-Protestant"[11] voting majority on the Court, then it is time to say that this complaint is at least unfair and, in the ultimate I think, untrue. On the issue of appeals from the Quebec Civil Code, for example, though one could hardly suggest that the common-law judges on the Supreme Court have shewn a great deal of understanding of or feeling for the basic principles and underlying philosophy of the Code, it is certainly not true of recent years that the civil-law judges have been outvoted or outweighed on civil-law matters of substance by their common-law brethren. On the one hand, indeed, the common-law judges seem to have been developing the merits of a Frankfurterian policy of judicial self-restraint in civil-law matters at least: on the other hand, it may be suggested that, on the record, the prime civilians on the Court, Chief Justice Taschereau and Mr. Justice Fauteux, seem to have no especial enthusiasm for assuming the mantle of watchdog of the purity of the Civil Code.

[10]*Tremblay Report*, III, p. 292.   [11]*Ibid.*, II, p. 40.

When we come to public law matters, of course, the areas of ethnic-cultural division on the Court tend to become more clear and obvious. One must recognize, frankly, that a number of what common-law jurists would characterize as the great civil liberty cases of the decade of the 1950's, all of them arising originally from Quebec, were decided by narrow, sometimes 5 to 4, majorities on the Court with the French-speaking judges invariably dissenting from the essentially "Anglo-Saxon" common-law majority. One can recognize the sense of constitutional outrage that certain Quebec jurists may be disposed to feel at Supreme Court decisions given upon a fact-situation arising originally from Quebec, in which the "Anglo-Saxon" judges are regarded, so to speak, as having sought to impose their own particular ethnic-cultural values upon the French-Canadian judges' values. There is certainly something, for example, that seems politically rather unfortunate in the common-law majority, in the *Roncarelli* case in 1959,[12] rooting its decision solely in common-law precedents and authority; though Continental European civil-law doctrines and jurisprudence seemed readily available to reach the same end result and actually to be even more persuasive than the common-law authority. Perhaps Mr. Justice Abbott, as a civil-law judge who is nevertheless an "Anglo-Saxon," adds to the gravamen of the offence in Quebec eyes by consistently siding with the common-law majority in these civil liberties cases of the 1950's, in contraposition to his French-Canadian judicial colleagues.

One recognizes, of course, in a plural federal society the possibility, indeed the desirability at times, of different jurisprudential characterizations of the same fact-situations arising from different provinces. And even when the characterizations are made the same way, and the different interests that are present are properly identified, it is necessary to remember that different ethnic-culturally-based (in Roscoe Pound's terms) "civilization areas" might strike the balance of the competing interests in different ways. In a competition between interests in public order on the one hand and interests in free speech and communication on the other, an "Anglo-Saxon" society, with its commitment to "open society" values would tend normally to give the benefit of the doubt, and consequently the authoritative community preference, to the free speech and communication interests. Quebec, on the other hand, with its commitment in ethnic-cultural terms, as the Tremblay Report notes, to the "sense of order"[13]—in priority or hierarchical superiority, as it seems

[12]*Roncarelli* v. *Duplessis*, 16 DLR (2d) 689 (1959); discussed in 37 *Canadian Bar Review* 503 (1959).
[13]*Tremblay Report*, II, p. 35.

from the Report, to the "sense of liberty" and the "sense of progress"[14] —might often, if not usually, tend to prefer the interests in public order over the interests in free speech and communication.

One recognizes—indeed no one committed to sociological jurisprudence teachings, as we are so largely in the common-law world today, could deny this—that law must be a reflection, in measure, of societal facts, and we do accept the existence of two major and distinct civilization areas in Canada. It is proper that in large areas of the positive law —not merely the more obvious areas of private law covered by the Quebec Civil Code, such as family law and matrimonial property law— there can be, and must be, large-scale, if not indeed fundamental, differences as to substantive principle and application as between the French-speaking and the English-speaking civilization-areas, such divergencies stemming both from Quebec's distinctive European civil-law heritage and also, in the family-law area at least, its predominantly Roman Catholic religious culture. It is also proper that Quebec's special claims in these areas, if once demonstrated to be inadequately protected under existing constitutional machinery arrangements, should receive some further special institutional protection. The real problem, particularly when one leaves the private law and goes on to public-law issues, must be as to the possible area and ambit of permissible divergency on ultimate philosophic key concepts between the different civilization-areas, if a federal state is to be viable.

One is aware that it is not unique, in terms of comparative constitutional law experience, for one constituent unit within a federal or plural legal system to claim, and actually to receive, special legal privileges and status in comparison to the other constituent units. The general assumption, in the English-speaking federal systems at least, that all constituent units within a federal system must, as between themselves, have equal status and powers, is neither historically true nor logically necessary. The examples usually cited for this condition of, in effect, authoritatively sanctioned inequality of status and powers as between the various constituent units within a federal or plural legal system—Bavaria in relation to Imperial Germany in the federal constitution of 1871, and Hungary in the Austro-Hungarian Empire after the *Ausgleich* of 1867—are a little more ambiguous in their actual record as law-in-action than Quebec constitutional spokesmen would seem to admit. Bavaria's special status was overshadowed, from the first, by Prussia's political hegemony in Imperial Germany, and the constitution of 1871, as law-in-action, soon ceased to be truly federal, if it ever was that. I would be sorry,

[14]*Ibid.* at pp. 35–7.

also, if Quebec spokesmen should seek too much to use Hungary, after the *Ausgleich* of 1867, as a precedent on which to base their own claims for a rewriting of their own privileges and status in the Canadian federal system. The uninhibited demands of Magyar nationalism, which were vindicated so often at the expense of other ethnic-cultural minorities (for example, the various Slavic groupings) in the multinational Austro-Hungarian Empire, were one of the reasons for the political foundering of the Austro-Hungarian dual monarchy; for without a revision of Magyar intransigeance vis-à-vis the Slavs, it is difficult to see how the dual monarchy could have survived much longer than it did, even without the disasters of military defeat in the First World War. It is precisely because of a feeling that it is a sort of "Magyar intransigeance," involving the pressing of legitimate demands of national (in the sense of ethnic-cultural) self-consciousness to the point, however, where those demands cease to be reasonable in relation to other groups making up the nation-wide federal community, that there has developed recently in English-speaking Canada so much opposition to Quebec's claims for constitutional revision, such opposition stemming from groups which are neither exclusively "Anglo-Protestant" in the sense identified by the Tremblay Report nor even exclusively "Anglo-Saxon" in the strict sense of that word.

The real issue must be, as I have said, the limits of permissible dissent and disagreement on political, social, and economic fundamentals if a federal state is to be viable. Fortunately, we are all of us far less categorical today in our insistence on what is such a necessary minimum philosophical consensus than we were a few years ago. I can remember, in seminars on comparative federalism that I gave with Continental European students in Europe several years ago, raising the issue of whether a *viable* federal association would be possible between the two Germanies, in the event that they should ever by big-power, "summit meeting" agreement, be reunified; and I remember that the European students' conclusion at the time was that you just could not combine, in one state, a predominantly Christian Democratic and a predominantly Communist political philosophy. Yet, as Senator Claiborne Pell, the young Democratic Senator from Rhode Island, has recently reminded us, in a statement with an almost Fulbright-like ring in its insistence on studying the realities of the political here-and-now, West Germany and East Germany have been co-operating extensively over a period of years in matters ranging from common sporting teams for International Olympic competitions to extensive trade dealings and commercial intercourse generally. The philosophic gap, such as it is, between Quebec and English-speaking Canada today must surely be easier to bridge than that!

A lot of the intellectual difficulties which now exist between Quebec and English-speaking Canada—and I need only refer, now, to such incidents as the dark outbursts of purely irrational prejudice in Ontario over the comparatively trivial issue of converting the CBC radio network station CJBC in Toronto to a French-language station, or to the noisy clamouring of self-appointed "jingoists" over the issue of a new and distinctive national flag for Canada and a new and distinctive national anthem—would probably be dispelled in large measure if Quebec's intellectuals would take the time and trouble to spell out what it is that today's "revolution" in Quebec really involves. For we in English-speaking Canada envy you your revolution in Quebec, and the exciting opportunity that it presents for dramatizing in the public mind that testing of old ideas and old institutions by their utility in action today that is so vital to any society that wishes to remain in continuing growth and development. By comparison, I have the feeling that the Tremblay Report, even though it be itself only a decade old, with its at times almost mystical insistence on a largely undefined and uncon-cretized "national genius" as a factor guiding and controlling constitu-tional development, has lapsed somewhat into the juristic pessimism and historical fatalism of von Savigny's nineteenth century concept of *Volks-geist*. There is, besides, too great an element of generality and abstrac-tion in the Tremblay Report's formulations for them to be operationally useful in themselves at the present day.

In the absence of any substantial spelling out by Quebec spokesmen of the political-institutional implications of the revolution in Quebec and its general ideological base, the intellectual face of Quebec today, for a great many people in English-speaking Canada, is still largely that of Premier Duplessis' authoritarianism. The image of paternalistic sometimes benevolent despotism, with its occasional very ugly aspects of a police-state arbitrariness for those who crossed it, colours and con-ditions, in measure, the response in English-speaking Canada to de-mands pressed by Quebec spokesmen today, despite the fact that the era of Duplessis is long past and the Lesage Revolution under way. And if we may revert for the moment to the area of constitutional juris-prudence and specifically to the role of the judges of the Supreme Court of Canada, then in so far as Quebec's present-day constitutional spokes-men would insist on viewing the civilian judges on the Court as, in effect, partisan representatives of Quebec particularism, I cannot avoid expressing my misgivings at the trends in the civil-law voting on the Court in concrete cases over the past decade and a half. While I have elsewhere, and at the time the Supreme Court judgment was actually handed down in 1959, criticized certain aspects of the common-law majority's approach in the *Roncarelli* case to rationalization of the actual bases of decision, I cannot really see how any other end result was possible—speaking now of strictly civil law precedents. More than that, I would suggest, it is hardly possible judicially to tolerate constitutional *voies de fait* of the nature that Premier Duplessis himself admitted to committing against Roncarelli, and still to maintain a democratic polity. Looking at the record of the civil-law judges' dissents in the great civil liberties cases of the 1950's like the *Roncarelli* case, and taking note also of the uninhibited quality of the Civilian dissents in more recent *causes célèbres*, of the nature, for example, of *Reg.* v. *Brodie*[15] which seem to very many Common lawyers—and I have no doubt, also, to very many European-trained civil lawyers—quite unnecessarily to seek to defer to interests in public order and to apply censorship controls to long-accepted literary classics, one can feel very little sympathy at the moment for current Quebec proposals for changing the structure of the Canadian Supreme Court so as to give Quebec in effect 50 per cent of the voting power in judicial determinations of public law matters. One of the major tasks of Quebec's intellectuals, and especially of the lawyers, may therefore be to correct the currently rather conservative, backwards-looking image which Quebec jurisprudence presents outside the province. If it could be convincingly demonstrated to the general public in English-speaking Canada that the Quebec revolution, so far from being a purely xenophobic reaction against the English-speaking sections of the country, is really a movement for fundamental social reform and modernization of political and legal institutions both inside and outside the province—something which the legal establishment, at least, in English-speaking Canada, taking note of such recently announced law reform measures as Premier Lesage's proposals for removing ancient disabilities in the legal status of women under the Quebec Civil Code, have already concluded—then a great deal of the intellectual opposition, outside Quebec, to Quebec proposals for revision of the Canadian constitution would tend to diminish, if not to disappear altogether. But, by the same token, the need, on Quebec's part, for direct, formal changes in the Canadian constitution might tend to disappear also, leaving it to developing custom and convention, as of now, to effect changes as the need emerges in concrete situations, without the necessity for noisy and prolonged, and ultimately divisive, public controversy.

[15]*Reg.* v. *Brodie*, 32 DLR (2d) 507 (1962), a 5 to 4 decision, with Kerwin C.J.C., Taschereau J., and Fauteux J. each dissenting specially, and Locke J. dissenting without filing a formal opinion.

COMMENTARIES / COMMENTAIRES

P. AZARD

Je voudrais prendre la liberté de vous faire une remarque qui pourrait
s'intituler d'une manière fort large en apparence: « Le rôle du juriste dans
le monde d'aujourd'hui » ; elle nous ramène immédiatement à la tâche que
le Canada de 1964 doit confier à ses professeurs de droit et juristes prati-
ciens. On a souvent signalé l'attitude conservatrice des juristes dans la société.
Dans cet auditoire même, beaucoup de personnes, en particulier des spécialistes de la science politique, ont dû pouvoir, au cours des précédentes
séances, constater une certaine gêne des juristes, de la majorité d'entre eux
du moins, devant l'ampleur de l'effort qui leur était proposé. Ce sentiment
de réserve et de gêne est bien compréhensible. Gardien de la loi écrite ou des
règles coutumières, selon le système de droit auquel il appartient, le juriste
ne peut considérer toute proposition de changer le droit positif en vigueur
que comme une vue de l'esprit, laquelle vue appartient au monde des hypo-
thèses et doit être bien distinguée de la réalité du droit. Cette attitude a,
d'ailleurs, valu de cinglants reproches au monde du droit.

Un juriste français, extrêmement au courant du droit établi, le Professeur
André Tunc, a reproché à ses collègues d'avoir maintenu sciemment leur
discipline à l'âge de la pierre éclatée. Pourtant, on est bien obligé d'admettre que le juriste doit adhérer au droit existant et en assurer la protection parfaite aussi longtemps que ce droit n'aura pas été changé. Malgré
cela, je n'ai nullement l'intention de considérer comme des fauteurs de troubles
et des ennemis de l'ordre économique, politique, et social établi les juristes
qui viennent de présenter leurs communications. En effet, leurs efforts et
leur science n'ont pas seulement pour résultat de mieux faire connaître des
problèmes d'une brûlante actualité, ceux que le droit constitutionnel du
Canada présente, mais aussi de nous démontrer que, dans la société moderne,
on accorde au juriste un tout autre rôle que celui d'être le gardien nécessaire
et naturel des droits existants. On souhaite de plus en plus, on a souhaité
expressément ici, que le juriste propose à la société des suggestions qui
permettent de faire progresser le droit. Au premier abord, il y a une
certaine opposition ou antinomie entre les deux tâches envisagées. Comment, serait-on tenté de dire, peut-on être un bon gardien de la loi et
un conseiller fidèle de son application, si l'on s'intéresse aussi à d'éventuels
changements ? A cette objection, la réponse est beaucoup plus facile qu'elle

ne le paraît au premier abord. C'est précisément celui qui veille avec soin à l'exacte application de la loi existante qui est le mieux à même de déceler les difficultés fonctionnelles d'application et de proposer les meilleurs remèdes. Objectivement et socialement parlant, les nécessités de l'époque doivent d'abord recevoir satisfaction et cela aussi vite que possible.

Au surplus, le meilleur moyen de défendre un système juridique n'est-il pas de veiller avec soin à éviter toute sclérose génératrice de rupture et de bouleversement grave ? En 1964, partout, dans un monde en évolution technique, économique et sociale effrénée, et plus particulièrement au Canada où l'on enregistre un véritable séisme politique, le juriste doit proposer à la société des projets et des schémas d'évolution du droit. Ces schémas permettront à l'homme politique, auteur des lois, au journaliste qui façonne l'opinion publique, à l'homme de la rue même, de choisir avec plus ou moins de bonheur et d'intuition les solutions juridiques qu'indiqueront les facteurs sociaux pour le plus grand bien commun. De tels bureaux d'études juridiques — et c'est un tel bureau qui a fonctionné ici, dans un cadre particulièrement propice — exercent une fonction bienfaisante, non seulement, nous croyons l'avoir montré, sur l'évolution du droit mais il faut bien aussi comprendre que l'examen de schémas de réforme juridique est un facteur de stabilité sociale et politique. Un révolutionnaire auquel on soumet les conséquences de ses idées, et que l'on fait réfléchir aux moyens pratiques et techniques de leur réalisation, n'est plus révolutionnaire à vrai dire — c'est déjà le bâtisseur d'un monde futur.

W. A. MACKAY

It is perhaps fitting that someone from Nova Scotia should participate in our discussions on federalism. As Professor Beetz has reminded us, my province was the first home of a separatist movement in the new Canada. The movement began almost immediately after the passage of the BNA Act. Though short-lived as a political force, it, and the passage of the era of wooden ships manned by iron men, left a lingering dissatisfaction with Confederation in Nova Scotia for years. Indeed, it is only since the province moved into the twentieth century, and this in the years since the Second World War, that we have ceased to use the appellation "Upper Canadian" as a term without disparagement in referring to anyone who hails from the area west of the Quebec-New Brunswick border to the Lakehead. Not unlike Quebec, there is a marked feeling in my own province in very recent years that economic problems can be solved largely to our satisfaction by our own efforts, although, admittedly, we lack the resources and the apparent dynamism of our compatriots in "la belle province."

Perhaps another reason justifies my presence here today. Nova Scotians, if not all Maritimers, though pragmatic enough when problems raise their ugly heads and finally scream for solutions, tend to be very conservative in outlook, tied, as perhaps the people of Quebec are still, to traditions and to a past perhaps less glorious than it now appears. It was useful for me that Professor Laforest outlined the view which Maritimers have always taken of economic policies and problems of this region in this nation.

I mention all of these matters to emphasize that there are perhaps more interpretations of Confederation than Professor Morin dealt with this afternoon, that of a unitary state and that of union of two peoples with distinct cultures. Perhaps this also indicates my own belief that the interests of Canadians outside Quebec are much more diverse than would appear from the assumptions underlying Mr. Morin's thesis, and that these interests do not now tend towards strong central control by the federal government, though admittedly they might at one time have been so considered with justification. I would also question any assumption that all French Canadians across this land look to Quebec as their national home, an assumption that underlies some of the thinking about binational developments in this country. Certainly, this does not appear to be true of the Acadians who live in this region, though admittedly their cultural aspirations are reviving and have elements in common with those of our brothers in Quebec. And this is as it should be.

If I am right in questioning assumptions of unanimity of interests among French Canadians and among non-French Canadians and in suggesting to you that, in any revision of the Constitution, factors other that the existence of two ethnic and cultural groups must be considered, then there are limits which circumscribe the areas in which binational control of policies is likely to be acceptable.

In the economic field at least our colleagues in the CPSA have made clear the magnitude and the importance of the shift in power—particularly in relation to fiscal matters—to the provinces. It seems clear that, if we wish a viable Canadian market to continue with sufficient stability, substantial changes ought to be made in the co-ordination of policies among the provinces and between them and the central government—and they ought to be made soon. Management of economic affairs would appear to require provincial or at least regional co-operation with the central government.

Incidentally, I suspect, as Professor McWhinney emphasized earlier, that we lawyers outside Quebec have generally paid too little attention to the proceedings and the fruits of federal-provincial conferences, and we paid none at all to the more recent innovation, initiated by Premier Lesage, of annual conferences of provincial premiers. And yet these are the fundamental institutions now giving new dimensions to federalism in this country.

Let me hasten to suggest that one cannot fault the thesis of binational control, at least in certain areas of government responsibility. This seems to me to be an important matter which we must consider, and soon, in a thorough way. As Professor McWhinney has pointed out, some areas are now by custom, if not by convention, already subject to such control. His concept of dualistic federalism already has some validity. But, as I have already suggested, I am not at all sure that there is yet any consensus of the range of interests that ought to be subject to this control. Nor am I at all sure that it is enough to leave such matters to convention, common-law trained though I am. Perhaps, as agreement is reached on one matter or another, written constitutional change should be undertaken. For example, most of us would concede that a consensus is likely to be achieved quickly on constitutional guarantees of collective and individual rights, or at least on many of them; and there is much to be said for amending the constitution as quickly as possible in this regard. Again, I doubt that much difficulty lies in the way of insulating private-law disputes arising in Quebec under the Civil Code and related statutes against the "corrupting influence" of common-law trained judges in the Supreme Court of Canada. Surely appropriate changes in that institution can be agreed upon. Yet, as Mr. McWhinney has pointed out, public law questions (and what any such question is will give rise to dispute) may not be so readily dealt with.

Again, I am sanguine enough—perhaps naive enough—to think that providing our own procedure for amendment of the constitution, to be used whenever a consensus for any change is attained, is not as insurmountable a task as our past fruitless efforts would seem to suggest.

Finally, let me comment on a few general suggestions made by Mr. McWhinney. Rightly, he points out that federalism is as dynamic an organization as we wish it to be, and that there is nothing sacrosanct about the equality of status for constituent units within a federation. The latter suggestion underlies Mr. Morin's proposals and it is, it seems to me, worthy of fullest consideration. After all, we have never really had a federation of equals, either in the ethnic groupings of peoples in this land or among the provinces. And yet our constitution, at least the written version if not the constitution in action, has thus far failed to take full account of inequalities. Neither the French fact nor the non-French fact should be ignored in our constitution. Nor should other differences among us be ignored—for example, the relative strengths of provinces—and yet a complete consensus of how these differences should be accorded recognition even for the time being has yet to be attained. There is need for discussion among us all. We can only presume that there is time for it to take place.

Mr. McWhinney is right, in my view, when he suggests that our colleagues in Quebec, must spell out in concrete terms, as Mr. Morin has tried to do today for us, changes which they would deem essential in the constitution. One of the difficulties of living in this part of the country, as in many other areas, is that one must rely largely on newspapers which report, accurately or inaccurately, some of the statements of some of the leading spokesmen in some parts of the country. One does not always get any clear view of the positions which are being criticized.

Yet, it seems to me Mr. McWhinney was wrong in suggesting this afternoon, if I understand him correctly, that the burden of proof is upon those, primarily in Quebec, who seek change to convince the rest of us of the need. Far too few people in the common-law provinces of Canada have been considering constitutional questions now in the air in anything like sufficient depth. If I am wrong, you may correct me; but I suggest this is true not only of our politicians but of us law teachers as well. All of us can take a leaf from the book of universities in Quebec, and particularly from the University of Montreal, and we should all begin *now* to consider these questions in depth. If we do not, we shall probably never be convinced of the real need for change and we shall certainly not be prepared for the dialogue which must take place soon. Our "rendezvous with the BNA Act," to use Dean Scott's phrase, is at hand. And we must be prepared—or the opportunity will be gone before we know it is upon us.

MAXWELL COHEN

Any serious discussion concerning the constitutional and institutional framework for a reconstructed Canadian federalism must be caught between the tensions of our history with its established political habits and forms, and the not-yet-defined future that barely can be sensed but certainly not really apprehended. Caught between past and future the observant scholar, whatever his behavioural discipline, must function responsibly even though he may often seem to be giving expression to preferences or values that may or may not be reconciled easily with the analytical lessons derived from his discipline. In the present "revolutionary setting, at least where Quebec is concerned, there is little doubt therefore that political scientists, constitutional lawyers, and historians will view the reshaping of Canadian federalism not merely from the vantage of their own technical areas but also from their presuppositions as to the kind of life and society envisaged for Canada or for a region of Canada to which the observer in question may be particularly devoted. Scholarship, caught in the midst of the present Canadian debate—as it is always with ideas and those who promote them—becomes both mirror and catalyst. Given, therefore, the present fluid situation in accommodating the new Quebec, and the English-speaking response to it, any allegedly "scientific" statements about federalism must be viewed with a good deal of reserve. To put it bluntly, we are all advocates, one way or another of our prejudices or values about Canada or Quebec, and under these conditions scholarship often becomes a means for rationalizing with footnotes a complex of preferences.

Let me begin, therefore, by admitting that I have preferences, that I am a prisoner more than I am the master of my own value system, and that I will view Professor Morin's remarks as having no lesser or greater scientific pretensions than my own. For he, too, is a creature of choices, conscious or concealed, choices that are essentially more visceral than cerebral in their origins and rationale. By saying this I do not minimize the interplay between preference and discipline, between thought and conviction, between so-called scientific judgment and the shaping of values. I mean simply to recognize that in discussing the probable and desirable shape of our future federalism I am aware that goals and images already held rank very high on the scale of scholarly motives and judgment.

For these reasons I wish to set out at once some of my own prejudices:
1. I favour a strong, united Canada where there is an abundance of federal power to achieve economic and social wellbeing and a sense of nationhood within Canada as well as an effective place for Canada as a middle-power

making its contribution in the world outside. For me, the consequences of this general prejudice or conception, must be that any future constitutional arrangements are unacceptable unless they provide for such a united, effective Canada.

2. Since general principles do not decide very much—whatever my civil-law colleagues say—this first major prejudice must now be translated by me into very concrete statements of power-allocation. I therefore believe that any federal government, to be effective at home and abroad, must have at least the following:

a. General taxing powers, as at present;

b. Monetary and fiscal powers, as at present;

c. The right to spend in any direction, as at present, subject however to specific consultation with the provinces wherever spending directly affects the power of the province or any of its major interests or institutions.

d. Defence and foreign policy, as at present;

e. An improved treaty implementation power, but hopefully designed so as not to permit treaties to be used by the federal Parliament as a means to modify in any way language, education, religion, and the cultural autonomy of Quebec and elsewhere.

f. Federal control over banking, interest rates, currency and coinage, inter-provincial and foreign trade, interprovincial and foreign transportation, with joint immigration and agricultural control as at present, etc.

3. I am in favour also of strong self-respecting provincial authority where the increased educational and welfare burdens and the opportunity for important measures of regional planning all make it necessary and desirable to improve the revenue position and general economic role of the provinces. Since, however, the provinces have large powers of direct taxation, which they often have not fully exploited as yet, and since they also have very substantial powers over expropriations, prices, production, wage policy and the labour market, as a result of eighty-five years of favourable interpreta-tions of the BNA Act, there are very few other important areas that could be allocated to the provinces. If it is remembered also that they have control over their own natural resources, the scope for intensive resource planning and development here is limited only by economic realities on the one hand and available bureaucracies on the other. Even the constitutional effects of Chief Justice Lett's judgment in the *B.C. Power Case* do not really intrude materially into this large area of existing provincial authority. Indeed, striking evidence of the range of local economic authority is to be seen in the fact that anti-combines policy in Canada, apart from the limitation of being confined in its constitutional justification to "criminal law," is perhaps even more confined by the ability of the provinces to withdraw industries from the effect of the policy through giving price control and cartelized behaviour, within the province, some legal status which the Courts will then respect—as they did in the *Canadian Breweries Case*.

4. I am in favour of the New Quebec, completely and unreservedly, where the words "New Quebec" mean a massive cultural advance, economic self-confidence, political morality, an educational revolution, and a vast improve-ment in the public service and in the public services. This means to me also an acceptance of the "quiet revolution" projected beyond Quebec to include

language and school rights for French-speaking Canadians, and constitutionally provided for, in all those provinces where there is any density of French-speaking citizens to demand it. The concept of a culturally dual Canada is here to stay. It may take quite a long time before French is a meaningful experience for many English-speaking Canadians outside of Quebec; but consciousness of the dualism nevertheless will precede the skills required to make it a personal experience. Without that consciousness we shall have the worst of the two-nation theory; namely, Quebec and the other Canada, living across the gulf of language and resentment. In federal terms the dual culture already expresses itself and must increasingly do so, in Parliament, in public documents and soon in the ease with which both languages under appropriate conditions may find an automatic application to the work of the public service. No doubt for some time, at the federal level, mistakes will be made both ways for some governments may lean over backwards to appear to be more "Quebecois" than even French-Canadians themselves would expect. But that is a posture far more likely to lead to harmony than one where English-speaking Canada appears resistant to the idea of the cultural dualism wherever that dualism presses on toward some new equilibrium.

5. I have a prejudice against doing violence both to persons and to history and there is a not a little in the Quebec revolution, on its extreme side, that may be harsh to the "outsider" as it sometimes already is brutal to history. For that history, of Confederation's origins, surely is much more than Professor Morin's paper suggests. The pressures to unite also were linked with the common desire of the provinces to protect a common Canadian life against the immense pull of the United States and to have a strong enough central government so as to avoid what appeared to be pitfalls of American federalism. Professor Morin does not say much about this in his paper, yet it is important to remind ourselves that the Quebec leaders of his day did not envisage a weak national government and were able to reconcile substantial local autonomy with a strong federal authority. It is brutalizing our history to pretend that there has been a deliberate violation of a compact between the founding cultures. Indeed, the reverse may be true, namely, that with the Judicial Committee of the Privy Council as a guide, we moved farther away from the original conceptions—conceptions shared by some important French-Canadian leaders of the day—to the point where provincial power before the Second World War cut across much effective economic policy-making at the national level. It is true of course that the depression, the Second World War, and post-war reconstruction shifted the administrative balance heavily in favour of central power, a shift made more significant and durable also by the growth of a first-class federal public service. That balance is now moving in some important sectors back to the provinces; but that shift really has far less to do with the constitution than it has with provincial economic and welfare realities on one hand and new federal-provincial administrative arrangements on the other. There is very little in the constitution to blame either for these shifts to the provinces by judicial interpretation on the one hand, or shifts to the federal government since 1930 by political or administrative arrangements on the other. To a very large extent, therefore, modernizing the constitution must

be for Canadians more a matter of form and symbol than of substance—
although a new charter of powers may be valuable for the educational
consequences of the exercise and the dramatic symbolism of the result.

Let us now leave my prejudices and values and political-legal choices and
turn to those of Professor Morin.

Professor Morin has divided his paper into four general areas: (1) the
new division of powers; (2) the new federal institutions; (3) the protection
of collective and individual rights; and (4) the amending process. Let me
deal briefly now with each although I have, by stating my own "prejudices,"
really shot my bolt. But before discussing Mr. Morin's four-part analysis
and proposals, let me first state *his prejudices* for him as I understand them
from his paper.

1. I suggest he believes that federalism in Canada must assume a strong
independent Quebec able to advance with a high degree of autonomy on the
economic and cultural levels and that constitutionally it is possible to have
such arrangements without real injury to a federal Canada.

2. There is a crisis, and the crisis can be best solved by a grand redesigning
of Canadian federalism, since federal systems can move from highly centralized models to decentralized ones and he prefers one that is substantially
decentralized to fit present Canadian needs, particularly in Quebec.

3. He believes that a dominant social fact is the role of state intervention
in the economy and he favours powers for Quebec to enable it to plan and
intervene in the economy as the social philosophy of the new Quebec may
require.

These beliefs have led to Mr. Morin's four main groups of recommendations.

1. He is concerned to have a new division of powers to achieve, for
Quebec at least, a kind of economic independence as well as rights of
consultation in other areas even where there are no actual legal powers.
Indeed, he confines the scope of future federal power to "external affairs,
common defence, interprovincial commerce and transportation, monetary
policy, customs and immigration." Though he refers to other federal systems
to demonstrate the range of options, I doubt whether a study of Australian
and United States constitutional development would justify a narrow view
of federal power. Indeed, the reverse is true. Beginning as "states" with
extensive local powers both countries have moved towards even greater
degrees of central authority. Moreover, Mr. Morin implies that the new
division of powers should be designed to assist the other provinces in uniting,
presumably in some regional merger, e.g., the Prairies and the Maritimes;
and this program would make more palatable a binational theory of alloca-
cation of powers with Quebec "on an equal footing with the central government." He does not mention the equality of the newly merged regions but
presumably he would accord them some higher status than now they have,
if not as "high" as Quebec.

It seems to me quite daring of Mr. Morin to advise English-speaking
provinces to lose their identity when he is so anxious for Quebec to retain
its own. And while there are profound differences—since Quebec is the
homeland of all French Canadians in Canada, and for the English-speaking
Ontario, thank God, is not—it is quite possible that Nova Scotia and Alberta
feel as strongly about their identity for their own reasons and have no

desire to lose it. Whatever the merit of this aspect of his argument the plain truth is that we have probably gone as far as we should go in economic decentralization with expropriation powers, resource control, prices, production and labour relations, including wage policy, all substantially under provincial jurisdiction, and I would see no practical good in trying to find further economic areas of action to be conferred upon the provinces. Finally, in this connection, I am not impressed with Mr. Morin's treaty-making recommendations on the West German analogy, namely, giving power to the provinces, or to Quebec, to engage in direct treaty-making within their own areas of jurisdiction. For obvious reasons this opens the door to the achievement of international personality by provinces or by Quebec that under Canadian conditions might hasten the day toward the disintegration of the federal personality. Even the West German model does not go quite that far.

2. Mr. Morin urges the reformation of the Senate as a kind of chamber of nationalities with half the members from the French-speaking population from all provinces and they would not represent provinces but rather they would provide "equal representation of the two nations." Cabinet members would also be selected from the Senate. Similarly, he would introduce the binational concept into new federal boards to be created to control policy in a number of areas, defence, monetary questions, external affairs, etc. And he concludes this recommendation with the suggestion that the new legislation in these areas would be considered by such boards before being put to Parliament.

There is no doubt Mr. Morin is more optimistic about the future of the Senate than many Canadians are willing to be after so much has been said about so little over many years of discussing the Senate as a staple of Canadian political humour. To convert the Senate now into something almost more important than the House of Commons—since as Mr. Morin admits by its very nature the House will remain as at present with an English-speaking majority—would go far beyond any range of acceptable reforms in the name of our bicultural future. At a time when parliamentary democracy faces, in many countries, increased criticism for its weakness, inefficiency and built-in stalemates, it would surely be inviting trouble to design a second chamber that would transform responsible government as we know it into something quite different and quite unpredictable except for the likelihood of increased deadlock. Similarly, cabinet government could hardly function if policies were to be cleared by binational boards made up of equal numbers from the two language groups. I should have thought that this clearing procedure already takes place, at all times, through the realistic operation of our political processes with parties, caucuses, compromise, and regional interests all at work and influencing every issue of any importance.

3. Mr. Morin argues for a bill of rights, collective rights and individual rights, the effect of which would confirm the use of the French language for courts, boards, legislatures, schools, in all the provinces where there is a French-speaking population. At the same time individual rights would be partly protected by a federal bill of rights, partly by a provincial one, the latter to deal with "civil rights proper" (marriage and property) and economics rights . . . under provincial competence. . . ." I have no quarrel with these general notions but I am somewhat surprised that any lawyer would

propose a bill of rights for such things as marriage and property when these presumably are already part of the well-established law of the land both within the language of the existing "constitution" and in more general concepts of law as well. I do not see the value of this reiteration, but if it makes a group of Canadians happier to spell out in greater detail and in something called a bill of rights certain matters now protected in other ways, I can see no objection to a new constitution so doing. Nor do I object to a reshuffling of minor powers, e.g., "marriage and divorce," in favour of the provinces. Of course, if Mr. Morin is suggesting a "due process clause" to protect property does he think Quebec's planners will take kindly to such a juridical shadow cast across their Diceyan dreams?

4. Mr. Morin proposes that the amending process be such that "all provisions dealing with the autonomy of Quebec and its participation in the federal parliament and administration" be entrenched and not be subject to amendment without the consent of Quebec.

Frankly, I am unable to understand the full significance of this proposal without a good deal more elucidation than appears in Mr. Morin's very brief and somewhat discouraging statement. It is one thing to entrench a number of key subjects such as language, religion, education, direct taxation powers, etc. It is quite another to put forward as a concept, "the autonomy of Quebec," so general that it could embrace as many ideas and policies as an extremist might wish to assert thereby subjecting the whole amending process to the veto. Mr. Morin believes this power would "create a climate of confidence," but it would also create an amending quagmire out of which proposals for changes would rarely emerge.

Mr. Morin has also stated that he believes the Supreme Court of Canada as a federal court should not be the court of final appeal on matters touching the Quebec Civil Code, while on constitutional matters a further court should be established presumably equally divided between the two language groups. There is a good deal to be said for the reconstitution of the Supreme Court for civil law appeals. But is there as much to be said for a constitutional court permanently reflecting a "two-nation" theory in numbers, if not in viewpoint?

The real question, in the end, is whether Mr. Morin really desires a viable federal Canada in economic and political terms or whether he is seeking a loose arrangement, transitional in character, which in fact becomes an intermediate zone between classical Canadian Confederation and outright independence for Quebec—with the likelihood that if the modified federalism did not work then the transition to a separate state could be made without great difficulty. His other, not fully articulated, premise is to the effect that there is a view of state intervention in the new Quebec which does not exist to the same extent in the rest of Canada, federally or provincially, and Quebec therefore needs powers different from the other provinces to implement its new social objectives. I think this is a quite unrealistic assessment of the present scope of planning and intervention, federally and in several of the provinces, and it misses the point I made before, namely, that if Quebec is now concerned to achieve a post-capitalism welfare state, with neosocialist characteristics, there is little in the present constitutional arrangements to prevent it from moving as far along that road as it may wish to go.

What is required is the creation of a joint federal-provincial secretariat to manage all of the on-going problems, financial and programatic, that will now mark the new forms of co-operation and authority. Such a realistic administrative framework can be more important than constitutional refinements. On both grounds, therefore, I reject the distinction between Quebec's so-called constitutional needs and the powers that it already has; and I reject the view that Canada, federally, or outside of Quebec, resists the kind of state intervention in the economy to the degree that Quebec now desires to have it.

There are many aspects to, and aspiration of, the new Quebec within the new Canada with which many Canadians of goodwill already are in substantial measure of agreement. What is loosely called "repatriation" of the Constitution; a more effective amending process at home; a redrafted national charter that symbolizes the present and eliminates the obsolete and the anachronistic; a bill of rights within the Constitution; French-language and school rights in all the provinces concerned; more realistic treaty implementation powers; all of these and more may not be too difficult to agree on. But Mr. Morin has given us a design for fragmentation and possible deadlock, not one for effective union, and he has given it to us with a body of reasons that are unconvincing as a matter of economic description and therefore also unconvincing as a question of constitutional need. By all means let us find symbols and powers that dignify the new Quebec and unite us all within a two-culture society. As Mr. Morin insists, there are many roads leading to a federal state, but I regret that his map leads elsewhere to some ideological wilderness where a modern effective federal Canada will not be found.

Address / Allocution

delivered at the Joint Dinner of the Association of Canadian Law Teachers and the Canadian Political Science Association at Charlottetown, PEI, on Thursday evening, June 11, 1964

prononcée lors du dîner conjoint de l'Association canadienne des professeurs de droit et de l'Association canadienne des Sciences politiques à Charlottetown, Ile du Prince Edouard, le jeudi 11 juin 1964

F. R. SCOTT

Messieurs les deux co-présidents :

C'est exactement de même dans la Commission royale sur le bilinguisme et le biculturalisme : je me trouve entre deux entités égales. On dit de notre commission que nous ne sommes pas seulement bilingues et biculturels, mais aussi bizarres.

I have not yet reached such a stage of senility that I cannot take a hint. I promise not to stand between you and the women of Confederation.* I also doubt whether the Canadians of this day and age have the stamina of the Fathers of Confederation. If you read that delightful book by Professor Waite, *The Life and Times of Confederation*, you will find that on a certain Thursday—today is Thursday—the Fathers and their companions visited the North Shore all day, bathed in the warm waters thereof, came back, went to a grand ball at Province House at 10:00 p.m., had supper that began at 1:00 a.m. and was followed by nearly three hours of speeches, and then all went down to that good ship *Queen Victoria* to start their journey to Halifax.

Speaking of Queen Victoria and being in the Maritimes, I am reminded that there was the great Cape Breton bard who, in an outburst of loyalty, wrote:

*It had been announced that immediately after the dinner there was to be a pageant of "The Women of Confederation," to which the dinner guests were invited.

> Here's to Queen Victoria
> Dressed in all her regalia
> With one foot in Canada
> And the other in Australia.

I shall not touch further on the question of the Monarchy tonight.

Of course, I could take up the whole time this evening just telling you my twelve bilingual stories. Human stories give quite an insight into social attitudes. I think perhaps I might tell you two. I once complained to my co-commissioner, Jean Marchand, that all the stories I could collect were against the English. He said: "They ought to be too."

The first story is of the *Time* reporter sent out to the Prairies to find out some grass roots opinion about bilingualism. He stopped an old farmer in Alberta and said: "My man, what do you think about bilingualism?" The man replied: "I will tell you what I think about it; if the English language was good enough for Jesus Christ, it's good enough for me." You know, I have a horrible suspicion that that story is true.

Then there is the story of the extreme French-Canadian nationalist and separatist—let's say just by accident his name was Barbeau; I don't know what it was really. To the amazement of his friends, he suddenly introduced a bill in the Quebec Legislature to change his name to Smith; and they asked "What has come over you?" He replied: "My doctor has just told me that I have an incurable cancer, so when I die there will be one less Englishman." I told that story, when I was down in Louisiana about a month ago at the Louisiana State University—also a school that teaches the civil law in the English language—whereupon one member of the faculty said he had heard it in Ireland in 1918. These stories go around the world in all minority situations like atrocity pictures which are used by both sides in world wars.

If I have any serious idea tonight (I am beginning to wonder whether I have) and in view of the fact that, being a member of the Commission, I cannot express my opinions—I don't mind that so much, but the real problem is I cannot express any biases—I thought I would remind you that learned gatherings such as this and the Royal Society which preceded you, where similar questions were discussed at a very high level, come up with many good and fine ideas and are an essential part of the process by which a nation rethinks its basic beliefs. But somebody ultimately has got to make the decisions. Somebody has to take these various ideas and put them into somewhat more official form. In other words, there has to be machinery to formulate what is going to be decided, to reduce it to manageable proportions, to offer it to governments.

Now of course, the Royal Commission, of which I am a member, is one such body. I want to point out to you that we have not been given the whole job. We have been given more than we can bite off, I think, but it is certainly not the whole job. What is it in fact that we are doing as a federal royal commission? I promise not to read the whole of our terms of reference, but still there's this sentence, including that word biculturalism which, you know, in a recently published French-English dictionary especially prepared for Canadians, does not even exist. We are to inquire into and report upon the existing state of bilingualism and biculturalism in Canada (well, that's not perhaps too difficult), to recommend what steps should be taken to develop the Canadian Confederation on the basis of an equal partnership between the two founding races (in the French text, "les deux peuples qui l'ont fondée": "peoples," which is better. I may say, the Commission prefers "peoples" to "races") taking into account, of course, the contribution of the other ethnic groups. So the notion of an equal partnership is dominant, and that is a pretty pregnant notion; we shall think about that for a long time. We then have to go and look upon the whole use of the two languages in the federal civil service, including Crown corporations, on the use of the two languages in public and private organizations, e.g., the Canadian Political Science Association and Association of Canadian Law Teachers, and then, recognizing that education is essentially a provincial matter, to discuss with the provinces the situation in regard to the uses of the two languages in their schools, and the opportunities Canadians have of learning the two languages. That is a pretty large order. But may I point out it does not cover all the big issues that are before us in Canada. We don't have to concern ourselves with the basic problem of fiscal relationships between Ottawa and the provinces. There may be some fiscal implications in recommendations we shall come to make, but that is a very small part of the total economic and fiscal problem which was discussed so largely this morning.

Neither is it our business to talk about the "repatriation" of the constitution, or to recommend the nature of the amending process which we must decide upon if we are to repatriate it. I consider this, Ladies and Gentlemen, to be absolutely crucial and, as you know, the Fulton formula was produced some time back; it is still there; I openly opposed it then and I am able to oppose it now, since it is not within the terms of reference of my commission, though it has, I think, some very interesting ideas in it. But there is an issue we must take up again. Our Commission is not instructed to do it.

Some people are talking about drafting a new constitution, almost as though we started again; that is certainly not our job. It may well be that some recommendations of our Commission may involve some constitutional amendment. I don't think we, as a Commission, will go into the question whether there need be an amendment; we will leave that to others. But if it is to be any overhaul of the total constitution, we are not the body to do it, nor are we to look after present distribution of legislative powers, to see whether there are inadequacies or inconsistencies. There are certainly lots of varied interpretations around such subjects as insurance, marketing, and other areas I could mention, but that is not our concern.

Further, while we do our work on the Commission, changes are constantly going on in Canada around us. A very active program of introducing bilingualism into the federal civil service is under way by the present government, which is not hesitating to make changes, just because it has asked a Royal Commission to look into the problem. So we see these things altering while we are supposed to be observing and reporting. Certainly a great many new fiscal relationships have been developed, and these affect greatly the total climate in the country and the intensity of the antagonism—because there is always a good deal of antagonism—that exists. The arrangements governments make in their daily contacts with one another affect that climate and change therefore the opportunities we have of working out our own particular solutions. And of course, the air is full of new concepts of federalism.

These have been discussed here. What does it mean, a special status for Quebec? Speaking as an English Canadian resident in Quebec, I am very glad Quebec has some special status, because it is very useful to me. There are very many other aspects of this: all the opting-out provisions, the once radical idea that the province that opts out should be paid as much money as if it opted in. I think we are surprising ourselves how flexible can be the concepts of federalism, and it is only because we are habituated to concepts existing in the past that we are apt to feel when a new idea is put forward that it cannot work or it is too radical or something. We just do not know what we can do until we sit down and think it out and try it. There is an extraordinary flexibility within this rigid constitution of ours in the relations between governments: delegation of powers, changes of fiscal concepts, and so forth. But what I am pointing out to you is not the business of my commission. It is all going on around us.

Now apart from my Commission, Quebec has a parliamentary committee, which has under way a very considerable program of research, under Professors Morin and Patry. It is hearing witnesses, and many very interesting ideas are being put forward before that committee. Is it true, for example, that there are only 8 per cent of the people of Finland who speak Swedish, and yet Swedish is an official language throughout Finland? What is the relationship between Puerto Rico and the United States in terms of an associated state? What happened to the Austro-Hungarian Empire? A dual monarchy? Is it true that a canton in Switzerland can have international relations with bodies outside, and the *Länder*, in Germany equally, with permission from Bonn? The world is full of very interesting variations. Our Canadian reformers can obtain, I think, benefit from looking all about. This is going on before this Quebec parliamentary committee.

There may well be called in Quebec, in the indefinite future, by the initiative of the St. Jean Baptiste Society, the *Etats généraux*—the Estates General. Now that is an old term; I never thought Quebec would think up the Estates General! Nevertheless, the project is to call a great big kind of constitutional convention—this will be unofficial I assume—and see whether it can work out proposals. There have also been in the provinces of Manitoba and Saskatchewan two committees appointed by the governments, on bilingualism and biculturalism, to look at the provincial aspects of this matter. One thing is quite certain: the problems of bilingualism and biculturalism are not just federal problems, they are also intra-provincial problems.

These seem to me to be the official or quasi-official committees—the machinery which is at work trying to come up with answers. They are not just discussing, as learned societies do, but discussing first and trying professionally to arrive at a conclusion and a recommendation. My first point is that I do not think we have quite enough of these. Who is going to do the repatriation? Who is going to look at the amending process? It has been promised, I think, by Mr. Pearson, that something further will be done and perhaps when we first fly our new flag, we shall take a deep breath and go on to Stage Two, whatever it is going to be. But these are matters knocking on the door. I used to say to my classes in constitutional law, "We have a *rendez-vous* with the BNA Act. It's going to come some day!"

There are times when I do not know whether my Commission is going to be the most influential thing in the picture; I sometimes doubt it. But there are two things we can do that are very well worth doing, and they are not miracles. The first is that we have an excellent program of research now under way. A national advisory committee, bilingual, has thought out the various different areas of research, and if we do what we plan to do, we should be able to produce for all the Canadian people the most complete analysis of the development of this society, not only economically and politically (which is mostly what the Sirois Commission did) and not only just almost exclusively from the point of view of Quebec (which is what the Tremblay Commission did) but in its entirety. I think we can do that; it is under way; it will be a lasting benefit to scholars, students, as well as citizens wanting to make up their minds. For whatever Confederation may have been, it has lasted 100 years; it has existed; it has produced results; and those are worth examining and analysing.

The second thing, I think, which is important, is that we shall look at many bilingual and bicultural situations of majority and minority. They are lasting situations. Suppose Quebec goes independent. There is an English minority in Quebec. We'll stop talking about the French fact, and start talking about the English fact. You don't get rid of the question by independence. Nor do you get rid of the question in the other provinces by independence. It is a permanent thing, and it is worth studying, because here in Canada we face exactly the kind of problem— basically the same kind of problem with its own modifications—that almost every large state in the entire world faces. The whole human race is being thrown together more closely now. England has many negro immigrants. How will they behave? The Common Market in Europe brings Greeks into Germany and Italians into France and so forth. What happens? Russia is full of these problems. Many countries will be interested in what this Royal Commission is doing. This, it seems to me, is the problem and there is no easy solution for it. There is no gimmick that is going to make it easy. And independence or dependence or federalism or associated state is going to leave the problem still with us.

Now, messieurs les deux co-présidents, I haven't any message for this great gathering. Our Royal Commission is just in what we call Stage 3. Stage 1 was the ten commissioners (has there ever been a Royal Commission with ten people on it before?) meeting one another, getting certain headquarters and a certain staff together, and trying to get at least a tentative definition of bilingualism and biculturalism. Stage 2 was the visit, by the two co-presidents, to the premiers of every province —a private visit—to talk about the educational aspects in a general way. And Stage 3 is that unusual operation, on which we are now engaged, of regional visits. It is not in our terms of reference that we are supposed to travel around the country, asking people to come and talk about Canada's problems, but, about last November, when we had our first experimental regional meeting in the City of Ottawa and sixty different organizations or individuals came before us (we did not think we would get twenty), many of them said to us: "What you are supposed to be doing is so difficult, so hard to explain, and the issues that your terms of reference raise are so fundamental, that it is useless for you to ask for submissions, 'mémoires,' at this point, because people don't know what to put in them. You have got to go about the country and give localities an opportunity of being confronted with some of these issues." We cannot suggest any answers, of course, when we go to these meetings, and, of course too, an evening meeting open to the public brings out all the extremists and the crackpots, although they may do some good. They can give the challenging point of view, though I must say that some pots are more cracked than others. There was a wild woman in Fredericton who, when the chairman said: "Now we have simultaneous translation and everybody can pick up a transistor at the door and hear either English or French," said: "We don't want transistors, we want the English language."

Anyway, we find them in all areas. Also, on the other side, I shall not forget one student in Sherbrooke saying: "There is only one minority in the whole of Canada that matters at all, and that is the English minority in Quebec. The sooner they go west, the better."

If we have time, I think we can do this job, and I think we can do it well, and I think we can add some new principles to those principles already in the present Canadian Constitution, most of which surely have stood us in pretty good stead. The monarchic principle? Well, I said I would not say anything about that; it is in the constitution. There is the principle of federalism, of the type that gives co-ordinate powers to central and local legislatures; the principle of judicial review, so the courts can say either of a federal law or of a provincial law: it is *ultra vires*. Maybe we shall have to modify the constitutional court; that is a detail as long as the principle of judicial review remains. The principle of responsible government—who would want to change that? I must say, however, I am a little frightened of certain strains of thought in a certain minority in Quebec, which is very anti-democratic, largely I think because they associate democracy with the present domination of Quebec by large corporations.

Besides these principles, we have in the present Act only the glimmerings of bilingualism and biculturalism. By glimmerings, I mean that there is only one province wholly bilingual, that is Quebec. Ottawa is bilingual in the language used in the publication of the statutes; it has not been bilingual in the day-to-day administration up to now. There have been only glimmerings upon the cultural side, which is harder to work out. Also, of course, we have not had in the constitution fundamental, basic human rights really guaranteed.

Can we carry forward these new principles and formulate them and put them in the constitution so that everybody likes it? Can we make people not only like their province but even conceivably like Ottawa? This is the challenge we have before us.

CANADIAN UNIVERSITY PAPERBOOKS

Milton Keynes UK
Ingram Content Group UK Ltd.
UKHW031028291024
450383UK00001B/36